**Oryx Sourcebook Series
in Business and Management**

Small Business
An Information Sourcebook

Oryx Sourcebook Series in Business and Management

1. Small Business

Oryx Sourcebook Series
in Business and Management

Small Business
An Information Sourcebook

by Cynthia C. Ryans
Paul Wasserman, Series Editor

ORYX PRESS
1987

The rare Arabian Oryx is believed to have inspired the myth of the unicorn. This desert antelope became virtually extinct in the early 1960s. At that time several groups of international conservationists arranged to have 9 animals sent to the Phoenix Zoo to be the nucleus of a captive breeding herd. Today the Oryx population is over 400, and herds have been returned to reserves in Israel, Jordan, and Oman.

Copyright © 1987 by
The Oryx Press
2214 North Central at Encanto
Phoenix, AZ 85004-1483

Published simultaneously in Canada

Printed and Bound in the United States of America

∞ The paper used in this publication meets the minimum requirements of American National Standard for Information Science—Permanence of Paper for Printed Library Materials, ANSI Z39.48, 1984.

Library of Congress Cataloging-in-Publication Data

Ryans, Cynthia C., 1933–
   Small business.

   (Oryx sourcebook series in business and management)
   Includes indexes.
   1. Small business—Management—Bibliography.
   2. New business enterprises—Management—Bibliography.
   I. Title. II. Series.
   Z7164.C81R92   1987   [HD62.7]   016.658'022   86-23565
   ISBN 0-89774-272-9

Contents

Introduction

Starting and operating a small business often involves considerable risk and effort on the part of the entrepreneur. In the first half of 1984, approximately 325,000 small businesses were started in the United States, while during this same period of time, 15,235 existing small businesses failed and 33,167 went into bankruptcy.* Why are so many new businesses starting while others are not able to succeed? What can be done to prevent these new businesses as well as the existing ones from failing? An obvious place to start would be careful planning and management. While this may seem easy, there are many factors involved in planning and managing a small business and few certainties.

For example, the economic trends of both the national and local economic situations as well as the way the entrepreneur adjusts his/her business to meet these trends, has a pronounced effect on the success or failure of a business. For example, in areas where there is high unemployment, there is unlikely to be a need for a personal limousine service.

Careful planning is a key factor to starting and running a successful business. Initially, the person who is thinking of starting his/her own business must determine if the particular business under consideration fits the individual's needs, aspirations, experience, and talents. A business is not likely to succeed if the owner has not picked a business compatible to his/her talents and interests.

Location is another very important aspect to consider. Can a small high-tech operation succeed in a rural community? Perhaps it can, but its chances may not be as good as locating it in a more urban area where supplies are more easily available and demand is greater for the product and/or service.

In addition, the availability of qualified personnel is important to the success of a business. The business needs to be located where there are qualified people who can work for the company, or where the area is attractive enough so that the people needed to operate the business would be willing to relocate.

---

*The State of Small Business: A Report of the President Transmitted to Congress May 1985. Washington, DC: U.S. Government Printing Office, 1985. pp. xi, 13.

IMPORTANCE OF THE BUSINESS PLAN

Preparing a workable business plan is a vital step to starting and operating a business, perhaps one of the most difficult functions for the small business entrepreneur. For example, the unique nature of a business can create difficulty in developing a plan to fit it. It is also necessary to develop specific goals and objectives. However, a good business plan can facilitate performance and success within the firm and is essential for funding. While some may consider a business plan merely a tool to use to obtain financing, it should also be used as an organizational and developmental plan for the business.

No venture can get underway without financial backing. Many businesses can be started with little or no capital. However, others may need considerable funding. Some entrepreneurs may know the most efficient and profitable way to obtain this funding, while others may need assistance from banks, consultants, accountants, or others in the financial arena of business.

Very few people have all the answers to every question that comes up in the operation of a small business and there are numerous experts who are more than willing to assist. This includes the services of site location experts, financial experts, lawyers, and tax accountants.

Frequently, new companies turn to venture capitalists for first- or second-stage funding. As noted earlier, this is where a well-developed business plan is essential. Venture capitalists have provided much of today's start-up funding but tend to follow a most sophisticated screening approach in determining which new companies to support.

One important factor when starting and managing a business is moving deliberately, i.e., avoiding the temptation to rush critical decisions. Often some very important aspects of potential success in the business can be overlooked. For example, the time taken to hire the right blend of personnel, those who work well with each other and for the company, can pay off in the long run. In addition, satisfactory benefits for the employees can go a long way toward maintaining good employee relations and toward employee retention. The continued evolution of technology is another aspect to recognize. With the ever-present advancements in the computer field, employee tasks and work flow are constantly changing, and this factor should be taken into consideration. Even the small business can take advantage of the "computer age" to increase production in the business.

THE BOOK'S DESIGN

The information in this guide is designed to provide the small business person with sources to use in every aspect of starting and operating a business. While the citations in this book cover the period from 1975 to the present, the emphasis is placed on more recent material. The earlier material has been included in areas of business that are relatively timeless or where the book (or article) is considered a "classic." There is an abundance of material written on the various aspects of small business. However, no attempt has been made to include every piece of information that has been published recently on the topic, but, rather, the material that would be most valuable to the small business person was selected. This book offers some material on every aspect of small business, indicates to the reader what is available, and suggests the types of information the various publishers and organizations offer. These organizations and publishers can be contacted for further information.

Some of the books cited in this bibliography are of a general nature or are written with the large corporation in mind. The information contained in them, however, can be extremely useful to the small business person in many aspects of the business operations.

One of the most current innovations in the business world is the use of the various online databases now available to small businesses. This topic is much too broad to be developed in this book. However, several general reference books on this topic are included.

For the reader's convenience, a directory of publishers is included in the Appendices. The addresses used are those that were available at the time the individual books were published. Some of the publishers may no longer be in business, while other addresses were unavailable at the time of publication. This does not mean that the books are not available; all the books listed in this bibliography can be obtained through local libraries.

The Appendices also contain several lists of names, addresses, and phone numbers that can be helpful to the small business person.

The author wants to thank Mike Cole, Carol Mandolin, and Judy Cannon of the Kent State University Interlibrary Loan Department for their efforts in obtaining much of the material that was used in this book. Linda Poje spent many hours putting this book on a computer disk. Her efforts are greatly appreciated. A special thanks goes to Dr. John K. Ryans, Jr., for his help and encouragement on this entire project.

Literature

1. ACCOUNTING

1. Baker, C. Richard, and Hayes, Rick Stephan. *Accounting, Finance, and Taxation: A Basic Guide for Small Business.* Boston: CBI Publishing Co., Inc., 1980. 438 p.
   The authors have provided a brief version of modern accounting and its relationship to capital and taxes.

2. Baker, C. Richard, and Hayes, Rick Stephan. *Accounting for Small Manufacturers.* New York: John Wiley & Sons, Inc., 1980. 197 p.
   Starting with illustrations of forms needed for small manufacturing enterprises, this book also includes information on financial statements, bookkeeping, assets, liabilities, cost accounting and pensions, and executive compensations.

3. Berger, Robert O., Jr. *Practical Accounting for Lawyers.* New York: John Wiley & Sons, Inc., 1981. 357 p.
   This book is designed to increase the professional horizons of practicing attorneys who desire a working knowledge of accounting.

4. Briggaman, Joan S. *Small Business Record Keeping.* Albany, NY: Delmar Publishers, 1983. 337 p.
   This book can help you develop the recordkeeping and management skills necessary for owning and managing a small business.

5. Camillus, John C. *Budgeting for Profit: How to Exploit the Potential of Your Business.* Radnor, PA: Chilton Book Co., 1984. 168 p.
   Numerous illustrations supplement this book as it enables the reader to set up his/her own method for developing a profit-oriented budget system.

6. Chilton, Carl S., Jr. *The Successful Professional Client Accounting Practice: A Complete Guide to Profit-Opportunities and Techniques.* Englewood Cliffs, NJ: Prentice-Hall, Inc., 1983. 217 p.
   This book is geared specifically toward accountants who serve professional clients—doctors, dentists, lawyers, etc., and offers practical suggestions and ideas on how to provide a range of services for these clients.

7. Dyer, Mary Lee. *Practical Bookkeeping for the Small Business.* Chicago: Contemporary Books, Inc., 1976. 265 p.
This book tells the small business owner and manager how to keep accurate financial records through an easy-to-learn system that can be easily adapted to any kind of business.

8. Hutchinson, Susan. *All about Bookkeeping: A Guide for the Small Business.* Boulder, CO: Capricornus Press, 1982. 74 p.
The instructions in this book introduce you gradually to bookkeeping in a small company.

9. *Identifying Client Problems: A Diagnostic Review Technique, With Selected Working Capital Illustrations.* New York: American Institute of Certified Public Accountants, 1983. 16 p.
This pamphlet describes a review technique to assist a practitioner in identifying potential opportunities for improving clients' financial activities.

10. Keeling, B. Lewis, and Bieg, Bernard J. *Payroll Accounting.* Rev. ed. Cincinnati, OH: South-Western Publishing Co., 1985. 364 p.
This book stresses the various methods for computing wages and salaries, the methods of keeping records, as well as the preparation of government reports.

11. Kirsner, Laura, and Taetzsch, Lyn. *Practical Accounting for Small Businesses.* Rev. ed. New York: Van Nostrand Reinhold Company, Inc., 1983. 254 p.
Some of the topics covered in this book are: initial tax planning, how to set up journals and ledgers, purchasing and accounts payable, preparing financial statements, computerizing your business, and retail store accounting.

12. Leven, Merwin. *Accounting for Owners and Managers.* New York: Boardroom Books, 1981. 152 p.
This book provides information on the balance sheet fundamentals of bookkeeping, flow of funds and cash flow, how to analyze the financial sheet, inventories, capitalization, cost accounting and cost control, and adjusting for inflation.

13. Lipay, Raymond J. *Accounting Services for Your Small Business: A Guide for Evaluating Company Performance, Obtaining Financing, Selling Your Business.* New York: John Wiley & Sons, Inc., 1983. 258 p.
The evolution, objectives, and nature of an accounting compilation and review are included in this book along with how those accounting services differ from an audit.

14. Miller, Donald E. *The Meaningful Interpretation of Financial Statements: The Cause-and-Effect Ratio Approach.* New York: AMACOM, 1979. 232 p.
This book explains how to prepare balance sheets and profit and loss statements.

15. National Society of Public Accountants. *Portfolio of Accounting Systems for Small and Medium-Sized Business.* Rev. ed. Englewood Cliffs, NJ: Prentice-Hall, Inc., 1977. 1,392 p.
Accounting procedures and the latest professional practices are discussed in this book for such businesses as architects, automobile dealers, florists, etc.

16. Perry, William E. *What to Ask Your Accountant: A Reference for Those in Business and Those about to Begin: The Small Businessman, the Self-Employed, and the Individual.* New York: Beaufort Books, Inc., 1982. 231 p.
This book tells how to best utilize your accountant's services. A series of questions that you can ask your accountant about each of these services follows a narrative on that particular subject.

17. Rachlin, Norman S., and Cerwinske, Laura. *Eleven Steps to Building a Profitable Accounting Practice.* New York: McGraw-Hill Book Co., 1983. 287 p.
The eleven steps discussed in this book are building the structure, the fees, a partnership, the staff, the promotional plan, a profitable tax department, an estate planning specialty, opportunities in litigation, acquisitions and mergers, the long-range plan, and building for the future.

18. Ragan, Robert C. *Financial Recordkeeping for Small Stores.* Rev. ed. Washington, DC: Small Business Administration, Office of Management Information and Training, 1976. 135 p. (For sale by U.S. Government Printing Office).
This book is for the owner-manager without a full-time bookkeeper.

19. Ragan, Robert C. *Step-by-Step Bookkeeping.* Rev. ed. New York: Sterling Publishing Co., Inc., 1983. 134 p.
This book describes a system for the small store owner whose business does not justify hiring a trained, full-time bookkeeper.

20. Ragan, Robert C., and Zwick, Jack. *Fundamentals of Record-Keeping and Finance for the Small Business.* Fairfield, CA: Entrepreneur Press, 1978. 63 p.
This book shows ways to maintain records to develop and implement a financial action plan.

21. Raiborn, D. D. *Audit Problems Encountered in Small Business Engagements.* New York: American Institute of Certified Public Accountants, 1982. 109 p.
This book takes an empirical look at the nature, frequency, and importance of the problems that are encountered when setting auditing standards in small business audits.

22. Rea, Richard C., ed. *Operating a Successful Accounting Practice: Collection of Material from the Journal of Accountancy Practitioners Forum.* New York: American Institute of Certified Public Accountants, 1979. 320 p.
This collection of articles published in the *Journal of Accountancy* consists of personal essays on such topics as growth, fees, relations with

clients, staff recruiting and training, and the relations between partners in the business.

23. Sharma, Jitendra J. *Managerial Controls for Small Business.* New York: Vantage Press, 1976. 96 p.
Based on business management in England, this book shows how managerial control is affected by those in charge of small business accounts. The final chapter covers American practices of management accounting in small business.

24. Slater, Jeffrey. *RX for Small Business Success: Accounting, Planning, and Recordkeeping Techniques for a Healthy Bottom Line.* Englewood Cliffs, NJ: Prentice-Hall, Inc., 1981. 198 p.
This book contains a basic how-to-do-it approach to taxes, accounting, cash management, and other recordkeeping concerns of small business.

2. ADVERTISING/PUBLIC RELATIONS

25. *A.N.A. Tie-In Promotion Service.* New York: Association of National Advertisers Inc., 1985. 47 p.
This annual listing of companies interested in using tie-in promotions with other companies gives the names of 285 people with over 250 companies involved in this service.

26. *Advertising Doesn't Cost...and Other Lies.* Miami, FL: L. S. Enterprises, 1977. 113 p.
This loose-leaf book offers data on planning, budgeting and advertising media. A glossary of advertising terms is also included.

27. Anthony, Michael. *Handbook of Small Business Advertising.* Reading, MA: Addison-Wesley Publishing Co., 1981. 207 p.
The purpose of this manual is to help the small business person develop an effective advertising program.

28. Beach, Rita A., ed. *Ad Guide 1978.* New York: American University Press Services, Inc., 1978. 456 p.
Arranged alphabetically by discipline, this book includes entries on domestic and foreign scholarly periodicals.

29. Bellavance, Diane. *Advertising and Public Relations for a Small Business.* Boston: Diane Bellavance, 1980. 75 p.
This handbook includes methodologies useful to the small business person in planning and implementing promotional campaigns. Examples of advertising artwork, rate cards, contracts, etc. are also provided.

30. Benn, Alec. *The 23 Most Common Mistakes in Public Relations.* New York: AMACOM, 1982. 257 p.
This book talks about some of the 23 most common mistakes in public relations.

31. Benn, Alec. *The 27 Most Common Mistakes in Advertising.* New York: AMACOM, 1978. 156 p.
Whether producing your own advertising or using the services of an agency, this book offers some practical advice on effective advertising.

32. Blake, Gary, and Bly, Robert W. *How to Promote Your Own Business.* New York: New American Library, 1983. 241 p.
This do-it-yourself guide to advertising, publicity, and sales promotion contains examples taken from real promotions and includes case histories, checklists, tips, and a list of promotional "do's and don't's" for the small business person.

33. Bogart, Leo. *Strategy in Advertising: Matching Media and Messages to Markets and Motivation.* 2d ed. Chicago: Crain Books, 1984. 406 p.
This book examines modern technology and describes how this can affect the advertiser's job.

34. Brannen, William H. *Advertising and Sales Promotion: Cost Effective Techniques for Your Small Business.* Englewood Cliffs, NJ: Prentice-Hall, 1983. 247 p.
This book provides a framework for building your own advertising and promotion strategy based on the knowledge and experience you have gained from your business.

35. Braun, Irwin. *Building a Successful Professional Practice with Advertising.* New York: AMACOM, 1981. 289 p.
Every aspect of advertising is covered in this book including a situation analysis, research, and developing an advertising message.

36. Carlson, Linda. *The Publicity and Promotion Handbook: A Complete Guide for Small Business.* Boston: CBI Publishing Co., 1982. 261 p.
This how-to book covers the various steps in marketing projects and tells where to get help and what you may expect to pay for this help.

37. Cassel, Dana K. *How to Advertise and Promote Your Retail Store.* New York: American Management Associations, 1983. 202 p.
This book is aimed at the established retailer who wants to improve marketing efforts, to improve ads or promotions and save advertising dollars without taking away the effectiveness of their campaigns.

38. Cook, Harvey R. *Profitable Advertising Techniques for Small Business.* Fairfield, CA: Entrepreneur Press, 1980. 133 p.
This book defines and describes the various types of advertising techniques that are most practical for small business.

39. Cutlip, Scott M.; Center, Allen H.; and Broom, Glen M. *Effective Public Relations.* Englewood Cliffs, NJ: Prentice-Hall, Inc., 1985. 670 p.
This basic book for practitioners covers such topics as staff, the origins and environment of public relations, the process of public relations, and much more.

40. Dailey, Andrea. *Advertising Small Business.* San Francisco, CA: Bank of America, 1978. 20 p.
This book offers suggestions and media analysis to the small business manager interested in developing an advertising campaign.

41. Dean, Sandra Linville. *How to Advertise: A Handbook for Small Business.* Wilmington, DE: Enterprise Publishing, Inc., 1983. 202 p.
    This handbook helps the small business owner build a knowledge of basic advertising concepts by explaining the jargon and methods used in buying advertising time and space.

42. *Direct Mail Advertising and Selling for Retailers.* New York: National Retail Merchants Association, 1978. 403 p.
    This book covers the entire scope of direct mail advertising.

43. Eicoff, Alvin. *Or Your Money Back.* New York: Crown Publishers, 1982. 151 p.
    The major focus of this book is that ads are supposed to sell something.

44. Goldman, Jordan. *Public Relations in the Marketing Mix.* Chicago: Crain Books, 1984. 165 p.
    This book presents a new approach to marketing-oriented public relations and shows how commonly used public relations vehicles can be converted into potent strategic weapons.

45. Gray, Ernest A. *Profitable Methods for Small Business Advertising.* New York: John Wiley & Sons, 1984. 285 p.
    This book covers every aspect of conducting an advertising program and enables the reader to prepare or judge the planning, developing, and direction of the advertising strategy.

46. *A Guide for Preparing & Releasing Industrial Publicity.* Easton, PA: Barry Jones Advertising, 1982. 30 p.
    This pamphlet tells just what industrial publicity is, how and when to use it, and provides information on how to write it and what it costs.

47. Holtje, Bert. *How to Be Your Own Advertising Agency.* New York: McGraw-Hill Book Co., 1981. 215 p.
    The author of this book points out the decisions that must be made before each step is taken in your advertising activities.

48. Holtz, Herman R. *The Secrets of Practical Marketing for Small Business.* Englewood Cliffs, NJ: Prentice-Hall, Inc., 1982. 192 p.
    The entire business situation for a wide variety of business enterprises is examined in this book including information on how to use your advertising dollar efficiently, how to use the media advantageously, and how to write advertising copy.

49. Johnson, Philip M. *How to Maximize Your Advertising Investment.* Boston: CBI Publishing Co., Inc., 1980. 224 p.
    The practicalities of how you can maximize your return on investment in marketing communications is covered in this book.

50. Klein, Ted, and Danzig, Fred. *Publicity: How to Make the Media Work for You.* New York: Charles Scribner's Sons, 1985. 262 p.
    This book outlines some basics of public relations, press releases, and pamphlets and tells how to pass information to the media through press conferences and seminars.

51. Kuswa, Webster. *Big Paybacks from Small-Budget Advertising.* Chicago: Darnell Corporation, 1982. 371 p.
This book tells how to eliminate costly mistakes and improve your advertising efforts.

52. Lewis, Herschell Gordon. *How to Handle Your Own Public Relations.* Chicago: Nelson-Hall, Inc., Publishers, 1976. 251 p.
This book tells how the amateur can succeed in public relations without serving an apprenticeship.

53. Lovell, Ronald P. *Inside Public Relations.* New York: Allyn and Bacon, Inc., 1982. 495 p.
This book offers the basics on how to set goals, originate programs, utilize the media/information networks and analyze results.

54. Maas, Jane. *Better Brochures, Catalogs, and Mailing Pieces.* New York: St. Martin's Press, 1981. 128 p.
This book gives helpful suggestions for the development of effective advertising literature design, as well as pointing out pitfalls to avoid for all types of businesses.

55. Nalickson, David L. *Advertising—How to Write the Kind that Works.* Rev. ed. New York: Charles Scribner's Sons, 1982. 220 p.
This book provides an orderly process for planning your advertising and some clear writing guidelines that can add advertising effectiveness.

56. Paetzel, Hans W., ed. *Complete Multilingual Dictionary of Advertising, Marketing and Communications.* Chicago: Crain Books, 1984. 606 p.
This reference manual covers more than 8,000 terms in advertising, marketing for print and electronic media, graphic arts and public relations.

57. Quinlin, Joseph C. *Industrial Publicity.* New York: Van Nostrand Reinhold Company, Inc., 1983. 258 p.
Hundreds of tips on how to fully exploit publicity opportunities are given in this book.

58. Ray, Michael L. *Advertising and Communication Management.* Englewood Cliffs, NJ: Prentice-Hall, Inc., 1982. 514 p.
Covering the details of advertising planning, creative and media decisions, this book uses advertising as the major component for outlining the steps toward effective communication.

59. Ridgway, Judith. *Successful Media Relations: A Practitioner's Guide.* Brookfield, VT: Gower Publishing Co., 1985. 214 p.
Some of the topics covered in this book include media relations programs, lists and contacts, releases, samples, ongoing information services, special offers, seminars for educating management, and much more.

60. Rust, Roland. *Advertising Media Models: A Practical Guide.* Lexington, MA: Lexington Books, 1986. 159 p.
This how-to-guide explains and analyzes media models and helps the reader find information necessary to make intelligent buys in a variety of media.

61. Salz, Nancy L. *How to Get the Best Advertising from Your Agency.* Englewood Cliffs, NJ: Prentice-Hall, Inc., 1983. 176 p.
This book tells how to achieve a healthy client-agency relationship. It explains just what goes on in every area where misunderstanding may occur.

62. Sawyer, Howard G. *Business-to-Business Advertising.* Chicago: Crain Books, 1978. 323 p.
Aimed at those involved in advertising or communications, this book is a collection of commentaries on business-to-business marketing and communications, from the development of advertising strategy to testing and measurement of results.

63. Schultz, Don E. *Essentials of Advertising Strategy.* Chicago: Crain Books, 1981. 131 p.
This book is written for both the newcomer as well as the established professional. It provides information on buyer behavior, understanding the buying process, and the difference between objectives and strategies.

64. Schultz, Don E.; Martin, Dennis; and Brown, William P. *Strategic Advertising Campaigns.* 2d ed. Chicago: Crain Books, 1984. 532 p.
A step-by-step approach for a powerful, successful advertising campaign is presented in this book. Examples of industry campaigns are included.

65. Schwaninger, Jim, and Aaron, Jan. *Tooting Your Own Horn.* New York: National Retail Merchants Association, 1978. 66 p.
Time tested techniques on good public relations that have been used by experts in retail public relations are included in this book.

66. *Selecting an Advertising Agency.* New York: Association of National Advertisers, 1977. 82 p.
This book discusses the many factors to look for when selecting an advertising agency.

67. Siegel, Connie McClung. *How to Advertise and Promote Your Small Business.* New York: John Wiley & Sons, Inc., 1978. 128 p.
This book provides a thorough and practical guide for small business promotion and advertising. Topics covered include media selection, budget planning, community relations, and ad creation.

68. Slutsky, Jeff, and Woodruff, Woody. *Streetfighting: Low-Cost Advertising/Promotion Strategies for Your Small Business.* Englewood Cliffs, NJ: Prentice-Hall, Inc., 1984. 240 p.
Some of the topics covered in this book include cross-promotions, publicity that is a free form of advertising, community involvement, in-store marketing, and off-premises promotions.

69. Smith, Cynthia S. *Step-by-Step Advertising.* New York: Sterling Publishing Co., Inc., 1984. 192 p.
This book includes ideas for effective, low-cost, practical promotion and campaigns, advertising, and public relations ideas.

70. Stewart, David W., and Furse, David H. *Effective Television Advertising*. Lexington, MA: Lexington Books, 1986. 178 p.
This comprehensive study of television advertising focuses on the aggregate responses of consumer audiences and evaluates the effects of 155 different factors on recall, comprehension, and persuasion.

71. *Top Management's Role in Directing, Budgeting and Evaluating Advertising Programs*. New York: The American Business Press, 1984. 29 p.
This book covers subjects such as adequate staffing, budgeting, research-based planning, trade shows, direct mail, and public relations.

72. Tuerck, David G., ed. *Issues in Advertising: The Economics of Persuasion*. Washington, DC: The American Enterprise Institute for Public Policy Research, 1978. 284 p.
This book discusses the issue of whether the expense of the increasing government regulation of advertising is justified by the benefits of the regulation.

73. Urdang, Lawrence, ed. *Dictionary of Advertising Terms*. Chicago: Crain Books, 1985. 209 p.
This mini-encyclopedia includes the working vocabularies of all parts of the advertising and marketing world. Contains over 4,000 terms.

74. Weilbacher, William M. *Choosing an Advertising Agency*. Chicago: Crain Books, 1983. 170 p.
This extensive checklist and in-depth analysis of every facet of the agency/client relationship was prepared by the president of Bismark Corporation.

75. *Work Book for Estimating Your Advertising Budget*. Boston: Cahners Publishing, 1985. 26 p.
This book is for advertising budget planners who study how factors such as market share, share of new product sales, market growth, product quality, etc., can affect the adequacy of their advertising budget.

3. BUSINESS LAW (BANKRUPTCY, INCORPORATION, LEASING, LICENSING, MERGERS, PATENTS, SUBCHAPTER S)

76. Adams, Paul. *The Complete Legal Guide for Your Small Business*. New York: John Wiley & Sons, Inc., 1982. 218 p.
This book shows the nonlawyer how to draft some of the agreements encountered in a small business.

77. Allen, Paul A. *How to Keep Your Company Out of Court*. Englewood Cliffs, NJ: Prentice-Hall, Inc., 1984. 282 p.
This text is a "do-it-yourself" book for those business owners seeking legal information regarding such topics as business contracts, product liability, patents, antitrust laws, tax problems, and the extension of credit.

78. Ash, Francesca, ed. *The International Licensing Directory 1985.* Southport, CT: Expocon Management Associates Inc., 1985. 224 p.
This book lists over 1,000 licensing companies worldwide offering over 3,000 properties. Each entry includes address, phone number, contact name and list of properties.

79. Augello, William J. *Freight Claims in Plain English,* 2d ed. Huntington, NY: Shippers National Freight Claim Council, Inc., Publishers, 1982. 691 p.
This book covers the legal aspects of freight claims including over 100 carrier declinations and what to do about them.

80. Baer, Walter E. *Winning in Labor Arbitration.* Chicago: Crain Books, 1982. 214 p.
This book covers the entire arbitration process from contracts to advocacy.

81. Brue, Nordahl L. *Retailer's Guide to Understanding Leases.* New York: National Retail Merchants Association, 1980. 202 p.
The special problems encountered by retailers operating in shopping malls are covered in this book.

82. Chatterton, William A. *Consumer and Small Business Bankruptcy: A Complete Working Guide.* Old Tappan, NJ: Institute for Business Planning, Inc., 1982. (Loose leaf)
This guide is designed to help the reader process a consumer or small business bankruptcy claim.

83. *Concise Explanation of the Subchapter S Revision Act of 1982: As Approved by Congress on October 1, 1982.* Englewood Cliffs, NJ: Prentice-Hall, Inc., 1982. 40 p.
This book discusses various aspects of the Subchapter S Revision Act of 1982 including elections, revocations and termination of the business, how to handle income, deductions and credits, how to handle distributions in the corporation and transitional rules.

84. Crumbley, D. Larry, and Davis, P. Michael. *Organizing, Operating, and Terminating Subchapter S Corporations: Law, Taxation, and Accounting.* Rev. ed. Tucson, AZ: Lawyers & Judges Publishing Co., 1980. 451 p.
This book provides a clear explanation of the complex provisions and case law governing the tax and accounting procedures involved in operating a small business corporation.

85. Dible, Donald M. *What Everybody Should Know about Patents, Trademarks and Copyrights.* Reston, VA: Reston Publishing Company, Inc., 1978. 254 p.
This book includes six steps to take when making a patent application, foreign registration and copyright notice.

86. Dunfee, Thomas W.; Ballace, Janice R.; and Rosoff, Arnold J. *Business and Its Legal Environment.* Englewood Cliffs, NJ: Prentice-Hall, Inc., 1983. 656 p.
The authors of this book tell how the legal system and public law affects business and business decision making.

87. Esperti, Robert, and Peterson, Renno. *Incorporating Your Talents: A Guide to the One-Person Corporation.* New York: McGraw-Hill Book Co., 1984. 243 p.
This book shows how to incorporate your particular talents. The 1982 Tax Equity Law and Fiscal Responsibilities Act are discussed.

88. Faber, Peter L., and Holbrook, Martin E. *Subchapter S Manual: A Special Tax Break for Small Business Corporations.* Englewood Cliffs, NJ: Prentice-Hall, Inc., 1983. 221 p.
Some of the topics covered in this book include how to handle income, deductions and credits, retirement plans, distributions, special tax savings, etc., all involving S Corporations.

89. *General Information concerning Trademarks.* Washington, DC: U.S. Department of Commerce, Patent and Trademark Office, 1984. 21 p. (For sale by U.S. Government Printing Office.)
This guide to the definition and functions of trademarks gives a discussion of application procedures.

90. Goldstein, Arnold S. *Basic Book of Business Agreements.* Wilmington, DE: Enterprise Publishing, Inc., 1983. 923 p.
This book offers a complete collection of ready-to-use agreement forms for most any personal or business situation.

91. Goldstein, Arnold S. *The Small Business Legal Problem Solver.* Boston: CBI Publications, 1983. 270 p.
This book not only states the law with regard to the small business owner but also tells the reader what to do and what not to do when specific legal problems arise.

92. Hancock, William A. *The Small Business Legal Advisor.* New York: McGraw-Hill Book Co., 1982. 258 p.
The author of this book has provided business people with a convenient and inexpensive way to have "conversation" with a lawyer regarding important legal aspects of starting and running a small business.

93. *Handbook on the Subchapter S Revision Act of 1982.* Englewood Cliffs, NJ: Prentice-Hall, Inc., 1982. 144 p.
This book includes a concise explanation of this act, the code selections as amended, and House and Senate committee reports.

94. Hearn, Patrick. *The Business of Industrial Licensing: A Practical Guide to Patents, Know-How, Trademarks and Industrial Design.* Brookfield, VT: Renouf USA, Inc., 1981. 626 p.
The legal and practical aspects of industrial licensing are explained in this book. It is intended for businesspeople rather than specialists.

95. Hilgert, Raymond, and Schoen, Sterling. *Labor Agreement Negotiations.* Cincinnati, OH: South-Western Publishing Co., 1983. 55 p.
The main theme of this book is how to negotiate a new labor contract that will govern future labor relations.

96. *How to Protect Your Ideas.* Los Angeles: American Entrepreneurs Association, 1981. 44 p.
For those in small business who need to protect innovative ideas or inventions, this book discusses the topic, including protection on paper, where to go for help, and patents.

97. Hughes, Theodore E., and Klein, David. *Ownership: How to Use the Various Forms of Ownership to Reduce Your Taxes, Preserve Your Assets, and Protect Your Survivors.* New York: Scribner's Sons, 1984. 182 p.
This book tells how to avoid unnecessary taxes by carefully managing your assets.

98. Hutzler, Laurie H. *The Regulatory and Paperwork Maze: A Guide for Small Business.* New York: Legal Management Services, Inc., 1979. 72 p.
The topics discussed in this book include how to find your way through the government maze, how to cope with your own paperwork maze, how to evaluate your regulatory and paperwork problems, and where to get more information on regulatory agencies.

99. *Impact of ERISA on Small-Scale Pension Plans.* Rye, NY: Reymont Associates, 1979. 24 p.
The effects of the 1974 Employee Retirement Income Security Act as it relates to more than 470,000 pension plans with fewer than 100 participants is discussed in this book.

100. Imundo, Louis V. *The Arbitration Game.* Cincinnati, OH: South-Western Publishing Co., 1982. 114 p.
This book tells how to increase effectiveness when preparing and presenting cases before arbitrators.

101. Jackson, Stanley G. *How to Proceed in Business—Legally.* Englewood Cliffs, NJ: Prentice-Hall, Inc., 1984. 232 p.
This book gives the reader a simple guide and sample forms needed to comply with federal regulations when starting a new business.

102. Jandt, Fred Edmund. *Win-Win Negotiating: Turning Conflict into Agreement.* New York: John Wiley & Sons, Inc., 1985. 300 p.
Written by a professional negotiator, this book discusses techniques used by people whose job is managing conflict.

103. Kamoroff, Bernard. *Small Time Operator: How to Start Your Own Small Business, Keep Your Books, Pay Your Taxes & Stay out of Trouble: A Guide and Workbook.* Rev. ed. Laytonville, CA: Bell Springs Publishers, 1983. 190 p.
Common types of laws and regulations that affect small businesses are discussed in this book.

104. Karrass, Gary. *Negotiate to Close: How to Make More Successful Deals.* New York: Simon & Schuster, 1985. 219 p.
The author of this book describes some of the strategies and techniques for successful negotiations.

105. Kelvin, Jeffrey B. *The Financial Planner's Handbook to Regulation and Successful Practice.* Rev. ed. Rockville Centre, NY: Farnsworth Publishing Co., 1983. 246 p.
This book looks at some regulatory acts that are pertinent to running a business including the Investment Advisors Act of 1940, state regulations, and federal regulations.

106. Lane, Marc J. *Legal Handbook for Small Business.* New York: AMACOM, 1977. 181 p.
This book includes checklists on trademarks, patents, copyrights, and contractual agreements.

107. Lane, Marc J. *Purchase and Sale of Small Businesses: Tax and Legal Aspects.* New York: John Wiley & Sons, Inc., 1985. 737 p.
This comprehensive book for the practitioner seeking the state of the law regarding small business includes checklists, forms, and examples.

108. Last, Jack. *Everyday Law Made Simple.* Garden City, NY: Doubleday & Co., Inc., 1978. 172 p.
In addition to providing general legal information, this book covers sales agreements, partnerships, corporations, real estate acquisitions, patents, copyrights, and other legal matters that are potentially important to the small business person.

109. Lowe, Julian, and Crawford, Nick. *Innovation and Technology Transfer for the Growing Firm.* New York: Pergamon Press, 1984. 226 p.
This book includes some general definitions and discussions on licensing, alternative licensing strategies, and some empirical evidence on a public policy approach that can be adopted by governments interested in using licensing in order to promote business development.

110. Lowe, Julian, and Crawford, Nick, eds. *Technology Licensing and the Small Firm.* Aldershot Hampshire, England: Gower Publishing Co., Ltd., 1984. 115 p.
This book examines the advantages and techniques of technology licensing for the small firm.

111. Lusterman, Seymour. *Managing Business State Government Relations.* New York: Conference Board, Inc., 1983. 50 p.
This book is intended for those who want to play a more effective part in public policy development in the states by providing information on how to interact with new laws and regulations affecting business.

112. McQuown, Judith H. *Inc. Yourself: How to Profit by Setting up Your Own Corporation.* Rev. ed. New York: Warner Books, 1981. 227 p.
This book serves as a guide to help you make the most of your professional help.

113. Mancuso, Joseph R. *Bankruptcy—How to Survive Chapter 11.* Worcester, MA: Center for Entrepreneurial Management, 1979. 38 p.
Information on the current bankruptcy act is included in this book as well as facts on how to prosper in economic turmoil.

114. Muncheryan, Hrand M. *Patent It Yourself.* Blue Ridge Summit, PA: Tab Books, 1982. 172 p.
This book shows how to prepare a patent application for your invention and successfully file the application with the patent office.

115. Nevitt, Peter K., and Fabozzi, Frank J. *Equipment Leasing.* 2d ed. Homewood, IL: Dow Jones-Irwin, 1985. 462 p.
The authors of this book provide essential, current information on every aspect of equipment leasing, covering current financial reporting and the tax aspects of leasing.

116. Nicholas, Ted. *How to Form Your Own Corporation without a Lawyer for under $50.00.* Wilmington, DE: Enterprise Publishing, Inc., 1978. 104 p.
Necessary forms for incorporating at the lowest possible cost are included in this book along with complete instructions on how to use them.

117. Nicholas, Ted. *How to Form Your Own Non-Profit Corporation without a Lawyer for under $75.* Wilmington, DE: Enterprise Publishing, Inc., 1980. 143 p.
This book covers such topics as corporation law, the role of the registered agent, tax exemptions, an organization plan and how to get underway after incorporation.

118. Norris, Kenneth. *The Inventor's Guide to Low-Cost Patenting.* New York: Macmillan Publishing Co., 1985. 233 p.
This guide for new-product marketers tells how to channel creativity, and how to avoid the high costs of a patent attorney and gives information on how to market a newly-patented product. Sample patent applications are included.

119. Posch, Robert J. *What Every Manager Needs to Know about Marketing and the Law.* New York: McGraw-Hill Book Co., 1984. 328 p.
This book offers pointers on how to recognize and avoid the legal pitfalls in product decisions.

120. Pressman, David. *Patent It Yourself! How to Protect, Patent, and Market Your Inventions.* New York: McGraw-Hill Book Co., 1979. 210 p.
This is a do-it-yourself book for those wishing to protect and/or sell their own inventions and includes both legal and commercial information to aid the inventor in licensing, protecting, and patenting the invention.

121. Pritchard, Robert E., and Hindelang, Thomas J. *The Lease/Buy Decision.* New York: AMACOM, 1980. 276 p.
This book includes financial tables, sample contracts and a step-by-step analysis on the topic.

122. Pritchett, Price. *After the Merger: Managing the Shockwaves.* Homewood, IL: Dow Jones-Irwin, 1985. 140 p.
This book offers insights into the people dynamics of a merger and provides some information on how to deal with postmerger problems.

123. Rice, Jerome S. and Keith, Libbey. *Making the Law Work for You: A Guide for Small Business.* Chicago: Contemporary Books, Inc., 1980. 131 p.
The author of this book shows the small business person how the law can strengthen the business. Some topics discussed here (with a minimum of legal theory and jargon) are negotiating loans, signing notes, collecting accounts, buying and selling, and personnel problems.

124. Rice, Michael Downey. *Prentice-Hall Dictionary of Business, Finance, and Law.* Englewood Cliffs, NJ: Prentice-Hall, Inc., 1983. 362 p.
This dictionary includes information in the field of business law, including federal legislation, administrative law, environmental law, pensions and profit sharing plans, bank and transportation regulations, and corporate law.

125. Roberson, Cliff. *Staying out of Court: A Manager's Guide to Employment Law.* Lexington, MA: Lexington Books, 1985. 177 p.
Written in clear layperson's language, this book shows how to avoid legal liability in employment decisions involving hiring, firing, and employment management.

126. Roberts, Duane F. *Marketing and Leasing of Office Space.* Chicago: Institute of Real Estate Management, 1979. 289 p.
The author provides a step-by-step account of how to lease vacant space in office buildings, how to negotiate the best leases for clients and how to improve your leasing commissions.

127. Rothenberg, Waldo G. *Tax and Estate Planning with Closely Held Corporations.* Rochester, NY: Lawyers Co-Operative Publishing Co., 1981. 698 p.
The basic rules of law in a closely held corporation is the theme of this book, including how to organize and finance the corporation, professional corporations, Subchapter S information, collapsible corporations, profit sharing plans, dividends, and liquidations.

128. Steingold, Fred. *Legal Master Guide for Small Business.* Englewood Cliffs, NJ: Prentice-Hall, Inc., 1983. 242 p.
This book is designed to give the small business owner or manager enough information to avoid legal problems. Topics discussed include partnership vs. sole proprietorships for tax breaks, legal fees, and using the legal system to your own benefit.

129. *Subchapter S Revision Act of 1982: Law and Explanation.* Chicago: Commerce Clearing House, Inc., 1982. 136 p.
This book provides coverage of the Subchapter S Revision Act of 1982 along with the texts of the amended Internal Revenue Code provisions.

130. Tarrant, John. *Perks and Parachutes.* New York: Linden Press/ Simon & Schuster, 1985. 315 p.
This book clarifies employment contracts and includes examples of standard employment contracts drafted by attorneys.

131. Unkovic, Dennis. *The Trade Secrets Handbook.* Englewood Cliffs, NJ: Prentice-Hall, Inc., 1985. 224 p.
The book gives strategies for protection of trade secrets, involving licensing, joint venturing, and international transactions.

132. Wasserman, Paul, and Wasserman, Steven, eds. *Law and Legal Information Directory.* 3d ed. Detroit, MI: Gale Research Co., 1984. 902 p.
This volume provides comprehensive coverage of both live and print sources of legal information.

4. THE BUSINESS PLAN

133. Aaker, David A. *Developing Business Strategies.* New York: John Wiley & Sons, Inc., 1984. 391 p.
This book provides an introduction and overview of business strategy and gives an external analysis of the industry, a self-analysis, business strategy alternatives, and finally the advantages and disadvantages of formal planning systems.

134. Argenti, John. *Practical Corporate Planning.* London: George Allen & Unwin, 1980. 221 p.
For the chief executive of the small- to medium-sized firm who has not yet adopted a corporate plan, this book provides a complete process. Cases are also included.

135. Bradway, Bruce M., and Pritchard, Robert E. *Developing the Business Plan for a Small Business.* New York: AMACOM, 1980. 50 p.
This book not only discusses how the small business person can improve many areas of the business but also provides a detailed outline of a business plan with many practical examples.

136. *Business Planning Guide.* Portsmouth, NH: Upstart Publishing Co., Inc., 1983. 115 p.
This book provides both prospective and present small business owners with a business plan and financing proposal outline.

137. Carruthers, William, ed. *The Little-Known Business Library: Final Report on 999 Successful, Little-Known Businesses.* Fort Worth, TX: Premier Publishers, 1980. 256 p.
This book contains accounts of business plans and ideas that have been successfully put into operation.

138. Dible, Donald M., ed. *How to Plan and Finance a Growing Business.* Fairfield, CA: Entrepreneur Press, 1980. 311 p.
This book contains information from company representatives about their experiences within the company.

139. Hosmer, LaRue T., and Guiles, Roger. *Creating the Successful Business Plan for New Ventures.* New York: McGraw-Hill Book Co., 1985. 213 p.
This guide explains the business plan, industry analysis, organizational

and financial planning, marketing production as well as the presentation of written reports. A sample business plan is included.

140. Kilpatrick, Michael. *Essential Programs for Small Business Planning.* New York: John Wiley & Sons, Inc., 1985. 266 p.
Computer programs necessary for the planning and analysis needs of the small business entrepreneur are discussed in this book.

141. McLaughlin, Harold. *Building Your Business Plan: A Step-by-Step Approach.* New York: John Wiley & Sons, Inc., 1984. 256 p.
Beginning with the company charter, this book offers a step-by-step process for creating a business plan covering market analysis, financial reporting, and a final suggested plan outline.

142. Mancuso, Joseph R. *How to Prepare and Present a Business Plan.* Englewood Cliffs, NJ: Prentice-Hall, Inc., 1983. 316 p.
All aspects of preparing and presenting a business plan are included in this book along with questionnaires, blank forms to use in planning, and examples of actual business plans.

143. Mancuso, Joseph R. *How to Write a Winning Business Plan.* Englewood Cliffs, NJ: Prentice-Hall, Inc., 1985. 344 p.
The author offers the reader a step-by-step system for writing a business plan that will attract the financing you need for your business. Checklists and key financial forms are included.

144. Nylen, David W. "Making Your Business Plan an Action Plan." *Business* 35 (October–November–December 1985): 12–16.
This author provides steps for developing a successful marketing plan.

145. Osgood, William R. *Basics of Successful Business Planning.* New York: AMACOM, 1980. 252 p.
A step-by-step approach to developing a business plan is included in this book along with the theory and practice of various types of successful business planning.

146. Osgood, William R. *How to Plan and Finance Your Business.* Boston: CBI Publishing Co., Inc., 1980. 165 p.
This guide to constructing a logically arranged and complete business plan and financing proposal is based on the evaluation of thousands of business plans and financial proposals. Sample worksheets are included in the appendix.

147. Osgood, William R. *Planning and Financing Your Business: A Complete Working Guide.* Boston: Inc/CBI Publications, 1983. 260 p.
This handbook shows how to prepare a logically arranged and complete business plan. It includes forms, tables, and charts to help in this process.

148. Person, Mary Jean, and Culligan, Matthew J. *Back to Basics: Planning.* New York: Facts on File, Inc., 1985. 225 p.
This book provides useful expositions on fundamental business planning in easy-to-understand language emphasized by diagrams, charts, and model plans that are structured for any business application.

149. *Planning Your Business.* Washington, DC: Price Waterhouse, 1985. 35 p.
This book deals with business planning to meet the business person's needs as well as those of outside lenders or investors.

150. Pring, Roger. *The Instant Business Form Book.* Reading, MA: Addison-Wesley Publishing Co., 1983. 160 p.
This book offers hundreds of forms from memo pads to sales spreadsheets that can be torn out and used in the business planning process.

151. Rich, Stanley R., and Gumpert, David. *Business Plans that Win.* New York: Harper & Row, 1985. 220 p.
These authors offer practical advice on writing a business plan that will sell your ideas. The book is based on the experience of the M.I.T. Enterprise Forum.

152. Williams, Edward E., and Manzo, Salvatore E. *Business Planning for the Entrepreneur: How to Write and Execute a Business Plan.* New York: Van Nostrand Reinhold Co., Inc., 1983. 200 p.
This book shows the practitioners of both small and large businesses exactly how to write a business plan as well as giving some insights on the methodology of planning and the mechanics of plan preparation.

5. BUYING AND SELLING A BUSINESS

153. Banning, Robert. *Zero Down: How to Buy a Closely Held Company without Using Any of Your Own Money.* Seattle, WA: Word Power, Inc., 1979. 159 p.
The author tells how to buy a small privately owned company without using your own money.

154. Bunn, Verne A. *Buying and Selling a Small Business.* 2d ed. Washington, DC: Small Business Administration, 1979. 122 p. (For sale by U.S. Government Printing Office.)
This book tells what the buyer (and seller) of a small business should know before the buy/sell decision is made, and where this information can be found.

155. Coltman, Michael M. *Buying (and Selling) a Small Business.* Seattle, WA: Self-Counsel Press, Inc., 1983. 137 p.
This book focuses on information for both the buyer and seller on buying or selling an existing business. The author includes information on getting started in the new business, finding a site, evaluation of the business, financing, contracts, leasing, and franchising.

156. Douglass, F. Gordon. *How to Profitably Sell or Buy a Company or Business.* New York: Van Nostrand Reinhold Co., Inc., 1981. 286 p.
The author includes information on how to determine the worth of your business, setting a price, how to make the decision to sell, where the buyer gets money, tax information, and how to close the deal.

157. Ford, Ian. *Buying and Running Your Own Business.* London: Business Books, Ltd., 1977. 210 p.
The purpose of this book is to make the reader aware of the pitfalls that are involved in buying a business and to show him/her how to recognize if they do exist.

158. Goldstein, Arnold S. *The Complete Guide to Buying and Selling a Business.* New York: New American Library, 1983. 273 p.
This book tells you how to pick the right business for you, how to distinguish between price and value, how to negotiate, how to use brokers, lawyers, accountants and bankers for your own good, and ways to finance a deal using very little of your own money.

159. Goldstein, Arnold S. *Own Your Own: The No-Cash-Down Business Guide.* Englewood Cliffs, NJ: Prentice-Hall, Inc., 1983. 208 p.
This book tells how to buy a business for a fraction of its worth, how to convince others to invest in you, how to buy a business with no cash down, and how to sell the seller your terms.

160. Greve, J. Terrence. *How to Do a Leveraged Buyout or Acquisition.* 2d ed. San Diego, CA: Buyout Publications, 1984. 416 p.
This step-by-step blueprint explains how to buy a company with very little capital.

161. Gustafson, Ray L. *Buying, Selling and Starting a Business.* Omaha, NE: Gustafson Horseshoe Corporation, 1982. 139 p.
Information necessary when you begin thinking about buying, selling, or starting a business is provided in this ready reference book.

162. Kirkpatrick, Frank. *How to Buy a Country Business.* Chicago: Contemporary Books, Inc., 1981. 248 p.
This book focuses on total simplification of the business-buying process which includes the search and research to make sure you have found the exact business you want.

163. McGaffey, Jere D. *Buying, Selling, and Merging Business.* Philadelphia, PA: American Law Institute—American Bar Association Committee on Continuing Professional Education, 1979. 591 p.
This book looks at the legal aspects of the purchase and sale of a business and the problems confronting the lawyer in a merger transaction.

164. Mangold, Maxwell J. *How to Buy a Small Business.* New York: Pilot Industries, Inc., 1976, 31 p.
With the use of tables, charts, and self-scoring checklists, this book provides a step-by-step explanation on how to buy your own business.

165. Miles, Raymond C. *How to Price a Business.* Englewood Cliffs, NJ: Institute for Business Planning, 1982. 133 p.
This book offers some suggestions on what you need to know when you want to sell your business such as how to arrive at the best selling price, as well as explaining the major steps involved in the pricing decision.

166. Quest, Miles. *How to Buy Your Own Hotel.* London: Northwood Books, 1979. 221 p.
This book provides information useful to those interested in buying a hotel or catering business, and includes some of the pitfalls in such a venture.

167. Rubel, Stanley M. *Guide to Selling a Business.* Chicago: Capital Publishing Corporation, 1977. 344 p.
This book lists 1,500 acquisitions-oriented businesses and 500 professional merger intermediaries.

168. Smith, Brian R., and West, Thomas L.*Buying Your Own Small Business.* Lexington, MA: The Stephen Greene Press, 1985. 118 p.
This book tells the right way to buy a small business. A simple step-by-step method on buying a business is included along with the forms for developing a three-year business plan.

6. COMMUNICATION (INTERNAL/EXTERNAL)

169. Aronoff, Craig E., et al. *Getting Your Message Across.* St. Paul, MN: West Publishing Co., 1981. 411 p.
The authors of this book discuss such areas as getting your message across through letters, memos, reports, face to face and through other media.

170. Avett, Elizabeth M. *Today's Business Letter Writing.* Englewood Cliffs, NJ: Prentice-Hall, Inc., 1977. 194 p.
This informative guide to letter writing discusses basic letter writing procedures and report writing.

171. Blicq, Ron S. *On the Move: Communications for Employees.* Englewood Cliffs, NJ: Prentice-Hall, Inc., 1976. 259 p.
The author takes the employee as a communicator through four stages: 1) the job applicant; 2) new employee; 3) junior supervisor; and 4) owner of a small or part-time business.

172. Blicq, Ron S. *Technically Write! Communicating in a Technological Era.* 2d ed. Englewood Cliffs, NJ: Prentice-Hall, Inc., 1981. 381 p.
The communication most frequently seen in industry is covered in this book. It stresses why communication skills are important and how to develop them.

173. Bogard, Morris R. *The Manager's Style Book.* Englewood Cliffs, NJ: Prentice-Hall, Inc., 1979. 179 p.
For middle management personnel, this book provides both the theory and technique to help create a management style that is effective as well as attractive.

174. Bormann, Ernest G., et al. *Interpersonal Communication in the Modern Organization.* Englewood Cliffs, NJ: Prentice-Hall, Inc., 1982. 287 p.
This book contains practical, nonacademic treatment of communication in the modern organization written by experts in the field.

175. Colby, Barnard L. *How to Write Like a Pro.* New London, CT: The Day, 1984. 69 p.
This book contains a list of words and pairs of words that are mistaken for one another or are misused.

176. De Mare, George. *Communicating at the Top: What You Need to Know about Communicating to Run an Organization.* New York: John Wiley & Sons, Inc., 1979. 270 p.
This guide for top-level executives offers hints on how to use communications techniques and media effectively to ensure successful dialog with clients, employees, the government, and the financial community.

177. Elsea, Janet. *The Four-Minute Sell.* New York: Simon & Schuster, Inc., 1984. 152 p.
The author presents a plan for making the first four minutes of a meeting a positive and effective experience through awareness of how one looks, sounds, and listens.

178. *Essential Telephone Communication.* Chicago: Edge Enterprises, Inc., 1985.
This individualized cassette training package teaches employees the fundamentals of business telephone communication. The cassettes cover listening/speaking, answering, message taking, holding/transferring, screening, and the negatives to avoid.

179. Fallon, William K., ed. *Effective Communication on the Job.* 3d ed. New York: AMACOM, 1981. 328 p.
The main theme of this book focuses on getting the message across.

180. Felber, Stanley S., and Koch, Arthur. *What Did You Say? A Guide to the Communication Skills.* 2d ed. Englewood Cliffs, NJ: Prentice-Hall, Inc., 1978. 365 p.
This book stresses the importance of clear thinking as a guide to communication skill—accurate expression of meaning.

181. Foreman, Robert L. *Communicating the Appraisal: Guide to Report Writing.* Chicago: American Institute of Real Estate Appraisers, 1982. 85 p.
This books is an aid to train and assist real estate appraisers in communicating the results of their efforts to their clients.

182. Forrester, Lynn S. *Experiencing Effective Communication in Business.* Cincinnati, OH: South-Western Publishing Co., 1986. 296 p.
This workbook covers such topics as writing letters, memos; and reports; how to listen, read, and speak; how to conduct meetings, conferences, and interviews; and much more.

183. Frank, Allan D. *Communicating on the Job.* Glenview, IL: Scott, Foresman & Co., 1982. 344 p.
Designed to help the entry-level employee improve his/her understanding and skill in various aspects of communication, this book contains a model consisting of four phases: analysis, prediction, action, and feedback.

184. Geffner, Andrea B. *How to Write Better Business Letters.* Woodbury, NY: Barron's Educational Series, 1982. 144 p.
More than 75 examples are included in this book that covers all of the typical kinds of written communications essential for small businesses. Especially important is the book's emphasis on the proper format for all types of letters.

185. Glatthorn, Allan A. *Writing for Success.* Glenview, IL: Scott, Foresman & Co., 1985. 134 p.
This book provides some guidelines for effective writing including advice on how to write sales letters, grammatical mistakes to avoid, and how to write under pressure.

186. Golen, Steven; Pearce, Glenn C.; and Figgins, Ross. *Report Writing for Business and Industry.* New York: John Wiley & Sons, Inc., 1985. 576 p.
This book covers the purposes, types, principles, processes, and techniques of both formal and informal business reports in both written and oral presentations.

187. Gootnick, David E., and Gootnick, Margaret Mary, eds. *The Standard Handbook of Business Communication.* New York: The Free Press, 1984. 479 p.
While mainly intended for educators, this comprehensive handbook covers such topics as written communication, interactional communication, and organizational communication.

188. Henze, Geraldine. *From Murk to Masterpiece: Style for Business Writing.* Homewood, IL: Dow Jones-Irwin, 1985. 120 p.
This clear, concise and to-the-point guide to the mechanics of practical business writing covers topics such as usage, format, and graphics.

189. *How Plain English Works for Business: Twelve Case Studies.* Washington, DC: Office of Consumer Affairs, U.S. Department of Commerce, 1984. 102 p. (For sale by U.S. Government Printing Office.)
This book tells how businesses can score successes by simplifying consumer documents. Includes information on easy-to-read warranties, credit contracts, insurance policies and product information booklets.

190. Iacone, Salvatore J. *Modern Business Report Writing.* New York: Macmillan Publishing Co., Inc., 1985. 380 p.
This guide to writing business reports gives advice for every step from planning and gathering of data to the organization and writing of the report.

191. Jackson, Clyde W. *Functional Business Writing.* Cleveland, OH: Association for Systems Management, 1977. 149 p.
The three-fold purpose of this book is to get the reader to think about business writing in a new manner; to analyze unique ways of writing taken from the business environment; and to provide simple methodologies, examples, and instructions to use in meeting these requirements.

192. Johnson, Bonnie McDaniel. *Getting the Job Done: A Guide to Better Communication for Office Staff.* Glenview, IL: Scott, Foresman & Co., 1984. 125 p.
This book serves as a manual for increasing office productivity through improving relationships between office employees and their managers and fellow employees, as well as contacts outside the organization.

193. Keithley, Erwin M., and Schreiner, Philip J. *A Manual of Style for the Preparation of Papers and Reports—Business and Management Applications.* 3d ed. Cincinnati, OH: South-Western Publishing Co., 1980. 118 p.
Designed as a reference and guide to written reports, this manual is divided into two parts: an explanation of report style and a complete model report.

194. Klauss, Rudi, and Bass, Bernard M. *Interpersonal Communication in Organizations.* New York: Academic Press, 1982. 232 p.
This book focuses on interpersonal information transfer, mainly verbal communication behavior of managers.

195. Leech, Thomas F. *How to Prepare, Stage and Deliver Winning Presentations.* New York: AMACOM, 1985. 417 p.
Some of the presentation aids that this book can help you become more familiar with include audio visuals, how to take clues from your audience, speaking style, confidence, and enthusiasm.

196. Linver, Sandy, and Taylor, Nick. *Speak and Get Results.* New York: Summit Books, 1983. 286 p.
This book focuses on more than the words we say, but also on the sound of our voices and the way we use our bodies when we speak, all providing a positive presentation and good business image.

197. Londgren, Richard E. *Communication by Objectives.* Englewood Cliffs, NJ: Prentice-Hall, Inc., 1983. 200 p.
Based on the MBO concept, this book provides a background and study of communication by objectives.

198. Martel, Myles. *Before You Say a Word—The Executive Guide to Effective Communication.* Englewood Cliffs, NJ: Prentice-Hall Inc., 1984. 215 p.
Many practical suggestions and strategies for communicating orally and communicating in tough situations are included in this book.

199. Nixon, Robert. *Practical Business Communications.* New York: Harcourt Brace Jovanovich, Publishers, 1984. 594 p.
This book tells how to write the business message, the business letter, a business report, as well as information on good oral communications in business.

200. Phillips, Gerald M. *Communicating in Organizations.* New York: Macmillan Publishing Co., Inc., 1982. 366 p.
The author of this book shows how people with technical and professional skills can learn to communicate effectively with others in order to succeed in his/her job.

201. Poe, Roy W. *The McGraw-Hill Guide to Effective Business Reports.* New York: McGraw-Hill Book Co., 1982. 208 p.
This author shows how to analyze other people's reports and tells how to become involved in an editorial process that ensures effective writing.

202. Poe, Roy W. *The McGraw-Hill Handbook of Business Letters.* New York: McGraw-Hill Book Co., 1983. 286 p.
This book includes model letters for more than 160 business situations including requests, transmittals, confirmations, and credit and collections.

203. Poe, Roy W., and Fruehling, Rosemary T. *Business Communication: A Problem-Solving Approach.* 3d ed. New York: McGraw-Hill Book Co., 1984. 400 p.
Some of the topics covered in this edition include a background for business writing, how to win and keep customers and solve their problems, hints on business reports, employment communications, general management communications, and much more.

204. Price, Jonathan. *Put that in Writing.* New York: Viking Press, 1984. 209 p.
This book tells how to make your letters and memos impressive and hard-hitting.

205. Reilly, Charles E., Jr., and Lynn, Dorothy A. *The Power of In-Person Communications.* New York: Hammond Farrell, 1982. 100 p.
This primer for the would-be public speaker is written in a straightforward, how-to format that breaks down the art of communicating into easy-to-understand segments.

206. Roddick, Ellen. *Writing that Means Business: A Manager's Guide.* New York: Macmillan Publishing Co. Inc., 1986. 120 p.
This book takes a structured look at communications and looks at such topics as composing your ideas, how to start and finish a letter, and sentence clarity.

207. Schermerhorn, Derick D. *Improving Your Business Communications: How to Speak, Write, Listen, and Observe More Effectively.* New York: Publications Division, National Association of Credit Management, 1984. 153 p.
This book attempts to illustrate more effective methods of communication between individuals, stressing the importance of listening as well as speaking, writing, and observing.

208. Smeltzer, Larry M., and Waltman, John L. *Managerial Communication: A Strategic Approach.* New York: John Wiley & Sons, Inc., 1984. 556 p.
This book offers a balanced coverage of communication theory as well as

written and oral communication. Managerial negotiations and technologically-mediated communications are featured.

209. Timm, Paul R. *Functional Business Presentations: Getting Across.* Englewood Cliffs, NJ: Prentice-Hall, Inc., 1981. 206 p.
This book begins by looking at a manager's critical competency and continues by offering information on conceptual planning, how to analyze your listeners, how to prepare your mind for proper communications, how to arrange your ideas, visual aids, and how to deliver your presentation and offer persuasive messages.

210. Vincler, James, and Vincler, Nancy. *Business Writing Made Easy.* Redwood City, CA: Persuasive Press, 1985. 220 p.
This guide shows you how you can cut your writing time and write powerful business communications.

211. Wohlmuth, Ed. *The Overnight Guide to Public Speaking.* Philadelphia, PA: Running Press, 1983. 149 p.
In addition to the six promises every audience wants to hear, the author also covers such topics as ten ways to avoid giving a bad speech, how to put your nerves to work for you, and when you should turn down a speaking engagement.

212. Wolf, Morris P., and Kuiper, Shirley. *Effective Communication in Business.* 8th ed. Cincinnati, OH: South-Western Publishing Co., 1984. 485 p.
While mainly concentrating on written communications, this book also offers some insights into good oral communications, word processing, and report writing.

213. *Words that Sell.* Westbury, NY: Caddylack Publishing, 1984. 128 p.
This thesaurus lists more than 2,500 words, slogans, and phrases that are used by profesional copywriters to sell an audience.

214. Zelazny, Gene. *Say It with Charts: The Executive's Guide to Successful Presentations.* Homewood, IL: Dow Jones-Irwin, 1985. 130 p.
This book provides the reader with suggestions and examples to help you "say it with charts."

7. COMPETITION

215. Birdzell, L. E., Jr. *Competing—The Enterprise of Business.* Washington, DC: National Chamber Foundation, 1981. 157 p.
Some of the topics discussed in this book include business opportunities for the small business person, competition, scale economies, database problems, and market share and profits.

216. Fuld, Leonard M. *Competitor Intelligence: How to Get It—How to Use It.* New York: John Wiley & Sons Inc., 1985. 479 p.
This comprehensive guide provides information on how to find the "95% of all necessary corporate data," information available in public sources regardless of whether the firm is privately owned or not.

217. Porter, Michael E. *Competitive Advantage.* New York: Free Press, 1985. 557 p.
The author of this book shows executives how to evaluate their own company's competitive position and create a competitive edge.

8. CONSULTING

218. Albert, Kenneth J. *How to be Your Own Management Consultant.* New York: McGraw-Hill Book Co., 1978. 207 p.
The author shows how to set up an internal problem-solving system and tells how to determine when an outside consultant is necessary. Information on how to select a consultant is also included.

219. Bell, Chip R., and Nadler, Leonard, eds. *The Client-Consultant Handbook.* Houston, TX: Gulf Publishing Co., 1979. 279 p.
Through a collection of articles, this book provides the client with information on how consultants function, their values, and strategies.

220. Blake, Robert J., and Mouton, Jane Srygley. *Consultation.* 2d ed. Reading, MA: Addison-Wesley Publishing Co., 1983. 596 p.
A systematic look at the scope of the consulting field is presented in this book. Emphasis is placed on the consultant/client interaction.

221. Deal, Terrence E., and Kennedy, Allan A. *Corporate Cultures: The Rites and Rituals of Corporate Life.* Reading, MA: Addison-Wesley Publishing Co., 1982. 232 p.
These authors discuss serious corporate culture problems they have encountered in their own management consulting experience.

222. *Directory of Management Consultants.* 3d ed. Fitzwilliam, NH: Consultants News, 1983. 392 p.
The types of services offered, name of president, size of staff, branches, geographical area served, etc. are all listed for management consultant firms.

223. *Directory of Personal Image Consultants.* New York, Fairchild Books, 1982. 94 p.
This book contains over 200 listings containing information on the services provided by image consultants located in 74 cities in 35 states and four foreign countries.

224. Fuchs, Jerome H. *Making the Most of Management Consulting Services.* New York: AMACOM, 1975. 214 p.
This book tells how to examine the value of outside professionals.

225. Hunt, Alfred. *The Management Consultant.* New York: Ronald Press, 1977. 159 p.
An overall view of the consulting profession is included here as well as the history and description of consulting and the services offered by management consultants.

226. Klein, Howard J. *Other People's Business: A Primer on Management Consultants.* New York: Mason/Charter, 1977. 202 p.
This easy-to-read overview of management consulting begins with a brief history of the topic and continues with analogies and examples of consulting.

227. Lant, Jeffrey L. *The Consultant's Kit: Establishing and Operating Your Successful Consulting Business.* 2d ed. Cambridge, MA: JLA Publications, 1984. 204 p.
The author of this book discusses such areas as how to determine if the consultant's world is right for you, contact networks, marketing and promoting your expertise, and how to go from leads to contract.

228. McLean, Janice, ed. *Consultants and Consulting Organizations Directory: A Reference Guide to Concerns and Individuals Engaged in Consultation for Business, Industry and Government.* 6th ed. Detroit, MI: Gale Research Co., 1984. 1,293 p.
The 8,000 listings in this book include principals, date founded, branch offices, descriptions of services and clients, and special services for consultants and consulting organizations.

229. Steele, Fritz. *Consulting for Organizational Change.* Amherst, MA: University of Massachustetts Press, 1975. 202 p.
Some of the general topics discussed in this book include how to learn from consulting, the client's role, and teamwork.

230. Stryker, Steven C. *Guide to Successful Consulting with Forms, Letters, and Checklists.* Englewood Cliffs, NJ: Prentice-Hall, Inc., 1984. 288 p.
The skills, practices, insights, and communications that are required to be a successful consultant are discussed in this book.

231. Wasserman, Paul. *Consultants and Consulting Organizations Directory.* 5th ed. Detroit, MI: Gale Research Co., 1982. 1,385 p.
This book provides an alphabetical list of firms, individuals and organizations active in the consulting field.

9. CREDIT AND COLLECTIONS

232. Biggar, Myron J. *Practical Credit and Collections for Small Business.* Boston: CBI Publications, 1983. 102 p.
Usage of tables and graphs helps to illustrate the development of skills necessary in setting up and operating a credit and collections system.

233. Goldstein, Arnold S. *Getting Paid: Building Your Powerful Credit and Collection Strategy.* New York: John Wiley & Sons, Inc., 1984. 274 p.
A step-by-step strategy for increasing profits using a proven two-pronged program to slash credit losses while at the same time maintaining or increasing sales is discussed in this book.

234. Hayes, Rick Stephan. *Credit and Collections: A Practical Guide.* Boston: CBI Publishing Co., Inc., 1979. 352 p.
For owners and managers of small- to medium-sized businesses, this book includes the financial and nonfinancial analysis necessary to judge the credit worthiness of a customer.

235. Kitzing, Donald. *Credit and Collections for Small Business.* New York: McGraw-Hill Book Co., 1981. 174 p.
This book was written to help small businesses without trained credit and collection personnel understand credits and collections and thus collect payments faster, have fewer bad debts and increase their profits.

236. Paulsen, Timothy R. *Collection Techniques for the Small Business.* Seattle, WA: Self-Counsel Press Inc., 1983. This book offers a "back to the basics" approach to successfully collecting money.

10. DATA PROCESSING

237. Baker, Richard H. *How to Run Your Business with dBase II.* Blue Ridge Summit, PA: Tab Books, Inc., 1984. 307 p.
This book tells just what a microcomputer can do in your small business and how well it will pay off. Suggestions are given on how to select a computer system and what programs are best.

238. Bencar, Gary. *Computer for Small Business: A Step-by-Step Guide on How to Buy.* Santa Barbara, CA: La Cumbre, 1983. 132 p.
Among the topics covered in this book are a discussion on the computer revolution, data processing systems, evaluating data processing needs, information on how to convert to software, and selection of hardware.

239. Bender, Jack. *A Layman's Guide to Installing a Small Business Computer.* New York: Petrocelli Books, Inc., 1978. 118 p.
The fundamentals of programing and computer operations are discussed in this book.

240. Best, Peter J. *Small Business Computer Systems.* Englewood Cliffs, NJ: Prentice-Hall, Inc., 1982. 296 p.
A detailed study of the design and implementation of computer systems for small businesses is covered in this book.

241. Bigelow, Robert P., ed. *Computers & the Law—An Introductory Handbook.* 3d ed. Washington, DC: American Bar Association, Section of Science and Technology, 1981. 343 p. (For sale by Commerce Clearing House News Bureau.)
More than 50 contributors have provided a general introduction to

computers and the law, including information on computers in law practices, governmental usage and regulation, contracts, software contracts, proprietary protection of software and much more.

242. Birnbaum, Mark, and Sickman, John. *How to Choose Your Small Business Computer.* Reading, MA: Addison-Wesley Publishing Co., Inc., 1982. 192 p.
This book can tell you if you really need a computer and gives you the right questions to ask to help you intelligently choose the right system.

243. Blumenthal, Susan. *Understanding and Buying a Small-Business Computer.* Indianapolis, IN: H.W. Sams, 1982. 157 p.
This introduction to computers for small business owners presents the basic concepts of computer technology, provides information on both hardware and software, describes hidden costs and pitfalls to avoid, and contains a glossary of computer terms.

244. Bly, Robert W. *The Personal Computer in Advertising.* Wayne, PA: Banbury Books, 1983. 197 p.
For the computer user in advertising, sales, or marketing, this book gives an overview of microcomputers and their applications.

245. Byerly, Greg. *Online Searching: A Dictionary and Bibliographic Guide.* Littleton, CO: Libraries Unlimited, 1983. 288 p.
This book provides concise and understandable definitions of online search terminology along with a selective annotated bibliography of journal articles, books, directories, bibliographies, annuals, and proceedings on the topic.

246. Canning, Richard G., and Leepre, N. C. *So You Are Thinking about a Small Business Computer.* Englewood Cliffs, NJ: Prentice-Hall, Inc., 1982. 203 p.
Designed for the person unfamiliar with computers, this book teaches how to successfully select a small computer system.

247. Christie, Linda Gail. *Managing Today and Tomorrow with On-Line Information.* Homewood, IL: Dow Jones-Irwin, 1985. 275 p.
This guide offers information on practical applications of online database sytems and tells how they can be used in growing and established corporations.

248. Cohen, Jules, and McKinney, Catherine Scott. *How to Computerize Your Small Business.* Englewood Cliffs, NJ: Prentice-Hall, Inc., 1980. 171 p.
This book is slanted toward the business executive rather than the technical expert and provides steps to computerize your business, focusing on the actual process for determining a company's specifications for computer implementation.

249. Cohen, Jules, and McKinney, Catherine Scott. *How to Microcomputerize Your Business.* Englewood Cliffs, NJ: Prentice-Hall, Inc., 1983. 180 p.
This book offers a step-by-step guide for selecting data processing equipment and services that will fit the exact requirements of your business and shows how to use them efficiently and profitably.

250. Curry, Jess W., Jr., and Bonner, David M. *Up and Running: The Small Business Computer Implementation Cookbook.* Englewood Cliffs, NJ: Prentice-Hall, Inc., 1984. 145 p.
This book presents in layman's terms a step-by-step procedure for installing a small mini- or micro-based computer system.

251. Daniels, Shirley. *All You Need to Know about Microcomputers: The Small-Business Manager's Advisory.* Oakland, CA: Third Party Publishing Co., 1979. 127 p.
This book, intended for the business manager who knows little or nothing about computers, describes computers and computer systems in simple terms.

252. Deutsch, Dennis S. *Protect Yourself: The Guide to Understanding and Negotiating Contracts for Business Computers.* New York: John Wiley & Sons, Inc., 1984. 223 p.
This book can help the small business person get on equal footing with the vender regarding the purchase of a computer system.

253. Edwards, Chris. *Developing Microcomputer-Based Business Systems.* Englewood Cliffs, NJ: Prentice-Hall, Inc., 1983. 224 p.
This book on the development of small computer systems for commercial data processing studies computer programing by showing examples and by explaining a single business in-depth.

254. Eischen, Martha. *Does Your Business Need a Computer?* Blue Ridge Summit, PA: Tab Books, Inc., 1982. 159 p.
This book helps you determine if computerization can augment your business procedures.

255. Elbra, Tony. *Database for the Small Computer User.* Manchester, England: NCC Publications, 1982. 177 p.
This book begins by explaining what database means and follows with discussions on choice of software, various aspects of minicomputers, information on shared-data machines and distributed databases.

256. Falk, Howard. *Handbook of Computer Applications for the Small or Medium-Sized Business.* Radnor, PA: Chilton Book Co., 1983. 331 p.
Based on the assumption that computers are a necessity for survival in today's business world, some of the topics covered here include business applications, various types of software and hardware, and installation.

257. Finn, Nancy B. *The Electronic Office.* Englewood Cliffs, NJ: Prentice-Hall, Inc., 1983. 143 p.
Written for the noncomputer person, this book is designed to help the small business person understand the technology available in this area.

258. Garetz, Mark. *Bits, Bytes, and Buzzwords: Understanding Small Business Computers.* Beaverton, OR: Dilithium Press, 1983. 139 p.
The five sections of this book are the basic computer system, the peripherals, the software, how to buy a computer, and a glossary.

259. Graham, Gordon. *Automated Inventory Management for the Distributor.* Boston: CBI Publishing Co., Inc., 1980. 234 p.
This book provides the fundamentals needed to get your automated system off the ground.

260. Green, James. *Automating Your Office—How to Do It, How to Justify It.* New York: McGraw-Hill Book Co., 1984. 245 p.
This step-by-step approach to integrating automation shows the reader how to understand an office automation study, justify the investment, and determine the appropriate types of implementation.

261. Greenwood, Frank. *Profitable Small Business Computing.* Boston: Little, Brown & Co., 1982. 165 p.
This book contains basic information on a number of key topics on computerizing a business. These include the benefits of computer utilization, system review, and suggestions on software and hardware.

262. Grieb, William E., Jr. *The Small Business Computer: Today and Tomorrow.* New York: Baen Enterprises, 1984. 287 p. (Distributed by Simon & Schuster.)
Starting at the most fundamental level, this book covers not just computers, but business requirements. It is designed for the businessman with no knowledge or experience in computers.

263. Hockney, Donald. *Personal Computers for the Successful Small Business.* New York: Macmillan Publishing Co., Inc., 1984. 202 p.
This book offers guidelines on what features to look for when buying a small business computer. A review of popular, proven personal computers is included.

264. Hoffman, Roger. *The Complete Software Marketplace, 1984–1985.* New York: Warner Software/Warner Books, 1985. 236 p.
This guide to developing and marketing software covers case studies on naming the company, structuring the business, getting insurance, legal matters, venture capital, advertising, promotions, and PR. In addition, lists of computer-industry lawyers, agents, and brokers are included as well as trade shows, consultants, market research firms, distributors, and trade publications.

265. Hoover, Ryan E. *Executive's Guide to Online Information Services.* White Plains, NY: Knowledge Industry Publications, Inc., 1984. 296 p.
This book tells you what some of the many online services are, how they can be used and their cost, and what they can mean for you.

266. *How Small Businesses Use Computers.* 3d ed. Cherry Hill, NJ: Management Information Corporation, 1982. 92 p.
This group of articles describes the reasons behind the decision to automate as well as descriptions of computer operations and plans to upgrade computer systems already in use.

267. Jong, Steven F. *Word Processing for Small Businesses.* Indianapolis, IN: H. W. Sams & Co., Inc., 1983. 190 p.
This author details over 50 hardware and software products and packages, the important features needed for word processing, the importance of user's manuals and training programs, how to combine word process-

ing and data processing into one system, and the future trends in word processing and microcomputers.

268. Koff, Richard M. *Using Small Computers to Make Your Business Strategy Work.* New York: John Wiley & Sons, Inc., 1984. 325 p.
This book provides information on how to make profitable business decisions on marketing, research and development, pricing, production, and finance by using sophisticated strategic managment techniques along with a personal computer.

269. Krutz, Ronald L. *Microprocessors for Managers: A Decision-Maker's Guide.* Boston: CBI Publishing Co., 1983. 135 p.
For the manager or executive who is in some way involved with microprocessors, this book covers such topics as a list of micro storage media, software, economics, and evaluation techniques.

270. Kutten, L. J. *Computer Buyer's Protection Guide: How to Protect Your Rights in the Microcomputer Marketplace.* Englewood Cliffs, NJ: Prentice-Hall, Inc., 1984. 142 p.
This book helps you in buying a microcomputer by answering questions and providing information on the legal points to consider.

271. McClellan, Stephen T. *The Coming Computer Industry Shakeout: Winners, Losers, & Survivors.* New York: John Wiley & Sons, Inc., 1984. 349 p.
This book provides the investor with a history of the transition of the computer world based on both large hardware systems and mini- and microcomputers as well as software.

272. McGlynn, Daniel R. *Personal Computing: Home, Professional and Small Business Applications.* 2d ed. New York: John Wiley & Sons, Inc., 1982. 335 p.
The personal computer revolution is discussed in this book along with a look at all aspects of personal computers, various aspects of interfacing, system applications, small business computer systems, and the future applications of computers.

273. McGlynn, Daniel R. *Simplified Guide to Small Computers for Business.* New York: John Wiley & Sons, Inc., 1983. 241 p.
This book includes an overview of the small business computer system marketplace and looks at computer hardware, peripheral devices in computer hardware, the concerns of small business computer system applications, and the acquisition process.

274. McWilliams, Peter A. *The Personal Computer Book.* Los Angeles: Prelude Press, 1982. 281 p.
Aimed at the first-time computer buyer, this book covers the entire spectrum of uses of the personal computer.

275. *Microcomputers: Market Strategies and Opportunities.* San Jose, CA: Creative Strategies International, 1982.
The critical issues that will impact the computer industry over the next five years are discussed in this book.

276. *Microcomputers—A Marketing Perspective.* Newport Beach, CA: MV Publishing, Inc., 1982.
Seventeen full-page microcomputer industry forcasts with annual breakouts through 1990 are included in this book.

277. Morris, Ralph. *Computer Basics for Managers: A Practical Guide to Profitable Computing.* 2d ed. London: Business Books, Ltd., 1984. 257 p.
This book looks at the various types of computers available, as well as their uses and applications.

278. Morris, Ralph. *Making the Most of Your Business Micro.* London, England: Business Books, Ltd., 1984. 153 p.
While this book is devoted to providing an overview of microcomputers and how they can be used in the business, the author stresses the importance of software throughout the book.

279. Perry, W. E. *So You Think You Need Your Own Business Computer.* New York: John Wiley & Sons, Inc., 1982. 201 p.
This book contains clear and comprehensive worksheets and checklists on the selection, installation and use of small computers in business.

280. Rosa, Nicholas, and Rosa, Sharon. *Small Computers for the Small Business.* Portland, OR: Dilithium Press, 1980. 334 p.
The authors of this book describe microcomputers and how they can be used in a small business, including information on hardware, timesharing, software, and word-processing.

281. Schadewald, Robert J., and Dickey, Bill. *dBase II Guide for Small Business.* Culver City, CA: Ashton-Tate, 1984. 350 p.
This book contains a collection of dBase II programs for business applications, primarily those useful for mail handling and accounting.

282. Schlueter, Louis, Jr. *User-Designed Computing: Free Enterprise Application Design.* Lexington, MA: Lexington Books, 1982. 145 p.
This book shows how computer applications that are designed by the user can be as useful as those that are produced by professionals.

283. Schulmeyer, G. Gordon. *Computer Concepts for Managers.* New York: Van Nostrand Reinhold Co., Inc., 1985. 285 p.
This book contains four major sections which discuss the importance of technical personnel, a summation of computer hardware, a discussion of various types of software, and how information processing can help managers.

284. Shaw, Donald R. *Your Small Business Computer.* New York: Van Nostrand Reinhold Co., Inc., 1981. 256 p.
Points such as cost and performance, storage, and information on various software systems are discussed in this book.

285. Simon, Alan R. *How to Be a Successful Computer Consultant.* New York: McGraw-Hill Book Co., 1985. 253 p.
The author of this book tells how to organize a computer consulting business, select the best services to offer, earn profits, and plan for the future.

286. Sippl, Charles J., and Dahl, Fred. *Computer Power for the Small Business.* Englewood Cliffs, NJ: Prentice-Hall, Inc., 1979. 306 p.
Beginning with the changes that are taking place in the computer world, this book looks at how and what computers can do, the array of equipment and programs sold, a step-by-step buying methodology, and much more.

287. Skees, William D. *Before You Invest in a Small Business Computer: Essential Information for First-Time Buyers.* Belmont, CA: Lifetime Learning Publications, 1982. 344 p.
For the business person considering small business computers costing from between $5,000 and $50,000, this book offers some practical information necessary in making this decision.

288. Slay, Joseph R. *Straight Talk on Computers for the Small Business Manager.* Richmond, VA: Center for Small Business Information, 1980. 84 p.
For the business manager with little or no familiarity with computers, this book provides advice on how to capitalize on the computer technology needed for the business.

289. *Small Business Computers to 1985.* San Jose, CA: Creative Strategies International, 1981. 120 p.
Information on various computers for small businesses is discussed in this book along with pictures of hardware and some price comparisons. A list of vendors is included.

290. Smith, Brian R. *The Small Computer in Small Business. A Guide to Selection and Use.* Brattleboro, VT: The Stephen Greene Press, 1981. 143 p.
This book provides a basic knowledge of computers with a limited use of technical language.

291. Smith, Brian R., and Austin, Daniel J. *Word Processing: A Guide for Small Business.* Lexington, MA: Lewis Publishing Co., 1983. 200 p.
This book discusses the use of word processing equipment in a small office or business.

292. Smolin, C. Roger. *How to Buy the Right Small Business Computer System.* New York: John Wiley & Sons, Inc., 1981. 156 p.
The design of small business computer systems, how they should operate, and what to expect of them is discussed in this book.

293. *The Software Catalog: Business Software.* New York: Elsevier Science Publishing Co., Inc., 1984. 696 p.
This catalog provides information on availability, price, applications, and compatibility of more than 50,000 software packages and the systems they run on.

294. *The Software Encyclopedia, 1985/86.* New York: R. R. Bowker Co., 1985. 2 v.
This two-volume set provides complete and detailed information on microcomputer software, containing over 22,000 microcomputer software packages from 3,000 publishers.

295. Strosberg, Linda. *Big Decisions for Small Business: What You Should Know Before You Buy a Computer.* New York: Harper & Row, 1984. 144 p.
This book begins by showing how to understand your needs for a computer and is followed by discussions on computer data, hardware, software, the impact of automation on the business, and how to find a solution to the computer dilemma.

296. Summer, Claire, and Levy, Walter A. *The Affordable Computer: Microcomputer Applications in Business and Industry.* New York: AMACOM, 1979. 179 p.
This book offers a case history that can be used to evaluate the value of a microcomputer for your business.

297. Traister, Robert J., and Ingram, Rich. *Making Money with Your Microcomputer.* Blue Ridge Summit, PA: Tab Books, Inc., 1982. 152 p.
The concepts, ideas, and software discussed in this book help the reader learn more about the microcomputer business and how it can relate to the home professional.

298. Tran, Thi Min-Chau, and Dan-Tan, Hau. *How to Automate Your Office: A Guide to Successful Implementation.* New York: AMA-COM, 1985. 357 p.
This book shows how to determine your automation needs, select vendors, hardware and software, how to justify costs, and how to get the best deal possible.

299. Warren, Carl, and Miller, Merl K. *From the Counter to the Bottom Line.* Portland, OR: Dilithium Press, 1979. 289 p.
The authors of this book guide the business manager through the accounting techniques that are needed to implement a microcomputer.

300. Watson, Hugh J., and Carroll, Arthie B. *Computers for Business: A Managerial Emphasis.* Dallas, TX: Business Publications, Inc., 1980. 530 p.
This book provides a broad managerial understanding of computers and their functions, applications, and implications for business.

301. Weidlein, James R., and Cross, Thomas B. *Networking Personal Computers in Organizations.* Homewood, IL: Dow Jones-Irwin, 1985. 250 p.
The authors offer managers who deal with PC networks, guidelines on the PC as a networking tool, organizational personal computing, and the human factor in automation.

302. Wiener, Norman. *Personal Computers: Gaining the Competitive Edge in Sales and Marketing.* New York: Alexander Hamilton Institute, 1983. 180 p.
Written primarily for sales managers, this book is a how-to book to make a microcomputer work in the job.

303. Wilcox, Russell E. *Computer and Microcomputer Systems for Small Businesses.* Phoenix, AZ: Oryx Press, 1984. 242 p.
This book gives a straightforward explanation of how to assess what is available today in the computer industry and tells how to automate the business successfully.

304. Woodwell, Donald R. *Managing Personal Computer Workstations: A Corporate Resource.* Homewood, IL: Dow Jones-Irwin, 1984. 208 p.
This book discusses the many questions business people have regarding how to manage and use a personal computer workstation in the business and tells how to handle computer expansion.

305. Woodwell, Donald R. *Using and Applying the Dow Jones Information Services.* Homewood, IL: Dow Jones-Irwin, 1985. 200 p.
This book shows how databases can be used in investing, corporate planning, education and communications, and how this data can be analyzed and interpreted.

11. DECISION MAKING

306. Bentley, Trevor J. *Making Information Systems Work for You.* Englewood Cliffs, NJ: Prentice-Hall, Inc., 1983. 178 p.
This test provides a concise, commonsense guide to the problem of providing information for making decisions in the workplace.

307. Donaldson, Gordon, and Lorsch, Jay W. *Decision Making at the Top.* New York: Basic Books, Inc., 1983. 208 p.
This book provides a look at how decisions are made inside the executive suite, based on interviews with top executives of a dozen leading corporations.

308. Henshaw, Richard C., and Jackson, James R. *The Executive Game.* 4th ed. Homewood, IL: Richard D. Irwin, Inc., 1984. 206 p.
This book shows the reader how to practice the art and science of planning and decision making at the level of top management. Two models of this game are included in this new edition.

309. Janger, Allen R., and Berenbeim, Ronald E.. *External Challenges to Management Decisions: A Growing International Business Problem.* New York: Conference Board, Inc., 1981. 68 p.
This book reports the results of a study by The Conference Board on the impact of outsider activity on company decision making.

310. Johnson, Rossall J. *Executive Decisions: Organization Development—Management Control—Executive Responsibility.* 3d ed. Cincinnati, OH: South-Western Publishing Co., 1976. 635 p.
By studying the 59 cases in this book, the reader can get a cross section of decision-making situations that have faced top management.

311. Makridakis, Spyros, and Wheelwright, Steven C., eds. *The Handbook of Forecasting: A Manager's Guide.* New York: John Wiley & Sons, Inc., 1982. 602 p.
This book stresses that the role of forecasting is not just a staff function but involves management tasks of planning and decision making.

312. Steiss, Alan Walter. *Strategic Management and Organizational Decision Making.* Lexington, MA: Lexington Books, 1986. 256 p.
A strategic management system that is applicable to all complex organizations is developed in this book.

12. ENERGY USE

313. *Auditing and Managing Energy Use in Small Industrial & Commercial Facilities.* Rye, NY: Raymont Associates, 1977. 25 p.
This brief report looks at some simple methods that management can use to analyze energy use, determine places where energy savings can be made, and estimate possible cost savings.

314. *Energy Management for Small Business.* Chicago: City of Chicago, 1982. 104 p.
This energy management manual is designed to help a company save significant amounts of money each year by using certain techniques to reduce energy consumption while at the same time maintaining sales volume and customer and employee comfort.

315. *Reducing Energy Costs in Small Business.* Reston, VA: Reston Publishing Co., Inc., 1983. 179 p.
This book serves as a guide to reducing energy costs for small business owners and focuses on the increased cost of energy in the 1980s. Topics range from lighting and temperature control to future sources of energy.

13. ENTREPRENEURSHIP

316. Ballas, George C., and Hollas, David. *The Making of an Entrepreneur: Keys to Your Success.* Englewood Cliffs, NJ: Prentice-Hall, Inc., 1980. 245 p.
Complete with humorous illustrations, this book is written in an effort to help the budding entrepreneur formulate a plan of action, put the idea or service into production, and make a profit at the same time.

317. Baty, Gordon B. *Entrepreneurship for the Eighties.* Reston, VA: Reston Publishing Co., Inc., 1981, 238 p.
This book focuses on the problems of a growth-oriented new enterprise.

318. Baumback, Clifford M. *Guide to Entrepreneurship.* Englewood Cliffs, NJ: Prentice-Hall, Inc., 1981. 235 p.
Directed toward business owner/managers, this book stresses the process of new business formation and discusses the trials and risks of business ownership.

319. Brandt, Steven C. *Entrepreneuring: The Ten Commandments for Building a Growth Company.* Reading, MA: Addison-Wesley Publishing Co., 1982. 193 p.
This book provides a business plan to map the winning course for the new entrepreneur.

320. Brodie, Earl D. *When Your Name Is on the Door.* New York: Books in Focus, Inc., 1981. 264 p.
This easy-to-read account of how to run your own business tells how the entrepreneur can see him/herself as a unique individual.

321. Brown, Deaver. *The Entrepreneur's Guide.* New York: Ballantine Books, 1980. 209 p.
This book can help you evaluate an entrepreneurial career by looking at new venture life-styles, describing entrepreneurial personality traits, and by outlining the risks involved in becoming an entrepreneur.

322. Buskirk, Richard H., and Vaughn, Percy J. *Managing New Enterprises.* St Paul, MN: West Publishing Co., 1976. 485 p.
This comprehensive reference book takes the reader from the initial planning stages through the financing, management, marketing, growth, and the sale of a business.

323. Christy, Ron, and Jones, Billy M. *The Complete Information Bank for Entrepreneurs and Small Business Managers.* Wichita, KS: Center for Entrepreneurship and Small Business Management, 1982. 293 p.
Divided into ten major sections of interest to the small business person, this book provides an annotated bibliography on all aspects of business, covering more than a 20-year period.

324. Church, Olive D. *Small Business Management and Entrepreneurship.* Chicago: Science Research Associates, 1984. 514 p.
Written primarily for those who plan, organize, finance, and operate their own businesses, this book discusses all these areas in detail.

325. Deeks, John. *The Small Firm Owner-Manager: Entrepreneurial Behavior and Management Practice.* New York: Praeger Publishers, 1976. 360 p.
The author of this book highlights the gap between theories about behavior and management practices of owner-managers.

326. Drucker, Peter F. *Innovation and Entrepreneurship: Practice and Principles.* New York: Harper & Row, 1985. 277 p.
One of America's leading management authors discusses the emergence of entrepreneurship as a relevant force in today's society. He emphasizes systematic management and focused strategies for the new entrepreneur.

327. Gevirtz, Don. *The New Entrepreneurs: Innovation in American Business.* New York: Penguin Books, 1984. 223 p.
Some of the topics discussed in this book include the entrepreneur and the establishment, how to make it as an outsider, and financing a business.

328. Hisrich, Robert D., ed. *Entrepreneurship, Intrapreneurship, and Venture Capital: The Foundations of Economic Renaissance.* Lexington, MA: Lexington Books, 1986. 160 p.
Some of the country's foremost experts tell what businesses and policymakers need to do in order to develop and nurture entrepreneurial success.

329. Hosmer, LaRue T.; Cooper, Arnold C.; and Vesper, Karl H. *The Entrepreneurial Function: Text and Cases on Smaller Firms.* Englewood Cliffs, NJ: Prentice-Hall, Inc., 1977. 484 p.
The authors of this book discuss the following topics as they relate to small business: marketing management, marketing research, operations management, financial management, product development, formation, consolidation, and expansion.

330. Kent, Calvin A., ed. *The Environment for Entrepreneurship.* Lexington, MA: Lexington Books, 1984. 191 p.
The material in this book, taken from a series of lectures, covers such topics as the entrepreneurial process, fiscal environment, taxation, regulation, patents, European environment and new entrepreneurs.

331. Kent, Calvin A.; Sexton, Donald L.; and Vesper, Karl H. *Encyclopedia of Entrepreneurship.* Englewood Cliffs, NJ: Prentice-Hall, Inc., 1982. 425 p.
This state-of-the-art book of research in entrepreneurship summarizes and categorizes material about the entrepreneur and examines research currently being done as well as telling what needs to be done.

332. Kets de Vries, Manfred F. R. "The Dark Side of Entrepreneurship." *Harvard Business Review* 63 (November–December 1985): 160–67.
This author describes the behavior patterns that entrepreneurs have in common and looks at how they affect their companies.

333. Krefetz, Gerald. *More than a Dream: Being Your Own Boss.* New York: American Management Associations, 1980. 10 p.
This book looks at some people who own small businesses and discusses their observations and insights.

334. Leavitt, Harold J. *Corporate Pathfinders: Building Vision and Values into Organizations.* Homewood, IL: Dow Jones-Irwin, 1985. 200 p.
This book provides information on how individuals at every level can shape their organizations through the development of their instincts, beliefs, and values.

335. MacFarlane, William N. *Principles of Small Business Management.* New York: McGraw-Hill Book Co., 1977. 534 p.
This book offers the entrepreneur everything he/she needs to know about small business ownership. It is presented in a question and answer format.

336. Mancuso, Joseph R. *A Diagnostic Test for Entrepreneurs.* Worcester, MA: The Center for Entrepreneurial Management, 1979. 16 p.
This book contains a series of questions and answers for the entrepreneur.

337. Mancuso, Joseph R. *No Guts, No Glory: How to Fight Dirty against Management.* Port Washington, NY: Ashley Books, 1976. 221 p.
This satirical book discusses internal techniques used by entrepreneurs in fighting dirty against management.

338. Mancuso, Joseph R. *The Small Business Survival Guide: Sources of Help for Entrepreneurs.* Englewood Cliffs, NJ: Prentice-Hall, Inc., 1980. 422 p.
A brief overview of how to handle the following areas of running a small business are included in this book: advertising, bankruptcy, business plans, franchising, data processing, marketing, minority businesses, patents.

339. Mancuso, Joseph R. *Sources of Help for Entrepreneurs.* Worcester, MA: Center for Entrepreneurial Management, 1979. 376 p.
This book contains an annotated list of little known places that help small business people.

340. Meredith, Geoffrey G.; Nelson, Robert E.; and Neck, Philip. *The Practice of Entrepreneurship.* Washington, DC: International Labour Office, 1982. 196 p.
This book provides help for would-be entrepreneurs and management advisers interested in developing their entrepreneurial skills.

341. Meyers, Herbert S. *Minding Your Own Business.* Homewood, IL: Dow Jones-Irwin, 1984. 128 p.
This book shows how owners of small businesses can capitalize on today's consumer environment through the use of intelligence and creativity.

342. Persons, Edgar A. *Be Your Own Boss: Introducing Entrepreneurship.* Arlington, VA: American Vocational Association, Inc., 1982. 23 p.
This book looks at ten basic questions for the person aspiring to be an entrepreneur.

343. Pickle, Hal B. *Small Business Management.* 3d ed. New York: John Wiley & Sons, Inc., 1984. 645 p.
By combining theory and practical applications, this book gives a conceptual view of small ownership.

344. Pinchot, Gifford, III. *Intrepreneuring.* New York: Harper & Row, 1985. 368 p.
While this book discusses entrepreneurship within the major corporation, many of its suggestions have applicability for the smaller firm. Particularly useful is its discussion of the planning cycle.

345. Posner, Mitchell J. *Executive Essentials.* New York: Avon Books, 1982. 627 p.
This approach to critical issues in business tells how to play the power game.

346. Ronen, Joshua, ed. *Entrepreneurship.* Lexington, MA: Lexington Books, 1983. 323 p.
A collection of writings by professionals, this book reasseses the role of creative entrepreneurship.

347. Rostadt, Robert C. *Entrepreneurship.* Dover, MA: Lord Publishing, 1985. This book provides information on new concepts, case histories, and resource information necessary for entrepreneurs.

348. Sexton, Donald L., and Smilor, Raymond W., eds. *The Art and Science of Entrepreneurship.* Cambridge, MA: Ballinger Publishing Co., 1985. 388 p.
This book focuses on the key practical and theoretical issues that define American business's fastest growing phenomenon.

349. Sexton, Donald L., and Van Auken, Philip M. *Experiences in Entrepreneurship and Small Business Management.* Englewood Cliffs, NJ: Prentice-Hall, Inc., 1982. 248 p.
This book provides an introduction to the process of starting and managing a small business. It includes 45 learning exercises that depict the daily events of entrepreneurs.

350. Shilling, Dana. *Be Your Own Boss.* New York: William Morrow and Co., Inc., 1983. 385 p.
This practical guide to owning your own business discusses such topics as how much money you need to start a business and how to get it, office space, employees and alternatives, recordkeeping, taxes, business forms, and much more.

351. Shook, Robert L. *The Entrepreneurs: Twelve Who Took Risks and Succeeded.* New York: Harper & Row, 1980. 181 p.
This book contains the stories of 12 men and women who succeeded in building successful enterprises.

352. Silver, A. David. *The Entrepreneurial Life: How to Go for It and Get It.* New York: John Wiley & Sons, Inc., 1983. 244 p.
The author of this book helps to answer three questions: 1. Do you have the heart to become an entrepreneur? 2. How do you become an entrepreneur? 3. How does an entrepreneur ensure success?

353. Siropolis, Nicholas C. *Small Business Management: A Guide to Entrepreneurship.* Boston: Houghton Mifflin Co., 1982. 570 p.
The entire spectrum of entrepreneurship, from the business plan to computers, from marketing research to social responsiblility, is covered in this book.

354. Smilor, Raymond W., and Kuhn, Robert Lawrence, eds. *Corporate Creativity: Robust Companies and the Entrepreneurial Spirit.* New York: Praeger Publishers, 1984. 148 p.
Included in this book are discussions on the entrepreneurial process,

sources of capital for small businesses, entrepreneurial activities and characteristics, and streamlining operations.

355. Stevens, Mark. *The 10-Minute Entrepreneur.* New York: Warner Books, 1985. 250 p.
Sources of management insight and information are included in this book along with some little-known strategies for making and saving money on business ventures.

356. Stevenson, Howard H., and Gumpert, David E. "The Heart of Entrepreneurship." *Harvard Business Review* 64 (March–April 1985): 85–94.
This article describes the anatomy of entrepreneurship by answering such questions as where the opportunities are and how you can capitalize on them, what resources are needed, and what structure is best.

357. Sullivan, Daniel J., and Lane, Joseph F. *Small Business Management: A Practical Approach.* Dubuque, IA: W.C. Brown, 1983. 527 p.
Focusing on the practical aspect of entrepreneurship, this book is divided into three major parts: starting a business, managing a business, and operating a business.

358. Van Voorhis, Kenneth R. *Entrepreneurship and Small Business Management.* Boston: Allyn and Bacon, Inc., 1980. 565 p.
This author has provided practicing managers with a book arranged in an "as needed" sequence.

359. Vesper, Karl H. *New Venture Strategy.* Englewood Cliffs, NJ: Prentice-Hall, Inc., 1980. 303 p.
This book describes the different kinds of entrepreneurial ventures and indicates the types of strategies needed.

360. Vesper, Karl H. *Review of New Venture Strategies.* Englewood Cliffs, NJ: Prentice-Hall, Inc., 1980. 303 p.
This book begins with an overview of entrepreneurship that concentrates on the human aspects of the entrepreneur as a person.

14. ESTATE PLANNING

361. Brogan, Frances B., Jr. *Estate Planning for Owners of Closely Held Corporations.* Englewood Cliffs, NJ: Institute for Business Planning, 1982. (Loose leaf)
This books provides information on all aspects of estate planning for the closely held business including how to transfer control and management at a minimum tax cost, information on using corporate funds to pay estate taxes, and estate planning benefits.

362. *Estate and Financial Planning for the Closely Held Business, 1983.* New York: Practising Law Institute, 1983. 848 p.
This book covers discussions on the Economic Recovery Tax Act, postmortem estate planning techniques for the closely held corporation,

corporate buy-sell agreements, life insurance, installment sales, and financial and estate planning for executives.

363. *Estate Planning for Interests in a Closely Held Business: Resource Materials.* Philadelphia, PA: American Law Institute-American Bar Association, Committee on Continuing Professional Education, 1981. 500 p.
An analysis of the problems that are encountered in connection with estate planning in a business.

364. *Estate Planning in Depth.* 6th ed. Philadephia, PA: American Law Institute-American Bar Association, 1981. 2 v.
This two-volume set outlines material written for a course of study on Estate Planning in Depth at the University of Wisconsin. Volume two deals with estate planning for the closely held business, the corporate executive, joint tenancy, and valuation problems that occur in a closely held business.

365. Howell, John C. *Estate Planning for the Small Business Owner: Avoid Personal Liability, Legal Fees, and Unnecessary Expenses.* Englewood Cliffs, NJ: Prentice-Hall, Inc., 1980. 153 p.
Topics discussed in this book include what estate planning is and some early steps in effective estate planning, information on the unified estate and gift tax schedule, joint ownership of property, how to write your own will as a part of your estate planning, and statutory provisions of all 50 states.

366. Looney, J. W. *Estate Planning for Business Owners.* Reston, VA: Reston Publishing Co., Inc., 1979. 291 p.
Some of the topics covered in this book include the probate problem, the taxation problem, the importance of early estate planning, life insurance, transfer of interest in the family owned partnership, and the merchant plan.

367. Weisz, Frank B. *An Estate Planner's Guide to Business Agreements and Estate Planning Documents.* Rev. ed. Rockville Center, NY: Farnsworth Publishing Co., 1981. 223 p.
This book covers such topics as sale of busines interests, deferred compensation and estate planning as well as insurance plans and employee benefit plans.

15. FINANCE (BANKING, TAXES, INSURANCE, PENSIONS)

368. Allen, Everett T., Jr.; Melone, Joseph J.; and Rosenbloom, Jerry S. *Pension Planning: Pensions, Profit Sharing, and Other Deferred Compensation Plans.* Homewood, IL: Richard D. Irwin, Inc., 1985. 900 p.
This book focuses on retirement plan objectives. The new edition has been updated regarding ERISA and other recent legislative developments.

369. Archbold, T. Ross. *Accounting for Pension Costs and Liabilities: A Reconciliation of Accounting and Funding Practice.* Toronto, Ontario: The Canadian Institute of Chartered Accountants, 1980. 226 p.
This book provides accountants and other users of financial information with an understanding of the underlying economic realities of actuarial science, accounting principles, and disclosures necessary in their business.

370. Aydon, Cyril. *How to Finance Your Company.* London: Business Books, Ltd., 1976. 206 p.
This reference book provides a source of ideas, advice and information on company financing, mainly for small- to medium-sized private companies.

371. *A Banker's Guide to Small Business Loans.* Washington, DC: American Bankers Association, Small Business Credit Committee, 1978. 53 p.
This booklet contains information on small business lending and processing small business loans. The final part discusses the various ways a small business can be assisted by the Small Business Administration.

372. Barker, Michael, ed. *Financing State and Local Economic Development.* Durham, NC: Duke University Press, 1983. 480 p.
The four main topics covered in this book are innovations in development finance, pension funds and economic renewal, venture capital and urban development, and banking and small business.

373. Bernstein, Leopold A. *Analysis of Financial Statements.* 2d ed. Homewood, IL: Dow Jones-Irwin, 1984. 381 p.
This book provides information on the tools and techniques necessary for analyzing financial statements.

374. Blackman, Irving L. *Your Business—America's Best Tax Shelter.* Chicago: Blackman, Kallick & Co., 1983. 46 p.
This book tells how to use your business as a tax shelter. It covers information on starting your business, the lifetime of the business, and ending the business.

375. Block, Julian. *Julian Block's Guide to Year-Round Tax Savings, 1985.* 5th ed. Homewood, IL: Dow Jones-Irwin, 1985. 343 p.
This book provides practical and effective legal tax angles that can reduce your tax bill.

376. Bradway, Bruce M., and Prichard, Robert E. *Protecting Profits during Inflation and Recession.* Reading, MA: Addison-Wesley Publishing Co., 1981. 224 p.
Suggestions on how to preserve your business in uncertain times are given in this book. In addition, the authors discuss such topics as automating the small business, marketing, advertising, taxes, and energy management.

377. Braverman, Jerome D. *Maximizing Profits in Small- and Medium-Sized Businesses.* New York: Van Nostrand Reinhold Co., Inc., 1984. 229 p.
This text focuses on the responsibility of the business manager to avoid profit erosion.

378. *Budgeting: A Tool for Planning Profit and Control.* Monterey, CA: Management Information Studies, 1985. 118p.
The framework provided in this book can help you coordinate operations, measure performance, and control results in line with company objectives.

379. Butler, David H. *An Income Tax Planning Model for Small Business.* Ann Arbor, MI: UMI Research Press, 1981. 324 p.
This revision of the author's 1978 thesis discusses the types of small business ownership and relates the tax laws to these types of organizations.

380. Butler, Robert, and Rappaport, Donald. *Money and Your Business: How to Get It, How to Manage It, How to Keep It.* New York: New York Institute of Finance, 1982. 6 v. in 2.
This series of guides is designed to assist the entrepreneur through the entire life cycle of the business.

381. *Buying Power: The Exercise of Market Power by Dominant Buyers; Report.* Paris, France: Organization for Economic Co-operation and Development, 1981. 178 p. (Available from OECD Publications and Information Center.)
This book studies the nature and existence of buying power with emphasis on giving and receiving unfair or discriminatory prices, terms, or conditions.

382. Campbell, Malcolm J. *Financial Directories of the World: A Guide to Information Sources in Finance, Economics, Employment, Property and the Law.* Guernsey, British Isles: Vallancy Reference Books, Ltd., 1982. 338 p.
This book contains a record of directory materials relating to financing or economic activities and financial information on specific organizations.

383. Channon, Derek F. *The Service Industries: Strategy, Structure and Financial Performance.* New York: Holmes & Meier Publishers, Inc., 1978. 292 p.
While mainly dealing with large service industries in Great Britain, this book examines the strategic and structural development of these industries and corrolates these with the firms' financial performances.

384. Chase, Anthony G., et al. *Small Business Financing: Federal Assistance & Contracts.* Colorado Springs, CO: Shepard's/McGraw-Hill, 1983. 398 p.
Some of the topics covered in this book include the Small Business Administration loan programs, long-term financing, government procurement, and special purpose assistance.

385. Coltman, Michael M. *Financial Control for the Small Business: A Practical Primer for Keeping a Tighter Rein on Your Profits and Cash Flow.* Seattle, WA: Self-Counsel Press Inc., 1982. 119 p.
This book discusses such topics of interest to the small business person as financial statements, depreciation, income statement and balance sheet analysis, cost management, fixed and variable costs, budgeting, cash management, and leasing.

386. Coltman, Michael M. *A Practical Guide to Financial Management: Tips and Techniques for the Non-Financial Manager.* Seattle, WA: Self-Counsel Press, Inc., 1984. 137 p.
This book illustrates some practical ideas and methods useful in improving the profitability of a small business.

387. *Computer Finance and Leasing: Recent Trends in Financing and Marketing.* New York: Practising Law Institute, 1982. 880 p.
The writings in this book discuss such topics as computer leasing, venture capital financing, R&D, partnerships, and protecting rights in employee innovations.

388. *The Corporate Finance Sourcebook 1985.* New York: Corporate Finance Sourcebook. (Annual)
This book lists over 2,500 firms and 12,000 individuals who can help answer questions on all aspects of business finance.

389. Costello, Dennis R.*New Venture Analysis: Research, Planning and Finance.* Homewood, IL: Dow Jones-Irwin, 1985. 190 p.
This book provides a framework on how to analyze investment opportunities in new ventures within existing firms.

390. Crestol, Jack, and Schneider, Herman M. *Tax Planning for Investors.* Homewood, IL: Dow Jones-Irwin, 1985. 241 p.
This book reflects the recent developments and changes in tax law.

391. Davey, Patrick J. *New Patterns in Organizing for Financial Management.* New York: Conference Board, Inc., 1983. 45 p.
This book reports on a survey of more than 240 companies on the financial management functions of their companies.

392. Day, Theodore, E.; Stoll, Hans R.; and Whaley, Robert E. *Taxes, Financial Policy, and Small Business.* Lexington, MA: Lexington Books, 1985. 167 p.
The authors of this book tell how small businesses set their financial policies and includes some facts about the effects of current tax policies on small business.

393. Diener, Royce. *How to Finance Your Growing Business.* Englewood Cliffs, NJ: Prentice-Hall, Inc., 1981. 387 p.
Some of the areas covered in this book include the different types of capital available, equity, unsecured borrowing for working capital, secured growth capital loans, time sales, packaging, acquisition, international finance, public stock issues, and much more.

394. *Economic Indicators.* Washington, DC: U.S. Government Printing Office. (Monthly)
This publication contains economic information on prices, purchasing power, credit, wages, money, production, and federal finance.

395. Ellerbach, Richard J. *Tax Reduction Strategies for Small Business.* Englewood Cliffs, NJ: Prentice-Hall, Inc., 1982. 145 p.
This book provides a step-by-step approach to wealth accumulation for small business owners through tax planning.

396. Ellis, John. *The New Financial Guide for the Self-Employed.* Chicago: Contemporary Books, Inc., 1981. 295 p.
This book discusses some common concerns for the self-employed, tells what specialists can do for you, discusses the importance of insurance, tells where to borrow money, find customers and make sales, covers time management, and collecting overdue bills.

397. Ernst & Whinney. *Deciding to Go Public.* Akron, OH: Privately Owned & Emerging Businesses, 1984. 139 p.
The process of going public is discussed as well as how to identify important planning considerations.

398. Ferner, Jack D. *How to Read, Understand, and Use Financial Reports.* New York: John Wiley & Sons, Inc., 1984. 256 p.
By using a self-teaching format, this author offers a concise guide explaining how to read a financial report and how to evaluate the figures and use them in decision making.

399 *Financial Records for Small Business.* San Francisco, CA: Bank of America, 1984. 19 p.
An overview of the flow of financial information through a business's accounting system is provided.

400. *Financial Studies of the Small Business.* Washington, DC: Financial Research Associates. (Annual)
The financial operations of approximately 50 types of businesses are included in this book. They are based on 25,000 financial statements of firms with capital under $250,000.

401. *Financing Your Business.* Washington, DC: Price Waterhouse, 1984. 65 p.
This guide, in the series for smaller businesses, covers information on how to obtain funds for a start-up situation or a going concern as well as for expansion.

402. Flesher, Dale L., ed. *Tax Tactics for Small Businesses: Pay Less Taxes Legally.* University, MS: Small Business Development Center and Bureau of Business Administration, University of Mississippi, 1980. 125 p.
This book brings together many tax-saving ideas that can be used by small business persons. It is written in nontechnical language.

403. Freiermuth, Edmond P. *Revitalizing Your Business.* Chicago: Probus Publishing Co., 1985. 171 p.
This author offers advice on how to manage your way out of several business crises, by using the bankruptcy process if all else fails.

404. *Futures Market Service.* New York: Commodity Research Bureau. (Weekly)
Known as the "blue sheet," this publication reports on the factors that influence commodity prices.

405. Fytenbak, I. M. *How to Obtain Financing and Make "Your Best Deal" with Any Bank, Finance or Lending Company!* Santa Clara, CA: Cambrian Financial Corp., 1980. 353 p.
This book offers solutions and practical ideas on how to improve your business finances, accounting, and planning for future growth.

406. Garcia, F. L. *Encyclopedia of Banking and Finance.* 8th ed. Boston: Bankers Publishing Co., 1983. 1,024 p.
Not only does this book cover the entire area of banking and finance, this new edition includes information on the rapid changes in this area.

407. Gargan, John Joseph. *Milking Your Business for All It's Worth: Tax-Saving Opportunities for Small Business.* Englewood Cliffs, NJ: Prentice-Hall, Inc., 1982. 137 p.
This book offers acccurate and authoritive information regarding tax saving opportunities for small business.

408. Garn, Harvey A., and Ledebur, Larry C. *The Role of Small Business Enterprise in Economic Development.* Washington, DC: U.S. Government Printing Office, 1981. 31 p.
This revision of a 1980 paper provides information on the economic development objectives of the small firm, employment potential, and cost/benefit ratios.

409 Gart, Alan. *The Future of Financial Services: Strategies for the Small Banks, Thrifts, and Insurance Companies.* Lexington, MA: Lexington Books, 1985.
This book looks at what will happen to small banks and insurance companies as more of the corporate giants buy into the financial services industry.

410. Gmur, Charles J., ed. *Trade Financing.* New York: Business Press International, Ltd., 1981 190 p.
This handbook describes the techniques available in trade financing and compares their advantages and disadvantages as well as giving suggestions on how and when they are best applied.

411. Goldberg, James M., et al. *Tax Planning for Small Business.* Washington, DC: James M. Goldberg, 1980. 51 p.
Suggestions on how to maximize returns from the business as well as how to minimize the amount paid to the government are covered in this book.

412. Goldstein, Arnold S. *Strategies and Techniques for Saving the Financially Distressed Small Business.* New York: Pilot Books, 1976. 48 p.
The author begins this book by evaluating a troubled business and follows with some remedies for the insolvent business; a discussion of creditors and credit, mergers, spin-offs, and consolidations.

413. Gourgues, Harold W., Jr. *Financial Planning Handbook: A Portfolio of Strategies and Applications.* New York: New York Institute of Finance, 1983. 443 p.

Beginning with a definition of financial planning as an ongoing process, this book goes on to present a segmented approach on how to use the financial planning process to achieve the accumulation, preservation, and distribution of wealth.

414. Green, Mark Richard. *Insurance and Risk Management for Small Business.* 3d ed. Washington, DC: U.S. Small Business Administration, Management Assistance Division. Support Services Section, 1981. 93 p. (For sale by U.S. Government Printing Office.)

This book discusses the various types of insurance and tells how to manage an insurance program for a small business.

415. Gup, Benton E., and Kitchin, Thomas W. *How to Ask for a Business Loan.* Richmond, VA: R. F. Dame, Inc., 1981. 34 p.

Divided into five main parts, this book shows the correct way to ask for a bank loan and includes information on several kinds of liens and their costs, the assets used for collateral, the terms used by bankers, and a list of further readings.

416. Hampton, John J. *Modern Financial Theory: Perfect and Imperfect Markets.* Reston, VA: Reston Publishing Co., Inc., 1982. 430 p.

This book makes difficult financial concepts understandable and covers the three most important areas of financial policy and theory: investment policy, capital structure/cost of capital, and dividend policy.

417. Hansen, Derek. *Banking and Small Business.* Washington, DC: Council of State Planning Agencies, 1981. 113 p.

This book discusses the performance and growth of small business and financing through private and public resources.

418. Hargrove, John O., ed. *Personal Tax Planning for Professionals and Owners of Small Businesses.* Berkeley, CA: California Continuing Education of the Bar, 1985. 434 p.

This book covers such topics as incorporation of professionals and executives; personal investments; tax planning; and going out of business.

419. Hayes, Rick Stephan. *Business Loans: A Guide to Money Sources and How to Approach Them Successfully.* 2d ed. Boston: CBI Publishing Co., Inc., 1980. 423 p.

This book is a practical guide to help the average business person learn about loans and be able to prepare loan applications for the company.

420. Heald, Stephen W. *How to Prepare and Use Cash Flow Projections.* Worcester, MA: Center for Entrepreneurial Management, 1979. 48 p.

The necessary knowledge on how to obtain loans and prepare budgets by the CPA-oriented small business are presented in this pamphlet.

421. Holtz, Herman. *2001 Sources of Financing for Small Business.* New York: Arco Publishing, Inc., 1983. 173 p.

This book provides names and addresses of agencies available to small business people who need money for the business, including lists of federal agencies and programs, state agencies, venture capitalists, and Minority Business Development Agency funded organizations.

422. Horvitz, Paul M., and Pettit, R. Richardson, eds. *Small Business Finance.* Greenwich, CT: Jai Press, 1984. 2 v.

This book consists of two volumes, with Volume A concentrating on financial problems and Volume B dealing with sources of finance.

423. *The INC. Executive Compensation Study.* Boston: INC. Executive Compensation Study. (Annual)

Important trends in executive compensation are covered in this book including salary, bonuses, benefits, and perks for CEOs, CFOs, and Chief Operating and Marketing Officers for small to mid-sized companies.

424. Joint Industry/Government Committee on Small Business Financing. *Small Business Financing.* Washington, DC: National Association of Securities Dealers, Inc., 1979. 91 p.

This report highlights the major problems associated with small business financing and offers viable solutions to these problems.

425. Jonovic, Donald J. *Someday It'll All Be Yours, Or Will It?* Cleveland, OH: Jamieson Press, 1984. 186 p.

This book shows how to minimize the family liabilities that drain the company's health while at the same time increasing the "equity" that is unique to family companies, i.e., mutual benefit.

426. Kibel, H. Ronald. *How to Turn around a Financially Troubled Company.* New York: McGraw-Hill Book Co., 1982. 182 p.

Intended for both the executive experiencing a business crisis as well as those with healthy companies who want to improve the company, this book shows how profit and loss control becomes less important in a crisis and how balance sheets take a front seat.

427. Kinsman, Robert. *Low Risk Profits in High Risk Times.* Homewood, IL: Dow Jones-Irwin, 1985. 318 p.

This author shows how to use risk-reducing investment techniques to avoid the dangers to your money caused by today's high risk times.

428. Krentzman, Harvey C. *Managing for Profits.* Washington, DC: U.S. Small Business Administration, 1981. 159 p. (For sale by U.S. Government Printing Office.)

Marketing, purchasing, financial management, taxation, insurance, and other areas of interest to the small business person are covered in this book.

429. Lane, Marc J. *Taxation for Small Business.* 2d ed. New York: John Wiley & Sons, Inc., 1983. 284 p.

Following closely on the heels of the Economic Recovery Tax Act of 1981, this second edition traces tax decision making from basic tax assumptions and organizational issues through the many operational tax opportunities and pitfalls.

430. Lazare, Linda, ed. *The Financial Desk Book.* New York: Simon & Schuster, Inc., 1985. 600 p.
This reference tool offers financial information for investors and financial professionals on tax tables, interest tables, tax law summaries, key dates, and historical charts.

431. Lee, M. Mark, ed. *ESOPs and the Smaller Employer.* New York: AMACOM, 1979. 79 p.
This book contains six articles on the implementation and use of employee stock ownership plans.

432. Levin, Dick. *Buy Low, Sell High, Collect Early and Pay Late: The Manager's Guide to Financial Survival.* Englewood Cliffs, NJ: Prentice-Hall, Inc., 1983. 192 p.
This lighthearted book gives some serious financial advice to the nonfinancial manager of a small business.

433. Loffel, Egon W. *Financing Your Business.* New York: Daniel McKay Co., Inc., 1977. 110 p.
Discusses some areas of financing your business such as are how to estimate your money needs, the financial records you will need, equity capital and venture capital, and money-building strategies.

434. Logue, Dennis E., and Rogalski, Richard J.. *Managing Corporate Pension Plans: The Impacts of Inflation.* Washington, DC: American Enterprise Institute for Public Policy Research, 1984. 68 p.
The authors of this book discuss the issues and problems created by the corporate pension system, including how inflation can affect pensions, its affect on capital asset markets, the performance of pension funds and what can be done about the effect of inflation on pensions.

435. Lynn, Robert J. *The Pension Crisis.* Lexington, MA: Lexington Books, 1983. 192 p.
This book provides an in-depth look at major pension systems, their advantages and disadvantages, how they work, and some thoughts on the future of these systems.

436. McConnell, John J., and Pettit, R. Richardson. *Application of the Modern Theory of Finance to Small Business Firms.* Washington, DC: U.S. Government Printing Office, 1980. 49 p.
This book reviews five basic areas in finance: capital budgeting, cash management, capital structure management, dividend policy, and pricing of financial contracts.

437. McQuown, Judith H. *How to Profit after You Inc. Yourself.* New York: Warner Books, 1985. 280 p.
Such problems as how to get maximum tax savings from your assets, how to profit from a net operating loss, how to rearrange your fiscal year for minimum taxes, and how to avoid the personal holding company trap, are all discussed in this book.

438. Madsen, Claudina, and Walker, John H. *Risk Management and Insurance; A Handbook of Fundamentals.* Washington, DC: National Association of College and University Business Officers, 1983. 76 p.

This book examines risk management as an emerging function in small business institutions and, more precisely, the institution's degree of exposure to the risk of loss, as well as the best method of dealing with that exposure.

439. Mamorsky, Jeffrey D. *Pensions and Profit Sharing Plans: A Basic Guide.* New York: Executive Enterprises Publications Co., Inc., 1977. 301 p.

This manual on the fundamentals of retirement plans describes the types of plans presently in use and discusses some factors to consider when establishing a plan.

440. Martin, Thomas J. *Financing the Growing Business.* New York: Holt, Rinehart and Winston, 1980. 372 p.

The little known financing alternatives that are open to small businesses are discussed in this book.

441. Martin, Thomas J. *Financing the Smaller Business.* Mount Kisco, NY: Center for Video Education, 1981. 330 p.

This course on how to finance a small business is written for the busy business person to take "at your own pace." It contains a video tape and a study guide.

442. Miller, Murray, and Serdahely, Franz. *How to Win the Battle against Inflation with a Small Business.* Wilmington, DE: Enterprise Publishing, Inc., 1980. 163 p.

The authors of this book provide some hints on how the small business person can cope with inflation and protect against inflationary forces.

443. Milling, Bryan E. *Financial Tools for the Non-Financial Executive.* Radnor, PA: Chilton Book Co., 1983. 201 p.

This book shows how to apply important formulas and ratios that serve as the basic tools for financial analysis.

444. Moffat, Donald W. *Concise Desk Book of Business Finance.* 2d ed. Englewood Cliffs, NJ: Prentice-Hall, Inc., 1984. 382 p.

This book was intended as a time-saving reference guide and contains an alphabetical listing of terms associated with business finance.

445. Moore, Geoffrey H. *Business Cycles, Inflation, and Forecasting.* Cambridge, MA: Ballinger Publishing Co., 1983. 504 p.

This analysis for managers tells how recessions affect business cycles and how inflation impacts growth cycles, the effect of federal deficit on business cycles, how price cycles affect profits, and how to forecast for maximum growth.

446. *NFIB Quarterly Economic Report for Small Business.* San Mateo, CA: National Federation of Independent Business. (Quarterly)

This statistical report includes information on price and earnings, dollar sales volume, and capital expenditures in the small business.

447. Nadler, Paul S., and Miller, Richard B. *The Banking Jungle: How to Survive and Prosper in a Business Turned Topsy Turvy.* New York: John Wiley & Sons, Inc., 1985. 447 p.

This book provides a means of survival for the professional American banker and the thrift executive, as well as those who are subject to the impact of banking.

448. Nunes, Morris A. *Operational Cash Flow Management and Control.* Englewood Cliffs, NJ: Prentice-Hall, Inc., 1982. 253 p.
This book is geared toward financial managers and is an attempt at helping them formulate a plan of action for financial operations. For easy reference, each chapter is named for a section of the balance sheet.

449. Oliver, Joseph R. *Big Tax Savings for Small Business.* Wilmington, DE: Enterprise Publishers, 1982. 276 p.
Some of the topics discussed in this book are the tax advantages of owning your business, deductions, losses, tax-sheltered retirement plans, tax tricks, inflation and taxes, incorporating, tax credits, and depreciations.

450. *Pensions and Retirement Planning for Small Businesses and Professionals.* Philadelphia, PA: American Law Insitute-American Bar Association, Committee on Continuing Professional Education, 1983. 651 p.
This course of study covers such topics as design and operation of cash and deferred arrangements, provisions of the Tax Reform Act of 1984, self-employed and S Corporations, interest-free loans, pension laws affecting women and marital rights, and provisions regarding insurance and loans.

451. Platt, Harlan D. *Why Companies Fail.* Lexington, MA: Lexington Books, 1985. 147 p.
This book offers information on the financial causes of business failure and provides some strategies that can be used to guide a company away from bankruptcy and liquidation.

452. Postyn, Sol, and Postyn, Jo Kirschner. *Raising Cash: A Guide to Financing and Controlling Your Business.* Belmont, CA: Lifetime Learning Publications, 1982. 309 p.
These authors offer advice on how to determine the amount of cash you need to operate a business as well as ways to negotiate the best deal for obtaining this cash.

453. Pratt, Shannon P. *Valuing Small Businesses and Professional Practices.* Homewood, IL: Dow Jones-Irwin, 1985. 250 p.
Some of the key issues discussed in this book include working with a business broker, some sources of financing, estate planning, and drafting a purchase agreement that is satisfactory to buyers and sellers.

454. Pring, Martin J. *Technical Analysis Explained.* 2d ed. New York: McGraw-Hill Book Co., 1985. 410 p.
This book is a guide on how to spot investment trends and turning points in business.

455. Purcell, W. R., Jr. *Understanding a Company's Finances: A Graphic Approach.* Boston: Houghton Mifflin Co., 1981. 143 p.
Through the use of diagrams, this book shows how to understand company financial reports in layman's terms.

456. Rao, Dileep. *Handbook of Business Finance and Capital Sources.* 3d ed. Minneapolis, MN: InterFinance Corp., 1982. 662 p.
This book provides names and phone numbers of people to contact in various financial institutions, plus their lending terms and limits.

457. Rausch, Edward N. *Financial Keys to Small Business Profitability.* New York: AMACOM, 1982. 166 p.
With a major focus on the earnings of the business and ways to improve earning, this book is divided into three areas: conservation of business cash, controlling production and costs, and enjoying the financial success of the business.

458. Rausch, Edward N. *Financial Management for Small Business.* New York: AMACOM, 1982. 184 p.
The five sections in this book are: "Your Profit Plan for Start-Up or Growth," "Sources of Money to Implement Your Profit Plan," "Your Fiscal Results Compared with Your Profit Plan," "Building an Estate from Your Business," and "Administering Your Firm's Profitability."

459. Ray, Graham H., and Hutchinson, Patrick J. *The Financing and Financial Control of Small Enterprise Development.* New York: Nicholas Publishing Co., 1983. 141 p.
Written by a British and Australian educator, this book covers such topics as the role of the entrepreneur in small business development, financial facilities, characteristics and control of the small business, and characteristics of growth.

460. Rayburn, Letricia Gayle. *Financial Tools for Marketing Administration.* New York: AMACOM, 1976. 310 p.
This book gives the manager information on financial controls for the administration of marketing cost that will provide a more efficient system for the distribution of products.

461. Robbie, Malcolm; Coulbeck, Neil; and Moulds, Tim. *Lending Packages for Small & Medium-Sized Companies.* London: Croom Helm, Ltd., 1983. 193 p.
This book provides practical guidance for bank managers when they deal with their business customers by offering a financing package to cover the legitimate cash needs of any small or medium-sized company.

462. Rowen, Joseph. *Planning and Budgeting Retail Marketing Communications.* New York: Sales Promotion Division, National Retail Merchants Association, 1981. 95 p.
This book provides a daily guide on how to develop a realistic marketing and promotion budget.

463. Rubin, Richard L., and Goldbert, Philip. *The Small Business Guide to Borrowing Money.* New York: McGraw-Hill Book Co., 1980. 265 p.
This step-by-step guide to raising capital spells out the best ways to get the financing you need at the best terms.

464. Schnepper, Jeff A. *The Professional Handbook of Business Valuation.* Reading, MA: Addison-Wesley Publishing Co., 1982. 346 p.
This book discusses in detail the valuation of assets in the closely held business, as well as the rules and techniques used by professionals in the business valuation field.

465. Silver, A. David. *Up Front Financing: The Entrepreneur's Guide.* New York: John Wiley & Sons, Inc., 1982. 245 p.
Some of the avenues for financing a business discussed in this book include leveraged buy-outs, private venture capital funds, SBICs and MESBICs, research and development grants, public offerings, government guaranteed loans, customer financing, and joint ventures.

466. *Small Business Financing.* Washington, DC: American Bankers Association, 1980. 58 p.
This book offers the small business person help in determining his or her financial needs and provides ways to explore alternative types and sources of financing.

467. Smollen, Leonard E.; Rollinson, Mark; and Rubel, Stanley M. *Sourceguide for Borrowing Capital.* Chicago: Capital Publishing Co., 1977. 440 p.
This book offers research information to help the business owner tap available resources for financing.

468. *Sole Proprietorship Returns.* Washington, DC: Department of the Treasury, Internal Revenue Service. (Annual) (For sale by U.S. Government Printing Office.)
This publication provides annual statistics on sole proprietorships, including receipts, cost of sales and operations, deductions, and net income or deficit.

469. Spiro, Herbert T. *Finance for the Nonfinancial Manager.* 2d ed. New York: John Wiley & Sons, Inc., 1982. 278 p.
This book explores the relevant financial concepts along with demonstrations of their application to the solution of problems that face financial managers.

470. Steinman, Ralph. *Tax Guide for Incorporating a Closely Held Business.* Rev. ed. New York: American Institute of Certified Public Accountants, 1978. 276 p.
This guide to the federal income tax structure as it relates to the incorporation of a closely held business includes discussions on sole proprietorships, partnerships, incorporation of subsidiaries, associations deemed taxable as corporations, and professional corporations.

471. Stevens, Mark. *Profit Secrets for Small Businesses.* Reston, VA: Reston Publishing Co., 1983. 197 p.
This book provides hints on how to slash operating expenses, boost profits, and improve the quality and money-making capabilities of your business.

472. *Studies of Small Business Finance Series.* Washington, DC: Interagency Task Force on Small Business Finance. (Irregular)
This series includes pamphlets on such topics as franchising, banking, credit cards and the financing of small businesses, access to capita

markets through pension funds, SBA loan programs, usury laws, and lease financing.

473. *Survey of Current Business.* Washington, DC: Department of Commerce, Bureau of Economic Analysis. (Monthly) (For sale by U.S. Government Printing Office.)
This publication includes statistical information on foreign and domestic investments and trade information.

474. *Tax Considerations in the Organization of Small Businesses.* Englewood Cliffs, NJ: Prentice-Hall, Inc., 1982. 31 p.
This book provides information on various tax-related decisions you will need to make when starting a business. Addresses sole proprietorship, partnership, regular corporations, and Subchapter S corporations.

475. *Tax Desk Book for the Small Business.* 3d ed. Englewood Cliffs, NJ: Institute for Business Planning, 1979. 511 p.
This book is one of the few tax reference books available for the small business entrepreneur. Some areas covered are Subchapter S, benefits, partnerships, fringe benefits, tax breaks, and depreciation.

476. *Tax Guide for Small Business.* Washington, DC: Department of the Treasury, Internal Revenue Service. (Annual)
The tax responsibilities of the four major forms of business organization are discussed in this publication: sole proprietorship, partnership, corporations, and S corporations.

477. *Tax Recommendations to Aid Small Business.* Washington, DC: AICPA, Federal Tax Division, 1980. 57 p.
This book provides information on the recommendations that developed from a three-year study on tax matters for small businesses.

478. Trotter, Samuel Eugene. *A Primer on Establishing and Financing Business.* Washington, DC: University Press of America, 1979. 53 p.
The basic operating principles and procedures necessary to establish and finance business organizations are included in this book.

479. U.S. Bureau of Economic Analysis. Department of Commerce. *Business Conditions Digest.* Washington, DC: U.S. Government Printing Office. (Monthly)
This publication includes charts and statistical tables useful to business analysts and forecasters on leading economic time series.

480. *Understanding Money Sources.* Washington, DC: U.S. Small Business Administration. Office of Management Assistance, 1980. 47 p. (For sale by U.S. Government Printing Office.)
This self-instructional manual identifies sources of capital, discusses prudent business management and shows how to recognize situations that require additional capital.

481. Valentine, Lloyd M., and Dauten, Carl A. *Business Cycles & Forecasting.* 6th ed. Cincinnati, OH: South-Western Publishing Co., 1983. 460 p.
This book provides the necessary framework for understanding those

factors contributing to the level of national income, as well as economic growth and stability.

482. Walker, Ernest W., and Petty, J. William. *Financial Management of the Small Firm.* Englewood Cliffs, NJ: Prentice-Hall, Inc., 1978. 384 p.
This book provides theoretical and practical information on the development of financial strategies and policies.

483. Walsh, Chapman; Henze, S. G.; and Kelleher, S. E. *Designing Cost-Effective Employee Health Plans.* Elmsford, NY: Pergamon Press, Inc., 1982. 63 p.
All aspects of setting up and fine-tuning an employee health plan successfully are included in this book.

484. Walsh, Francis J. *New Rules for Pension Accounting.* New York: Conference Board, Inc., 1983. 15 p.
This pamphlet reports on current concerns from the Financial Accounting Standards Board regarding pension accounting.

485. Welsh, John A., and White, Jerry F. *Administering the Closely Held Company.* Englewood Cliffs, NJ: Prentice-Hall, Inc., 1980. 350 p.
This book presents the cause and effect of various financial and administrative decisions.

486. Wood, Edward Geoffrey. *Bigger Profits for the Smaller Firm.* London: Business Books, Ltd., 1978. 211 p.
Aimed specifically at directors and senior managers of small and medium-sized firms, this book uses practical experience to illustrate the basic principles on how profits can be increased and maintained and to show how the small firm can survive and prosper.

487. Young, Michael, and Buchanan, Nigel. *Accounting for Pensions.* Cambridge, MA: Woodherd-Faulkner, 1981. 211 p.
This book deals with both the accounting and administrative facets of running a pension system and includes a glossary for terminology definitions.

488. Zwick, Jack. *A Handbook of Small Business Finance.* Washington, DC: U.S. Small Business Administration, Management Assistance Division, Support Services Section, 1981. 57 p. (For sale by U.S. Government Printing Office.)
This book on the principles of financial management provides ways to finance growth and working capital and explains ratio analysis.

16. FRANCHISING

489. Bond, Robert E. *The Source Book of Franchise Opportunities.* Homewood, IL: Dow Jones-Irwin, 1985. 509 p.
This book contains a list of over 1,400 franchise opportunities in the U.S. and Canada by type of business. Full financial and franchisor-service details are included along with a geographical index.

490. *Franchise Opportunities Handbook.* Washington, DC: U.S. Government Printing Office, 1982. 430 p.
This book identifies hundreds of companies in many industries that will grant franchises to qualified applicants. Detailed information about each franchise is included.

491. Friedlander, Mark P., Jr., and Gurney, Gene. *Handbook of Successful Franchising.* New York: Van Nostrand Reinhold Co., Inc., 1981. 458 p.
This comprehensive book provides detailed information about successful franchisors as well as key tips on how to start a franchise business.

492. Mendelsohn, M. *The Guide to Franchising.* 4th ed. Elmsford, NY: Pergamon Press, Inc., 1984. 325 p.
This book covers the entire scope of franchising. This edition includes two new chapters: "Issues in Franchising" and "The British Franchise Association."

493. *Representing the Franchisor and Franchisee.* New York: Practising Law Institute, 1979. 376 p.
This book looks at the legal aspects of franchising including facts on negotiating the franchise agreement and antitrust considerations in franchising.

494. Seltz, David D. *How to Get Started in Your Own Franchised Business: The Latest Shortcuts to Profit and Independence.* Rockville Centre, NY: Farnsworth Publishing Co., 1980. 325 p.
This book provides information on how to select the best franchise business for you.

495. Siegel, W. L. *Franchising.* New York: John Wiley & Sons, Inc., 1983. 206 p.
The author tells you how to make the right moves regarding buying and running a franchised business and how to find the right franchise for you.

496. Whittemore, Meg. "The Great Franchise Boom." *Nation's Business* 72 (September 1984): 20–24.
This article tells of the growth of franchises since the late 1950s. A box is included with questions one should ask before considering a franchise.

17. GENERAL

497. Albert, Kenneth J., ed. *Handbook of Business Problem Solving.* New York: McGraw-Hill Book Co., 1980. 850 p.
This book looks at various methods of professional corporate problem solvers use to solve business problems. These include planning, staffing, marketing, new products, and human resources.

498. Allsopp, J. Michael. *Survival in Business.* London: Business Books, Ltd., 1977. 139 p.
This book deals with business recovery and is concerned mainly with businesses that are failing. The author writes from personal experience and offers strategies for recovery.

499. Armstrong, Donald R. *Strategies for Success in Small Business.* Houston, TX: Bookman House, 1977. 221 p.
Divided into two major parts, this book first discusses management, finance, manufacturing controls, and the foundations of free enterprise. The second part looks at career options and the various aspects involved in success in running a small business.

500. Bannock, Graham. *The Economics of Small Firms: Return from the Wilderness.* Oxford, England: Blackwell, Ltd., 1981. 130 p.
This book discusses the political and economic aspects of small business in England. Suggestions are made for political reform which would encourage stronger governmental support of the small business entrepreneur.

501. Becker, Benjamin M., and Tillman, Fred A.. *The Family Owned Business.* 2d ed. Chicago: Commerce Clearing House, Inc., 1978. 393 p.
Problems and opportunities inherent in the family-owned business are discussed in this book. Two new chapters that have been added to this edition are "Human Behavior and the Family Business" and "Tax Incidences and Tax Techniques."

502. Blagrove, Luanna C. *Untold Facts about the Small Business Game: How to Be Competent in Business.* Manchester, CT: Blagrove Publications, 1980. 171 p.
Written in everyday language, this book looks at the varous aspects involved with operating a small business.

503. Bruchey, Stuart W., ed. *Small Business in American Life.* New York: Columbia University Press, 1980. 391 p.
This book contains essays on the history of small business in the United States.

504. Clifford, Donald K., Jr., and Cavanagh, Richard E.. *The Winning Performance: How America's High-Growth Midsize Companies Succeed.* New York: Bantam Books, 1985. 292 p.
This book reports on a study by McKinsey & Co. on how the nation's most successful midsize companies succeed.

505. Clifton, David S., and Fyffe, David E. *Project Feasibility Analysis: A Guide to Profitable New Ventures.* New York: John Wiley & Sons, Inc., 1977. 340 p.
This step-by-step approach for the preparation of project feasibility studies provides a methodology to answer three questions of the proposal: is the project profitable; how does the investment look in the eyes of society; and does the management have the necessary capabilities?

506. Costello, Dennis R. *Venture Analysis Research, Planning and Finance.* Homewood, IL: Dow Jones-Irwin, 1985. 189 p.
This book provides a framework to use in bringing together various forms of analysis including marketing research, competitor evaluations, cost studies, and the assessment of risks.

507. Curtin, Richard T. *Running Your Own Show: Mastering the Basics of Small Business.* New York: New American Library, 1983. 255 p.
This book is a step-by-step guide to charting your way past potential risks that arise when buying or building your own business.

508. Curtiss, Ellen T., and Untersee, Philip A.. *Corporate Responsibilities and Opportunities to 1990.* Lexington, MA: Lexington Books, 1979. 286 p.
This book looks at several key themes aimed at helping assess the kind of future you may face.

509. Danco, Leon A. *Beyond Survival: A Business Owner's Guide for Success.* Cleveland, OH: Center for Family Business, University Press, 1982. 196 p.
Some of the topics covered in this book include a portrait of the business owner, managing people and money, the gaining of commitments from outside advisors, managing your estate and time, and planning for the future.

510. Danco, Leon A. *Inside the Family Business.* Englewood Cliffs, NJ: Prentice-Hall, Inc., 1980. 248 p.
This book that guides the reader through the life cycle of a successful family business is designed for owners and managers of small, family-owned businesses. Special emphasis is placed on the transition from founder to heirs.

511. Delaney, William A. *Why Small Businesses Fail—Don't Make the Same Mistake Once.* Englewood Cliffs, NJ: Prentice-Hall, 1984. 208 p.
This author first looks at your chances for succeeding in business and includes information on how to avoid pitfalls in planning, legal aspects of the business, finance, operations management, growth, and mergers.

512. Edmunds, Stahrl W., et al. *Urban Small Business Development Report: A Literature Survey and Bibliography.* Riverside, CA: Graduate School of Administration, University of California, Riverside, 1980. 190 p.
This survey of over 400 references plus a 150-page literature survey of major articles on small business problems covers such topics as access to capital, taxation, government regulation, competition, inflation, technological innovation, job generation, and management effectiveness.

513. Gallup, George, Jr., and Gallup, Alec M. *The Great American Success Story: Factors that Affect Achievement.* Homewood, IL: Dow Jones-Irwin, 1985. 250 p.
The authors determine what factors (religion, education, parental influence, etc.) affect a person's success. A question and answer checklist to help the reader determine his or her own "success quotient" is included.

514. German, Paul M. *How to Win the Small Business Game.* Osterville, MA: Small Business Publications, Inc., 1980. 239 p.
The author of this book presents a general overview of how to win in running a small business. He covers such topics as how to determine if you are a winner, a discussion of the first three years in the business, as well as providing information on how to run a successful business.

515. *Guide for Occupation Exploration.* Washington, DC: U.S. Department of Labor, Employment and Training Administration, 1979. 715 p. (For sale by U.S. Government Printing Office.)
This book examines career options that are available in hundreds of career areas. The skill needed to succeed in these areas is also discussed.

516. Gupta, Brijen Kishore, and Lopatin, Arthur D. *Small Business Development in the Inner City Areas of Rochester.* New York: Council on International and Public Affairs, 1978. 241 p.
This book discusses and analyzes the needs, problems, and available resources for small business development in the Rochester area and identifies assistance for the needs of small businesses in the inner city areas.

517. Hahn, James, and Hahn, Lynn. *Aim for a Job in a Small Business Occupation.* New York: Richards Rosen Press, 1980. 156 p.
This book tells about jobs in all kinds of small businesses, what they are, how much you can earn, the necessary qualifications, what the future is, where the jobs are, the working conditions, and some schools where you can learn the job.

518. Hertz, Leah. *In Search of a Small Business Definition: An Exploration of the Small-Business Definitions of the U.S., the U.K., Israel, and the People's Republic of China.* Washington, DC: University Press of America, 1982. 454 p.
This book looks at the study and classification of the existing definitions and meanings of small business throughout the world in order to gain a knowledge and understanding for the formation of a uniform universal definition of small business.

519. *High Technology Industries: Profiles and Outlooks for "Robotics," "Telecommunications," "Computer Industry," and "Semiconductors."* Washington, DC: U.S. Department of Commerce, International Trade Administration, 1983. 4 v. (For sale by U.S. Government Printing Office.)
Information on certain futuristic industries for job hunters is included in this book.

520. Hollander, Edward D. *The Future of Small Business.* New York: Arno Press, 1979. 290 p.
This book examines small business in an economic context. It looks at small business through an analysis of the factors and institutions of the goods and services market as well as the capital and labor markets.

521. Holt, Nancy; Shuchat, Jo; and Regal, Mary Lewis. *Minding Your Own Small Business.* Belmont, MA: CDC Education and Human Development, Inc., 1979. (Loose leaf) (For sale by U.S. Government Printing Office.)
This book includes information on marketing, location, records, pricing, financing, and much more of interest to the small business person.

522. Johnston, J. Phillips L. *Success in Small Business Is a Laughing Matter.* Wake Forest, NC: Meridional Publications, 1982. 182 p.
The various details of transition to and ownership of a small business are looked at in a humorous but frank manner in this book.

523. Koch, Harry Walter. *A California Small Business Handbook.* San Francisco, CA: Ken-Books, 1980. 168 p.
Focusing on small businesses in California, this book is divided into six parts: starting a business, retail and mail order stores, running a business, taxes and government payments, California laws, and miscellaneous.

524. Lawriwsky, Michael. *Corporate Structure and Performance: The Role of Owners, Managers and Markets.* New York: St. Martin's Press, 1984. 286 p.
An anlysis of interacting roles of managers, stockholders, and markets is discussed in this book. The information is based on a ten-year research project involving 226 companies.

525. Levicki, Cyril, ed. *Small Business: Theory and Policy.* London: Croom Helm, 1984. 152 p.
Developed from a series of seminars in Italy and Britain, this book focuses on the examination of techniques needed to create successful small businesses. The three areas stressed are theoretical aspects of small business, economic conditions, and government policy toward small business.

526. Martin, Thomas John, and Bonner, Diane. *Protecting Your Business.* New York: Holt, Rinehart, and Winston, 1980. 183 p.
Written for owners and managers of small companies, this book helps you identify the "what ifs" that come up in running a business and offers suggestions for solving them.

527. Miles, Raymond C. *Basic Business Appraisal.* New York: John Wiley & Sons, Inc., 1984. 399 p.
Beginning with the basic concepts, this book contains 16 chapters that take the reader through the various steps of the appraisal process. Examples of actual appraisal reports are included.

528. Moskowitz, Milton; Katz, Michael; and Levering, Robert. *Everybody's Business: An Almanac.* San Francisco, CA: Harper & Row, Publishers, 1982. 916; 64 p.
This book provides answers to a wide range of questions concerning over 300 large companies, including sales figures, company history, employees, what they own, who owns the company, addresses, stock performance, etc.

529. Mucciolo, Louis. *Small Business: Look before You Leap.* New York: Arco Publishing, Inc., 1981. 290 p.
In addition to a list of publications on small business, this book takes a look at franchising, women as entrepreneurs, and finance in small business.

530. Pepper, Roger S. *Pressure Groups among "Small Business Men."* New York: Arno Press, 1979. 91 p.
This paper presents a preliminary analysis of the small business movement. It portrays the growth of the small business movement and discusses the position of small business as an independent political pressure group.

531. *Problems of Small, High-Technology Firms.* Washington, DC: National Science Foundation, 1981. 34 p.
This booklet summarizes the findings of a survey of 13,000 high-technology companies active in R&D, each with fewer than 500 employees, and discusses their overall perspectives, financial and personnel problems, and government regulations.

532. Rothwell, Roy, and Zegveld, Walter. *Innovation and the Small and Medium-Sized Firm: Their Role in Employment and in Economic Change.* Hingham, MA: Kluwer-Nijhoff Publishing, 1981. 268 p.
This book studies the contribution that small firms can make to technical progress in other cultures as well as their role in the economies of various countries. The author also suggests some new ventures and innovations available to the small firm.

533. Schmitz, Hubert. *Manufacturing in the Backyard.* London: Frances Pinter Publishers, 1982. 232 p.
This study on accumulation and employment in small businesses (ten employees or less) in Brazil offers some hints for any small business person involved in the manufacturing business.

534. Shuchat, Jo; Holt, Nancy; and Regal, Mary Lewis. *Something Ventured, Something Gained.* Belmont, MA: CRC Education and Human Development, Inc., 1979. (Loose leaf) (For sale by U.S. Government Printing Office.)
This book identifies the consumer and competition, break-even analysis, organization, and more.

535. *Small Business Enterprises for Workers with Disabilities.* Falls Church, VA: Institute for Information Studies, 1982. 114 p.
This self-help manual is designed to help workers with disabilities make appropriate small business decisions and to help them find the information and resources they need to seek out self-employment.

536. "Small Business Survival Kit." *Crain's Chicago Business.* 8 (September 16–September 22, 1985): 31–46.
This special section provides several articles of interest to the small business person in the Chicago area as well as tables on Chicago-area asset-based loans, 1985 minority enterprise small business investment corporations, venture capital firms, and small business investment corporations.

537. *Small Manufacturers.* Washington, DC: U.S. Government Printing Office, 1977. 44 p.
This pamphlet gives strategies for self-assessment for the small business person.

538. *Small Ventures: Tactics & Strategies.* Boston: Harvard Business Review Reprint Service, 1980. 80 p.
This book gives some ideas on how to understand and solve the special problems that face small, growing businesses. Topics covered are starting a new venture, planning strategy, financing, cutting costs, expanding marketing, and selling small companies.

539. Springer, John L., ed. *The Complete Guide for Business Owners.* Scarsdale, NY: TPR Publishing Co., 1982. 619 p.
This book tells what is needed to succeed in your own business, how to organize it, finance it, sell your product/service, money management, how to deal with employees, legal information, management, and much more.

540. Sroge, Maxwell. *Inside the Leading Mail Order Houses.* 2d ed. Colorado Springs, CO: Maxwell Sroge Publishing, 1984. 518 p.
This book provides the inside facts on 250 of America's largest mail order companies. Included is information on who owns the companies, who runs them, their history, the number of catalogs mailed, and average orders.

541. *The State of Small Business: A Report of the President Transmitted to the Congress.* Washington, DC: U.S. Government Printing Office. (Annual)
This annual report on small business includes statistics and information on industrial strategies and small firms, the effect of deregulation on small business, financing, employee benefits, women-owned and minority-owned businesses, and an update on the small business database.

542. Stern, Howard H. *Running Your Own Business: A Handbook of Facts and Information for the Small Businessman.* New York: Crown Publishers, 1986. 239 p.
This book includes information on every aspect of business operation.

543. Stevens, Mark. *36 Small Business Mistakes and How to Avoid Them.* West Nyack, NY: Parker Publishing Co., 1980. 191 p.
This book helps you steer around the obvious and the obscure dangers of running a business. The recommendations are all based on actual case histories.

544. Tate, Curtis E. *The Complete Guide to Your Own Business.* Homewood, IL: Dow Jones-Irwin, 1977. 384 p.
This book tells how to own your own business, how to avoid some of the mistakes involved in such a venture, how to get the most from limited economic and human resources, and guides you in the management and operation of the business.

545. *Urban Business Profiles: An Examination of the Opportunities Offered by 18 of the Most Common Types of Small Businesses, and a Guide to Their Establishment and Successful Management.* Detroit, MI: Gale Research Co., 1979. 388 p.
This book offers a profile of 18 studies on various businesses and the plan for preparing a business profile.

546. Vaughn, Roger J. *State Tax Policy and the Development of Small and New Business.* Washington, DC: Coalition of Northeastern Governors Policy Research Center, 1983. 144 p.
This book analyzes the role of both the small business and the new business in national and state economies. It also examines the relationship between federal and state economic policy and small business development. The use of tax policies to aid the small business person is also discussed.

547. Walker, Ernest W., and Petty, J. William. *Financial Management of the Small Firm.* Englewood Cliffs, NJ: Prentice-Hall, Inc., 1978. 382 p.
The authors of this book provide managers of small firms the financial theories used by large firms and some techniques and models that can be used in an analytical framework designed to improve the overall efficiency of the small business.

548. Walker, Ernest W., and Witt, Robert E., eds. *The Dynamic Small Firm.* Austin, TX: Austin Press, 1975. 484 p.
This book formulates a set of theories and principles relating to the successful operation and development of small businesses.

549. Weiner, Ed. *Five Chicks and a Small Business.* Ardmore, PA: Dorrance & Co. Inc., 1981. 143 p.
In relating his experiences of the struggles and successes as a small business person, this author includes some of the challenges he faced, some tried-and-true procedures to follow as well as some pitfalls to watch out for.

550. *Why S.O.B.'s Succeed and Nice Guys Fail in a Small Business.* San Diego, CA: Financial Management Associates, Inc., 1976. 337 p.
This author states that many rules in business are written by big government, big business, and big labor. The small business person has to bend or break these rules at times in order to survive. This book gives some pointers on how to survive in business and deal with these rules.

551. Winter, Elmer L. *Your Future in Your Own Business.* New York: Arco Publishing, Inc., 1977. 187 p.
This author discusses in this book such topics as how to decide whether to go into business, how to be successful in your own business, the best educational background to prepare you for your own business, and a number of other topics of interest to someone who owns their own business.

552. Zeigler, L. Harmon. *The Politics of Small Business.* New York: Arno Press, 1979. 150 p.
This book looks at the political life of American small business. Chapters include organized interest groups, ideologies and conflicts, and how to create a small business agency.

18. GOVERNMENT

553. Bequai, August. *Making Washington Work for You.* Lexington, MA: Lexington Books, 1985. 304 p.
Written by a Washington attorney, this book provides information on how to influence the federal government and use its services professionally, without hiring Washington experts. The book is written in nontechnical language.

554. Casy, William L., Jr.; Marthinsen, John E.; and Moss, Laurence S. *Entrepreneurship, Productivity, and the Freedom of Information Act: Protecting Circumstantially Relevant Business Information.* Lexingon, MA: Lexington Books, 1983. 240 p.
This complete study of the business disclosure practices of government agencies under the Freedom of Information Act combines legal, historical, and economic analysis and offers some policy alternatives.

555. Chappe, Eli. *Winning Government Contracts: A Complete 27-Step Guide for Small Businesses.* Englewood Cliffs, NJ: Prentice-Hall, Inc., 1984. 274 p.
This is a guide for small businesses bidding on government contracts, which enables the reader to learn the process while actually going through the procedure. This guide teaches the small business entrepreneur how to seek and obtain the services and facilities offered to small businesses by the federal government.

556. Cole, Roland J., and Tegeler, Philip D. *Government Requirements of Small Business.* Lexington, MA: Lexington Books, 1980, 174 p.
This book documents the nature of the costs that are imposed by federal, state and local government statutes and regulations on small businesses and suggests ways the small business person may reduce these costs.

557. Ebner, Judy, ed. *How to Sell to the United States Department of Commerce.* Washington, DC: United States Department of Commerce, 1984. 16 p. (For sale by U.S. Government Printing Office.)
This book is prepared especially for small, minority-owned businesses and female-owned businesses. It discusses the missions and functions of the DOC, what it buys, how it buys, and includes procurement information.

558. *Getting Government Help.* Washington, DC: Price Waterhouse, 1984. 63 p.
This book tells you what type of government help is available, where to go to get it, and who to talk to.

559. *Government Finance Statistics Yearbook.* Washington, DC: International Monetary Fund, 1980. 625 p.
Information on government units and accounts, the financial institutions and enterprises that are owned and controlled by the government and national sources of data on government operations are included in this book.

560. *Government Paperwork and Small Business; Problems and Solutions; Paperwork Measurement and Reduction Program.* Washington, DC: Small Business Administration, Office of Advocacy, 1979. 86 p.
This book reports on a study of over 1,000 firms which volunteered to help measure reporting burdens and point out problems in keeping a log of federal, state, and local forms that must be completed. Tables and flow charts are included.

561. *A Guide to Doing Business with the Department of State.* Washington, DC: Bureau of Management, Office of Small and Disadvantaged Business Utilization, 1984. (For sale by U.S. Government Printing Office.)
This book is designed to help the small, minority, and female-owned firms who are seeking to do business with the Department of State to identify procurement opportunities within the department.

562. *Guide to the Defense Acquisition Regulation for Small Business, Small Disadvantaged Business, Women-Owned Business.* Washington, DC: Department of Defense, 1981. 47 p. (For sale by U.S. Government Printing Office.)
This pamphlet explains the basic purchasing rules and regulations of the Department of Defense.

563. *Guide to the Defense Contracting Regulations for Small Business, Small Disadvantaged Business, Women-Owned Small Business.* Washington, DC: U.S. Government Printing Office, 1985. 51 p.
This guide explains the basic purchasing rules and regulations of the Department of Defense. While not intended to locate sales opportunities, the Appendix lists some sources of marketing information.

564. *Handbook for Small Business: A Survey of Small Business Programs of the Federal Government.* 5th ed. Washington, DC: U.S. Government Printing Office, 1984. 228 p.
Information on programs and services offered to small businesses by 25 federal agencies is included in this book.

565. Human Sciences Research, Inc. *Small Business Guide to Federal R&D Funding Opportunities.* Washington, DC: National Science Foundation, 1983. 136 p.
This guide provides the scientifically and technically competent small

business with information concerning opportunities on how to obtain federal funding for R&D activities.

566. *Ideas into Dollars.* Washington, DC: U.S. Small Business Administration, Management Assistant, Support Services Section, 1982. 24 p. (For sale by U.S. Government Printing Office.)
This book provides information on the government and private organizations, programs, and publications, aiding invention and innovation.

567. May, Eleanor G. *A Handbook for Business on the Use of Government Statistics.* Charlottesville, VA: Taylor Murphy Institute, 1979. 159 p.
This handbook provides information on how business people can use government statistics by offering a series of brief case descriptions of actual problem solving via public statistics.

568. Office of the Under Secretary of Defense for Research and Engineering. *Small and Disadvantaged Business Utilization Specialists.* Washington, DC: U.S. Government Printing Office, 1983. 57 p.
This book lists the locations of the Department of Defense procurement offices and gives the names and addresses of their small and disadvantaged business specialists.

569. *Selling to the Military.* Washington, DC: Department of Defense, 1983. 141 p. (For sale by U.S. Government Printing Office.)
This book provides those who have little experience with selling their products or services to the Department of Defense with basic information for locating sales opportunities.

570. *Small and Disadvantaged Business Utilization Specialists: Designed to Assist Small Business, Small Disadvantaged Business, Women-Owned Small Business, and Labor Surplus Area Business Firms.* Washington, DC: Department of Defense, Office of the Secretary of Defense, 1983. 57 p. (For sale by U.S. Government Printing Office.)
This booklet lists by state the offices of business utilization specialists that can provide information on defense procurement procedures, how to get your name placed on bidders' mailing list, and information on prime and subcontract opportunities.

571. *Small Business and Government Research and Development.* Washington, DC: U.S. Government Printing Office, 1978. 41 p.
This book assists the small business owner in determining if he or she qualifies for government R&D contracts and tells how to market these services to the government.

572. *A Small Business Guide to FDA.* Rockville, MD: U.S. Department of Health and Human Services, Public Health Service, Food and Drug Administration, 1982. 17 p.
This book is a ready reference book on how to deal with the FDA. It provides basic information on how to use the *Federal Register*, how to obtain agency documents and FDA statutes and regulations, how to petition the FDA, and how to participate in agency decision making.

573. *Small Business Guide to Federal R&D.* Washington, DC: National Science Foundation, 1980. 265 p.
This guide gives information on business opportunities to small firms working in the area of R&D. Names, addresses and phone numbers of people to contact regarding the programs are also included.

574. *Small Business Guide to Government.* Washington, DC: U.S. Small Business Administration, Office of Advocacy, 1980. 72 p.
In addition to a brief description of the Office of Advocacy, this booklet lists various SBA programs, small business investment companies and organizations, selected executive departments, and agencies of interest to small business.

575. *The States and Small Business: Programs and Activities.* Washington, DC: U.S. Small Business Administration, Office of Advocacy. Annual.
This book provides a list of state support structures, programs, and activities. The small business activities are listed in alphabetical order by state.

576. Stewart, Rodney D., and Stewart, Ann L. *Proposal Preparation.* New York: John Wiley & Sons, Inc., 1984. 319 p.
This book shows how to prepare a proposal or bid primarily for a government contract.

577. Stokes, McNeill, ed. *Conquering Government Regulations: A Business Guide.* New York: McGraw-Hill Book Co., Inc., 1982. 272 p.
This book is intended to create an awareness of the rights of small business owners in dealing with governmental regulations, whether federal, state, or local. Topics include business planning, lobbying, public relations, suing the government, and political action committees.

578. *United States Government Purchasing and Sales Directory: Who Buys What and Where; Who Sells What and Where.* Washington, DC: U.S. Small Business Administration, 1977. 204 p. (For sale by U.S. Government Printing Office.)
This directory is aimed at businesses interested in selling to the U.S. government and lists the purchasing needs of various agencies.

579. Young, Robert S., and O'Hern, Thomas M., Jr. *Small Business Guide to the Defense Acquisition Regulation.* Washington, DC: Logistics Management Institute, 1980. 47 p.
The basic purchasing rules and regulations of the Department of Defense are covered in this book. It does not give assistance in locating sales opportunities.

19. GROWTH

580. Bridge, John, and Dodds, J. C. *Planning and the Growth of the Firm.* London: Croom Helm, Ltd., 1978. 211 p.
This book looks at the economic theories of business behavior including both behavioral and managerial theories.

581. Daniels, Peter. *Service Industries: Growth and Location.* New York: Cambridge University Press, 1982. 100 p.
Provides an introduction to the growth, location, and character of service industries in the urban areas and regions of Great Britain.

582. Fenno, Brooks. *Helping Your Business Grow: 101 Dynamic Ideas in Marketing.* New York: American Management Associations, 1982. 225 p.
Based on the author's experiences with many different companies, this book offers a number of ideas on how to make your business grow.

583. Flink, Salomon J. *Equity Financing of Small Manufacturing Companies in New Jersey.* New York: Arno Press, 1979. 102 p.
This book reports on a study of small manufacturing companies that have experienced rapid growth or that have good prospects for expansion in the near future.

584. Hanan, Mack. *Fast-Growth Management: How to Improve Profits with Entrepreneurial Strategies.* New York: AMACOM, 1979. 145 p.
In addition to "Hanan's Laws," this book tells how to improve profits with entrepreneurial strategies.

585. Hanan, Mack. *High Tech Growth Strategies.* Englewood Cliffs, NJ: Prentice-Hall, Inc., 1983. 183 p.
Stressing market segmentation and key account selling strategies, this book also includes a discussion on the concepts of key account "partnering" and "premium pricing."

586. Hazel, Arthur Curwen, and Reid, A. S. *Enjoying a Profitable Business: A Practical Guide to Successful Growth Techniques for Small Companies.* London: Business Books, Ltd., 1976. 251 p.
This book takes a practical and realistic look at all the different things that happen every day in small companies and shows how to profit from them. It also includes examples of documents, forms, job specifications, budgets, and company manual material.

587. Hazel, Arthur Curwen, and Reid, A. S. *Rapid Company Growth: How to Plan and Manage Small Company Expansion.* London: Business Books, Ltd., 1979. 166 p.
This book begins with a look at market growth, the risks involved in rapid growth, assessing the need, and making decisions.

588. Naisbitt, John, and Aburdene, Patricia. *Re-Inventing the Corporation.* New York: Warner Books, 1985. 305 p.
This book offers a blueprint for building the corporation of the future.

589. Seltz, David D. *Branchising: Proven Techniques for Rapid Company Expansion and Market Dominance.* New York: McGraw-Hill Book Co., 1980. 228 p.
Intended for the manager involved in the growth of his or her organization, this book provides the concepts necessary for business expansion. It includes specimen agreements, forms, and charts necessary in such a situation.

590. "Small Is Beautiful: A New Survey of Hot Growth Companies." *Business Week* (May 27, 1985): 88–104.
This article provides a brief discussion on five entrepreneurs who started their own company and tells how they have succeeded. It also includes a table of the 100 best small growth companies listing important financial information on each.

591. Svigals, Jerome. *Planning for Future Market Events Using Data Processing Support: A Five-Step Growth Plan Process.* New York: Macmillan Publishing Co., Inc., 1983. 180 p.
The five steps discussed in this growth plan are setting up objectives; projecting marketplace events; anticipating system and development resources, reviewing implementation support, and assessing the results.

592. Swinton, David H., and Handy, John. *The Determinants of the Growth of Black-Owned Businesses: A Preliminary Analysis.* Washington, DC: U.S. Department of Commerce, Minority Business Development Agency, 1983. 129 p.
This study provides an empirical analysis of the growth experiences of Black-owned businesses and studies the rate of growth of Black business ownership.

593. Wingate, John W., and Helfant, Seymour. *Small Store Planning for Growth.* 2d ed. Washington, DC: Small Business Administration, 1977. 102 p. (For sale by U.S. Government Printing Office.)
In addition to discussing the management skills needed to realize growth, the author of this book outlines the pros and cons of physical expansion and the methods and sources of financing available to small businesses.

20. HOME-BASED BUSINESS (COTTAGE INDUSTRIES)

594. Atkinson, William. *Working at Home: Is It for You?* Homewood, IL: Dow Jones-Irwin, 1985. 162 p.
The psychological issues that face someone who works at home are addressed in this book.

595. Feldman, Beverly Neuer. *Homebased Businesses.* Los Angeles: Till Press, 1983. 215 p.
Some of the aspects of a home-based business discussed in this book include cash flow, how to plan your business, how to make the name legal. Also lists and discusses products and service businesses you can run from your home.

596. Feldstein, Stuart. *Home, Inc.: How to Start and Operate a Successful Business from Your Home.* New York: Grosset & Dunlap, 1981. 249 p.
This book tells how to use your home for an income-producing business. It describes how existing home entrepreneurs run their operations and shows how you can start your own business at home.

597. Hammer, Marian Behan. *The Complete Handbook of How to Start and Run a Money-Making Business in Your Home.* West Nyack, NJ: Parker Publishing Co., 1975. 252 p.
This book provides all you need to know to start and build your own successful money-making business including how to select a home business for profit, where to get the information you need, how to make money with time as your only investment, franchise businesses you can operate from your home, mail-order businesses, how to finance your home business, and much more.

598. Kishel, Gregory F., and Kishel, Patricia Gunter. *Dollars on Your Doorstep: The Complete Guide to Homebased Businesses.* New York; John Wiley & Sons, Inc., 1984. 183 p.
This book shows how to turn part of your home into a successful business, how to set up and furnish your business, how to allocate time for it, how to find customers, and finally how to get the sale.

599. Lieberoff, Allen. *Climb Your Own Ladder: 101 Home Businesses that Can Make You Wealthy.* New York: Simon & Schuster, Inc., 1982. 242 p.
This book tells how to put imagination and creativity into a number of different service businesses, from the in-home business, the part-time business, to the large, sophisticated full-time enterprise.

600. Masser, Barry Z. *$36,000 a Year in Your Own Home Merchandising Business.* West Nyack, NY: Parker Publishing Co., 1982. 217 p.
Dozens of case histories on how to start a merchandising business are included in this book.

601. Sharratt, Michael, and Sharratt, Suzanne. *No Job? No Sweat! Make a Potful of Money at Home in Your Own Business.* Littleton, CO: Sharratt and Co., 1983. 159 p.
This book provides seven steps to starting your own business in just 30 days.

602. Von Hoelscher, Russ. *A Treasury of Home Business Opportunities.* Rev. ed. San Diego, CA: Sterne Profit Ideas, 1985. 369 p.
This step-by-step guide on how to make big money in a cottage industry includes hundreds of low-cost, easy-to-start home businesses, tells how to write/publish for profits and how to operate a mail order business.

21. INTERNATIONAL BUSINESS

603. *American International Trade and Project Directory.* Washington, DC: North American Communications, Inc., 1985.
More than 3,000 listings of U.S. organizations that finance foreign projects are included in this reference guide.

604. Arpan, Jeffrey S., and Radebaugh, Lee H. *International Accounting and Multinational Enterprises.* 2d ed. New York: John Wiley & Sons, Inc., 1985. 370 p.
Topics in this book include dealing with foreign currency, audits, taxation, and environmental influences.

605. Axtell, Roger E., ed. *Do's and Taboos around the World.* Elmsford, NY: The Benjamin Co., 1985. 178 p.
This guide to foreign business and social manners provides information on gifts, gestures, jargon, protocol, and etiquette.

606. *Background Notes.* Washington, DC: United States Department of State, Bureau of Public Affairs. About 75 issues per year. (For sale by U.S. Government Printing Office.)
Profiles including up-to-date information on the economy, government, people, geography, history, and principal government officials. for countries throughout the world are included in this publication.

607. Bailey, Victor B., and Bowden, Sara R. *Understanding United States Foreign Trade Data.* Washington, DC: U.S. Department of Commerce, International Trade Administration, Trade Information and Analysis Trade Development, 1985. 189 p.
For those who have little or no experience with foreign trade data, this book gives an overview of U.S. foreign trade data and their uses.

608. Baker, James C., and Ryans, John K., Jr. *Multinational Marketing: Dimensions in Strategy.* Columbus, OH: Grid, Inc., 1975. 342 p.
This book of readings is organized within a framework that includes the traditional areas of marketing with three main aspects of international business: cultural, organizational, and financial.

609. *A Basic Guide to Exporting.* Washington, DC: United States Department of Commerce, International Trade Administration, 1981. 133 p. (For sale by the U.S. Government Printing Office.)
Information on what is needed by the small to medium-sized firm to be successful in international trade is included in this book. Also discusses ways to get assistance to reach these goals.

610. Becker, Carol A. *International Relations Directory.* Rev. ed. Washington, DC: Department of State Library, 1981. 80 p. (For sale by U.S. Government Printing Office.)
This book contains terms, phrases, acronyms, catch words and abbreviations that are used in international business.

611. Bentley, Philip, ed. *A World Guide to Exchange Control Regulations.* New York: Business Press International, Ltd., 1985. 371 p.
This book offers comprehensive details of currency regulations, permitted terms and payment mechanisms, remittance of profits, dividends, royalties, and much more.

612. Berenbeim, Ronald E. *Managing the International Company: Building a Global Perspective.* New York: Conference Board, Inc., 1982. 32 p.
This book reports on a study designed to identify managerial resources and practices that international companies use to help on the external and internal basis of internationalism.

613. Berger, Renee A. *The Small Business Incubator: Lessons Learned from Europe.* Washington, DC: Office of Private Sector Initiatives, Small Business Administration, 1984. 29 p. (For sale by U.S. Government Printing Office.)
This book is aimed at the small business person who is intending to enter into a foreign trade relationship or joint venture with European firms.

614. Blair, Frank E., ed. *International Marketing Handbook.* 2d ed. Detroit, MI: Gale Research Co., 1985. 3 v.
In-depth marketing and trade profiles for 142 nations are provided in this handbook. The data includes foreign trade outlook, industry trends, transportation and utilities, distribution and sales channels, credit trade regulations, and much more.

615. *Bottin International: International Business Register.* New York: International Publications Service. (Annual)
This worldwide classified directory lists more than 300,000 manufacturers, exporters/importers, producers, and traders in over 150 countries.

616. Briers, Roger. *How to Enter the Uncommon Common Market.* Princeton, NJ: Center for Marketing Communications, 1976. 14 p.
This pamphlet gives the more common assumptions and pitfalls in exploiting the overseas market. In addition, it discusses the role of research in export marketing and gives an overseas market checklist.

617. Cateora, Philip R. *International Marketing.* 5th ed. Homewood, IL: Richard D. Irwin, Inc., 1983. 801 p.
This book focuses on marketing management problems, techniques, and strategies needed to be successful in the world marketplace.

618. Cavusgil, S. Tamer, and Nevin, John R. *International Marketing: An Annotated Bibliography.* Chicago: American Marketing Association, 1983. 139 p.
This annotated bibliography is divided into five sections including review articles on international marketing, the environment of international marketing, area-oriented and comparative studies, issues in international management, and decision tools for international marketing.

619. Choi, Frederick D. S., and Mueller, Gerhard G., eds. *Frontiers of International Accounting: An Anthology.* Ann Arbor, MI: UMI Research Press, 1985. 313 p.
Eighteen articles from current American and international journals are analyzed in this book and questions are answered on various areas of international accounting.

620. Copeland, Lennie, and Griggs, Lewis. *Going International: How to Make Friends and Deal Effectively in the Global Marketplace.* New York: Random House, 1985. 288 p.
This guide to international business demonstrates what to do and what not to do when doing business abroad. A "must" for the international business traveler, it contains a country-by-country guide to the U.S.'s 30 major trading partners.

621. *Corporate Handbook to International Economic Organizations and Terms.* New York: United States Council for International Business, 1985. 63 p.
This glossary of terms provides a quick and convenient reference source for people doing business overseas.

622. Croner, Ulrich H. E. *Reference Book for World Traders: A Guide for Exporters and Importers.* Queen's Village, NY: Croner Publications, Inc., 1985. 3 v.
This book contains information for the business planning of exporting or importing as well as information on market research.

623. *Current Developments in U.S. International Service Industries.* Washington, DC: U.S. Department of Commerce. International Trade Administration, 1980. 131 p. (For sale by U.S. Government Printing Office.)
This book describes the international position of a number of service industries, identifies important issues affecting them, and discusses some development in these service industries.

624. Davidson, William Harley. *Global Strategic Management.* New York: John Wiley & Sons, Inc., 1982. 348 p.
This book gives frameworks for the development and analysis of global strategies as well as for the administration of multinational firms.

625. Day, Alan J., ed. *Government Economic Agencies of the World.* London: Longman, 1985. 546 p.
This directory includes a list of state-run and state-affiliated organizations and agencies concerned with the formulation and implementation of economic policy. A summary of tabulated economic indicators, economic, social, and political conditions, and directory or government economic agencies is included for each country.

626. Diamond, Walter H., and Diamond, Dorothy B. *Capital Formation and Investment Incentives around the World.* Albany, NY: Matthew Bender & Co., Inc., 1981. 2 v. (Kept up to date with loose-leaf supplements.)
The two-volume set provides in-depth coverage of 66 countries and how to organize a business regarding tax concessions and inducements.

Capital requirement tables and comparisons of the major capital formation vehicles for each country are also included.

627. Diamond, Walter H., and Diamond, Dorothy B. *Tax Free Trade Zones of the World.* Albany, NY: Matthew Bender & Co., Inc., 1977. (Kept up to date with loose-leaf supplements.)
This comprehensive guide to approximately 400 areas throughout the world covers such topics as free trade zones, free ports, transit zones, and free perimeters. The zones that are discussed here are those that offer the most favorable tax treatments.

628. *Direct Mail/Direct Response Advertising: An International Survey of Its Size, Regulation and Self-Regulation in 18 Countries.* New York: International Advertising Association, Direct Mail Marketing Association, 1981. 127 p.
Based on the responses to a worldwide survey dealing with the state of the direct-market industry, this book discusses government regulation, industry self-regulation, mail advertising, and much more.

629. *Directory of American Firms Operating in Foreign Countries.* 10th ed. New York: Uniworld Business Publications, Inc., 1984. 3 v.
More than 4,500 American companies that operate in foreign countries are listed in this book with the name of the president and the office in charge of foreign operations.

630. Dodge, F. W. *How to Develop a Big Money Making Export Business.* Albuquerque, NM: The Institute for Economic and Financial Research, 1984. 84 p.
Some of the topics on export businesses discussed in this book include the export manager and merchant, organization of the firm, financing, location, risks, contracts, pro-formas and letters of credit and correspondence.

631. Dunn, S. Watson; Cahill, Martin F.; and Boddewyn, Jean J. *How Fifteen Transnational Corporations Manage Public Affairs.* Chicago: Crain Books, 1979. 115 p.
This book provides an analysis of how to survive under volatile business conditions. It can be very useful to marketers responsible for overseas programs who are concerned with public issues management.

632. *Employment and Development of Small Enterprises.* Washington, DC: World Bank, 1978. 93 p.
This book studies employment problems in small businesses in developing countries, including information on the advantages and problems of small business development, institutional support, financial and technical assistance, and action by the World Bank.

633. *European Trade Fairs: A Guide for Exporters.* Washington, DC: U.S. Department of Commerce, International Trade Administration, 1981. 75 p. (For sale by U.S. Government Printing Office.)
Information on how to choose a market in Europe and how to identify the right fairs and make them productive for your company is included in this book.

634. *Export Directory/U.S. Buying Guide.* New York: Journal of Commerce. (Biennial)
This book profiles the business activities of over 37,000 exporters who sell products and commodities in world markets.

635. *Export Marketing for Smaller Firms.* 4th ed. Washington, DC: U.S. Small Business Administration, 1979. 84 p. (For sale by U.S. Government Printing Office.)
This book offers a step-by-step approach to determining the best markets for international trade. Pricing, distribution, foreign representative selection, and product promotion are also included.

636. *The Export Trading Company Act.* New York: Practising Law Institute, 1983. 408 p.
Among the topics covered in this book are the role of the international trading companies, the role of banks, antitrust and export trade, and taxation in international business.

637. *Exporters' Encyclopaedia.* New York: Dun and Bradstreet International. (Annual)
Some of the indexes included in this book are the export-order index, export markets index, and export know-how index. Each section contains detailed information on these topics for countries throughout the world and definitions of terms, statistical information, and important names and addresses.

638. *Exporting: Small and Growing Businesses.* New York: Deloitte Haskins & Sells, Small Business Services Department, 1981. 24 p.
The benefits and opportunities of the export market are discussed in this booklet along with steps necessary to formulate a successful export program.

639. *Foreign Markets for Your Products.* Phillipsburg, NJ: The Journal of Commerce. (Published on an ongoing basis.)
This information guide contains facts on more than 37,000 exporters and over 2,500 products. It is a supplement to *Exporter Directory/U.S. Buying Guide.*

640. Frank, Isaiah. *Foreign Enterprise in Developing Countries.* Baltimore, MD: The Johns Hopkins University Press, 1980. 199 p.
This book contains a compilation and analysis of corporate attitudes that are based on a series of in-depth interviews with 90 key individuals from industrial countries who have primary responsibilities for direct MNC investment in developing countries.

641. Haner, F. T. *Global Business: Strategy for the 1980s.* New York: Praeger Publishers, 1980. 229 p.
Mainly dealing with countries outside the Eastern Bloc, USSR, and the People's Republic of China, this book first describes a system for evaluating the potential level of human and physical resources and then applies this system to the 60 countries studied in this book.

642. Harper, Malcolm. *Consultancy for Small Businesses: The Concept, Training the Consultants.* London: Intermediate Technology Publications, Ltd., 1976. 254 p.
This manual reports the findings of experiments that were used to

provide economic on-the-spot consulting to small businesses in developing countries. It would be useful to those who are involved in promotion and development of small enterprises in developing countries.

643. Harper, Malcolm. *Small Business in the Third World: Guidelines for Practical Assistance.* New York: John Wiley & Sons, Inc., 1984. 211 p.
This book tells how to help small enterprises in the Third World.

644. Harrigan, Kathryn Rudie. *Strategies for Joint Ventures.* Lexington, MA: Lexington Books, 1985. 426 p.
This book gives a complete strategic framework on assessing, developing, and managing domestic joint ventures.

645. Hoopes, David S. *Global Guide to International Business.* New York: Facts on File, Inc., 1985. 847 p.
Divided into a worldwide section, a geographic region section, and a country-by-country resource section, this book covers general information services, finances, laws, regulations, marketing, transportation and shipping, and importing.

646. *How to Build an Export Business.* Washington, DC: U.S. Department of Commerce, Office of Minority Business Enterprise, 1984. 158 p. (For sale by U.S. Government Printing Office.)
This complete and informative guide gives information on how to build a competitive and viable exporting business.

647. Hunt, Robert W. *The Evaluation of Small Enterprise Programs and Projects: Issues in Business and Community Development.* Washington, DC: U.S. Agency for International Development, 1983. 59 p.
The four main sections in this book are a definition of small business development, the impact of small business development programs, effects of small business contributions to community development, and issues for impact evaluations.

648. *International Business Travel and Relocation Directory.* 3d ed. Detroit, MI: Gale Research Co., 1984. 978 p.
For personnel in companies doing business overseas, this book contains background information for employees going abroad as well as resources and reference materials for the five major areas of the world.

649. *International Financial Statistics.* Washington, DC: International Monetary Fund. (Monthly)
This publication arranges all aspects of international and domestic finance by country.

650. Johannsen, Hano, and Page, G. Terry. *The International Dictionary of Business.* Englewood Cliffs, NJ: Prentice-Hall, Inc., 1981. 376 p.
Covering the whole area of business and management, this book includes over 5,000 entries on international usage. Also included is information on nongovernment agencies, associations, trade unions, and stock exchanges.

651. Joyner, Nelson T., Jr., and Lurie, Richard G. *How to Build an Export Business: An International Marketing Guide for the Minority Owned Firm.* Washington, DC: U.S. Government Printing Office, 1981. 158 p.
Designed specifically for minority firms who are new-to-export, this step-by-step guide describes in detail what to do and how to do it. It also includes facts on where to go for information on specific international marketing help.

652. Kahler, Ruel. *International Marketing.* 5th ed. Cincinnati, OH: South-Western Publishing Co., 1983. 426 p.
The text in this book offers a basic look at international marketing from the viewpoint of an international marketing manager. Included are such topics as market analysis, marketing channels, physical distribution, trade promotion, pricing, and financing.

653. Kaynak, Erdener, ed. *International Marketing Management.* New York: Praeger Publishers, 1984. 386 p.
This readings book provides new developments in international marketing and international marketing research as well as industrial marketing, the internationalization process and cross-national marketing strategies.

654. Keegan, Warren J. *Multinational Marketing Management.* 3d ed. Englewood Cliffs, NJ: Prentice-Hall, Inc., 1984. 698 p.
This book provides the business person with the conceptual and analytical tools that will help him or her to take advantage of the overseas market opportunities and avoid the pitfalls that can arise in the venture.

655. Kennedy, Gavin. *The Businessman's Guide to Doing Business Abroad.* New York: Simon & Schuster, Inc., 1985. 224 p.
This book tells the reader what he or she needs to know for successful business negotiations, barter, trade, and business entertaining throughout the world.

656. Killing, J. Peter. *Strategies for Joint Venture Success.* New York: Praeger Publishers, 1983. 133 p.
From a British point of view, this book studies such aspects of joint ventures as how joint should the venture be, how to design a shared management joint venture, how to manage shared joint ventures, and using joint ventures as a mechanism for technology transfer.

657. Korth, Christopher M. *International Business, Environment and Management.* 2d ed. Englewood Cliffs, NJ: Prentice-Hall Inc., 1985. 580 p.
This textbook gives an overview of international business and stresses the opportunities, barriers, and economic environment involved. The author also discusses the multinational corporation, government(s), and international operations.

658. Leontiades, James C. *Multinational Corporate Strategy: Planning for World Markets.* Lexington, MA: Lexington Books, 1985. 228 p.
Guidelines for management on both the national and global level are provided in this book.

659. Lusterman, Seymour. *Managing International Public Affairs: Research Report from the Conference Board.* New York: Conference Board Inc., 1985. 34 p.
This book looks at staffing and organizational measures adopted by MNC to serve their public policy interests.

660. McCall, J. B., and Warrington, M. B. *Marketing by Agreement: A Cross-Cultural Approach to Business Negotiations.* New York: John Wiley & Sons, Inc., 1984. 274 p.
These authors provide the basics for the negotiator operating in foreign markets.

661. McDonald, Malcolm, and Ryans, John K., Jr. *Handbook of International Marketing Advertising Strategy.* Bradford, England: MCB Publications, 1982. 191 p.
This collection of readings contains information on international marketing planning, barter, advertising regulation, export strategy, and restrictive business practices.

662. *Metric Laws and Practices in International Trade: A Handbook for U.S. Exporters.* Washington, DC: U.S. Department of Commerce, International Trade Administration, Office of International Services, 1982. 113 p. (For sale by U.S. Government Printing Office.)
This book includes information on foreign laws and regulations pertaining to metric requirements for imported products. Names and addresses of foreign contacts are also given.

663. *Multinational Executive Travel Companion.* Boston: Multinational Executive, Inc. (Annual)
Over 140 business cities throughout the world are covered in this book listing details of major trade fairs, expositions, public and commercial holidays, business practices, and etiquette.

664. Neck, Philip A., ed. *Small Enterprise Development: Policies and Programmes.* Geneva, Switzerland: International Labour Office, 1977. 227 p.
The authors of this book have collected information on current policies and programs from both developing and industrialized countries.

665. Newbould, Gerald D.; Buckley, Peter J.; and Thurwell, Jane C. *Going International: The Experience of Smaller Companies Overseas.* London: Associates Business Press; New York: John Wiley & Sons, Inc., 1978. 247 p.
This book discusses the experience of managers in small firms that have overseas production subsidiaries. The authors attempt to identify what promotes success.

666. Ortiz-Buonafina, Marta. *Profitable Export Marketing: A Strategy for U.S. Business.* Englewood Cliffs, NJ: Prentice-Hall, Inc., 1984. 260 p.
An international perspective of export activities is provided in this book. It includes an original flow model to be used as a step-by-step blueprint

for successfully managing the export operation and providing a framework on which to develop a full marketing strategy.

667. *Overseas Business Reports.* Washington, DC: U.S. Government Printing Office. (Quarterly)
Current detailed marketing information for the export business is contained in this book as well as the economic and commercial profiles of many countries.

668. Parry, Thomas G. *The Multinational Enterprise: International Investment and Host-Country Impacts.* Greenwich, CT: Jai Press, Inc., 1980. 172 p.
This book presents a theoretical approach to the subject of MNC direct foreign investment in the Third World.

669. Peebles, Dean M., and Ryans, John K., Jr. *Management of International Advertising: A Marketing Approach.* Boston: Allyn and Bacon, Inc., 1984. 296 p.
The problems, opportunities, challenges, and successes of international marketing are discussed in this book. Many examples and insights as well as campaigns are taken from some of the world's largest corporations as well as some from smaller companies.

670. Perry, Simon, ed. *Euromoney Yearbook 1985.* New York: Business Press International, Ltd., 1985. 216 p.
This book offers an analysis and comprehensive data on the Euromarkets including a three-year history of exchange rates for 25 currencies. Also included is a comparable history of interest rates, yield and return data, country risk data, taxation, and accounting worldwide.

671. *Principal International Business: The World Marketing Directory.* New York: Dun and Bradstreet Inc. (Annual)
Over 50,000 businesses are listed in this book with information on their legal name, parent company, address, cable, sales volume, chief executives, and SIC number.

672. Ricks, David A. *Big Business Blunders: Mistakes in Multinational Marketing.* Homewood, IL: Dow Jones-Irwin, 1983. 158 p.
Much can be learned from a company's mistakes, whether they are a large corporation or a small business. This book contains some of the blunders made by large corporations while marketing their products overseas.

673. Roth, Robert. *International Marketing Communications.* Chicago: Crain Books, 1982. 353 p.
This book contains a blend of sound theory and solid practice addressing potential problem areas of international marketing communications. Information on market research, marketing plans, how to select an agency, scheduling, budgeting, and translations is included.

674. Ryans, Cynthia C. *International Business Reference Sources: Developing a Corporate Library.* Lexington, MA: Lexington Books, 1983. 195 p.
This book provides a single source of representative holdings of international business sources. Sections on government publications, journals,

annuals, loose-leaf services, directories, almanacs, handbooks, and international business books each contain annotated bibliographies.

675. Ryans, John K., Jr., et al. *International Advertising Strategy.* Bradford, England: MCB Publications, 1977. 569–84 p.
This pamphlet contains two articles reprinted from the *European Journal of Marketing*: "A New Perspective on Advertising Standardization" and "An Analysis of Headquarters Executive Involvement in International Advertising."

676. *Small Business Market Is the World.* Washington, DC: U.S. Small Business Administration, Office of International Trade, 198?
This publication lists programs designed to help small businesses enter into or expand in international markets.

677. *Small Enterprise: A Listing of U.S. Non-Profit Organizations in Small Enterprise Development Assistance Abroad.* New York: American Council of Voluntary Agencies for Foreign Service, 1982. 104 p.
This book contains a list of 91 U.S. nonprofit organizations involved in small enterprise development assistance programs overseas.

678. *Statesman's Year-Book.* New York: St. Martin's Press, Inc. (Annual)
This book includes a history, population statistics, information on constitution and government, defense, economy, energy and natural resources, trade, communications, and diplomatic representatives for countries throughout the world.

679. *Statistical Yearbook.* New York: United Nations Publications. (Annual)
Statistical data for member countries of UNESCO is included in this book.

680. Stopford, John M.; Dunning, John H.; and Haberich, Klaus O. *World Directory of Multinational Enterprises, 1982–83.* 2d ed. Detroit, MI: Gale Research Co., 1983. 3 v.
Corporate profiles and five-year financial summaries of approximately 550 multinational corporations are given in this book. An overview of MNCs surveys their history, growth, and development.

681. Storey, David J., ed. *The Small Firm: An International Survey.* New York: St. Martin's Press, Inc., 1983. 274 p.
This book reviews trends in the small-firm sector, covering the full spectrum of economic development. The majority of the text examines small firms in developed countries.

682. Streng, William P., and Salacuse, Jeswald W. *International Business Planning: Law and Taxation (U.S.).* Albany, NY: Matthew Bender & Co., Inc., 1982. 6 v. (Kept up to date with supplements.)
Divided into three major parts, this book outlines the framework of international business, discusses export transactions, foreign sales, export tax incentives, and analyzes foreign investment transactions.

683. Terpstra, Vern. *International Dimensions of Marketing.* Boston: Kent Publishing Co., 1982. 186 p.
Some of the topics on international marketing discussed in this book are research, product strategies, international distribution, pricing, and promotion.

684. Terpstra, Vern, and David, Kenneth. *The Cultural Environment of International Business.* 2d ed. Cincinnati, OH: South-Western Publishing Co., 1985. 242 p.
This book compares culture and business and discusses the effects of cultural differences such as religion, values, education, and language on business in the international arena.

685. Thorelli, Hans, and Becker, Helmut. *International Marketing Strategy.* Rev. ed. New York: Pergamon Press, Inc., 1980. 423 p.
This collection of readings on international marketing contains one section on international marketing from the point of view of the small to medium-sized firm.

686. Verduin, Paul. *Small Business Incubation: Successful Models from Abroad: A Special Report Designed for American Small Business Managers and Developers.* Washington, DC: Council for International Urban Liaison, 1984. 52 p.
This book is designed to help the small business person learn more about small business incubators and how they can benefit the entrepreneur.

687. Vorio, Virginia M. *Adapting Products for Export.* New York: The Conference Board, Inc., 1983. 40 p.
This report looks at what management needs to know to determine if their companies' domestic products need to be physically altered or adapted for export sale.

688. Walmsley, John. *Handbook of International Joint Ventures.* London: Graham & Trotman Limited, 1982. 161 p.
This book provides international practitioners with information necessary to justify their involvement in joint ventures and suggests some ways to improve results from this area of doing business.

689. Wasserman, Paul, ed. *Statistics Sources.* 9th ed. Detroit, MI: Gale Research Co., 1984. 2 v.
This subject guide contains information on industrial, business, social, financial, and other aspects of interest to the business person. Entries are under the name of the country as well as the subject.

690. Wortzel, Heidi Vernon, and Wortzel, Lawrence H. *Strategic Management of Multinational Corporations: The Essentials.* New York: John Wiley & Sons Inc., 1985. 460 p.
This readings book includes information on techniques, political environment, finances, marketing, production and innovation management, and corporate culture of interest to multinational corporations.

691. Wragg, L. de V. *Composite Currencies.* New York: Business Press International, Ltd., 1984. 168 p.
This training manual of foreign exchange dealing in the spot and forward markets includes information on major dealing centers, market partici-

pants, how markets are made, rates, how to approach dealers, dealing room, budgeting and staffing, and much more.

22. MANAGEMENT AND ORGANIZATION

692. *AMA Management Handbook.* 2d ed. New York: AMACOM, 1983. 1 v. various paging.
This volume is a complete business library offering proven profit making information on every conceivable business topic. It contains the expertise of more than 200 outstanding authorities.

693. Albert, Kenneth J. *How to Solve Business Problems.* New York: McGraw-Hill Book Co., 1983. 207 p.
This book shows the reader how to apply the management consulting approach to unstructured business problem solving.

694. Albert, Kenneth J., ed. *The Strategic Management Handbook.* New York: McGraw-Hill Book Co., 1983. 546 p.
The contributors of this book have presented how-to material on five basic topics: strategic thoughts and actions, strategic management; strategic planning, strategic implementations, and some key issues and resources on the topic.

695. Albrecht, Karl. *Successful Management by Objectives: An Action Manual.* Englewood Cliffs, NJ: Prentice-Hall, Inc., 1978. 226 p.
This book focuses on the basic concept of MBO and the fundamental principles of human behavior that support it. It provides a thorough treatment on the topic for those who want to know how to manage by objective.

696. Albrecht, Karl, and Zemke, Ron. *Service America! Doing Business in the New Economy.* Homewood, IL: Dow Jones-Irwin, 1985. 235 p.
New management ideas that emphasize the profitable corporate utilization of a "service mentality" are discussed in this book, and it shows how a service-oriented company can become "customer-driven."

697. Alcorn, Pat B. *Success and Survival in the Family-Owned Business.* New York: McGraw-Hill Book Co., 1982. 253 p.
This book brings out the problems facing family owned businesses and attempts to make the reader aware of organized and humanized approaches to special areas of business management. Real life examples of families in business are included.

698. Altman, Mary Ann, and Weil, Robert I. *Managing Your Accounting and Consulting Practice.* Albany, NY: Matthew Bender & Co., Inc., 1978. 1 v. various paging (Kept up to date by annual supplements.)
This book provides information you need to maintain an organized, profitable practice including fees and financial controls, personnel management, use of personal computers, and practical and legal aspects of forming a partnership or professional corporation.

699. Ames, Michael D., and Wellsfry, Norval L. *Small Business Management.* St. Paul, MN: West Publishing Co., 1983. 492 p.
Focusing on the most common problems encountered by owners and managers of a small business, this book uses a step-by-step approach to solving these problems.

700. Anthony, William P. *Managing Your Boss.* New York: American Management Associations, 1983. 197 p.
This book tells how to manage effectively by gaining the support and cooperation of your boss.

701. *Assisting Small Business Clients in Obtaining Funds.* New York: American Institute of Certified Public Accountants, 1982. 57 p.
This book provides some hints on management advisory service for a CPA's small business clients.

702. Baumback, Clifford M. *Basic Small Business Management.* Englewood Cliffs, NJ: Prentice-Hall, Inc., 1983. 540 p.
By studying the actual business cases included in this book, readers can learn basic concepts of small business management.

703. Baumback, Clifford M. *How to Organize and Operate a Small Business.* 7th ed. Englewood Cliffs, NJ: Prentice-Hall, Inc., 1985. 578 p.
This book is intended for people interested in small business management. It contains information on the importance of small business, its status, problems, and requirements for success.

704. Becker, Franklin D. *Workspace: Creating Environments in Organization.* New York: Praeger Publishers, 1981. 225 p.
This author discusses how the physical settings of an organization can have a significant impact on the quality of work life and the effectiveness of the business.

705. Berg, Norman A. *General Management: An Analytical Approach.* Homewood, IL: Richard D. Irwin, Inc., 1984. 204 p.
This book is intended to help managers develop skills in job performance through the application of strategy formulation.

706. Bhandari, Narendra C. *Cases in Small Business Management.* Cincinnati, OH: South-Western Publishing, Co., 1979. 200 p.
Twenty-six cases on a variety of decision-making problems from a cross section of small business are included in this book.

707. Blake, Robert Rogers, and Mouton, Jane Srygley. *Solving Costly Organizational Conflicts: Achieving Intergroup Trust, Cooperation and Teamwork.* San Francisco, CA: Jossey- Bass, Inc., Publishers, 1984. 327 p.
This book describes the Interface Conflict-Solving Model in enough detail to enable administrators to use it as a working management tool.

708. Blanchard, Kenneth, and Johnson, Spencer. *The One Minute Manager.* New York: William Morrow & Co., Inc., 1982. 111 p.
This practical guide to effective management is designed to help any manager assist his or her people to become peak performers.

709. Blanchard, Kenneth, and Lorber, Robert. *Putting the One Minute Manager to Work.* New York: William Morrow & Co., Inc., 1984. 112 p.
This companion book to the *One Minute Manager* shows how to implement the three secrets outlined in the first book: set one minute goals, give one minute praisings, and deliver one minute reprimands.

710. Blanchard, Kenneth; Zigarmi, Patricia; and Zigarmi, Drea. *Leadership and the One-Minute Manager.* New York: William Morrow & Co., Inc., 1985. 111 p.
This book focuses on situational leadership, demonstrates different management styles and shows how to shift from one to another according to the situation.

711. Bolman, Lee G., and Deal, Terrence E. *Modern Approaches to Understanding and Managing Organizations.* San Francisco, CA: Jossey-Bass Inc., Publishers, 1985. 356 p.
The authors demonstrate the strengths, weaknesses, and applicability of four approaches to management analysis: structural, human resources, political, and symbolic.

712. Brandt, Steven C. *Entrepreneuring in Established Companies: Managing Toward the Year 2000.* Homewood, IL: Dow Jones-Irwin, 1985. 250 p.
The problems of current management practices are discussed in this book along with suggestions for ways to solve them.

713. Broh, Robert A. *Managing Quality for Higher Profits: A Guide for Business Executives and Quality Managers.* New York: McGraw-Hill Book Co., 1982. 200 p.
This book is a guide for corporate executives and small business managers to help them make profits through product quality, as well as to help quality managers and engineers increase individual productivity and company productivity.

714. Broom, H. N.; Longenecker, Justin G.; and Moore, Carlos W. *Small-Business Management.* 6th ed. Cincinnati, OH: South-Western Publishing Co., 1983. 632 p.
The authors provide a thorough coverage of managerial activities needed for the successful operation of a small business. The sixth edition has put more emphasis on entrepreneurial opportunities and new-venture processes.

715. Brown, Arnold, and Weiner, Edith. *Supermanaging: How to Harness Change for Personal and Organizational Success.* New York: McGraw-Hill Book Co., 1984. 283 p.
This book deals with how to master change, first by having a good and objective description of the current environment, and to have an awareness of the priorities needed as well as respond to the elements that make up that environment.

716. *Business Basics.* Washington, DC: U.S. Small Business Administration, Office of Management Assistance, 198-. (For sale by U.S. Government Printing Office.)
This set of self-study booklets each contains texts, questions, and exercises that teach specific aspects of small business management. Some topics include cost control, capital planning, asset management, marketing strategy, consumer credit, and risk management.

717. Campbell, David P. *If I'm in Charge Here Why Is Everybody Laughing?* 2d ed. Greensboro, NC: Center for Creative Leadership, 1984. 164 p.
This easy-to-read book contains helpful tips for people in charge and tells how to take charge, make things happen, and have an impact on the world in general.

718. Carey, Omer, and Olson, Dean. *Financial Tools for Small Business.* Reston, VA: Reston Publishing Co., Inc., 1983. 269 p.
Written for owners and managers of small business, this book provides information on the skills necessary to manage a small business.

719. Clowes, Kenneth W. *The Impact of Computers on Managers.* Ann Arbor, MI: UMI Research Press, 1982. 190 p.
The impact that computer use has on managers, organization, and perceptions of work activity are discussed in this book.

720. Comer, James M., and Dubinsky, Alan J. *Managing the Successful Sales Force.* Lexington, MA: Lexington Books, 1985. 145 p.
By examining research through 1983, the authors have developed some specific operational guidelines for managers.

721. Culligan, Matthew J.; Deakins, Suzanne; and Young, Arthur H. *Back-to-Basics Management: The Lost Craft of Leadership.* New York: Facts on File, Inc., 1983. 157 p.
Written for the individual manager, this book stresses the fact that the key factor in motivation, productivity, profit, and successful management is the individual manager.

722. Danco, Leon A., and Jonovic, Donald J. *Outside Directors in the Family Owned Business: Why, When, Who and How.* Englewood Cliffs, NJ: Prentice-Hall, Inc., 1981. 216 p.
This survival manual for the owner of a family-owned business looks at boards of directors, analyzing what they are, why they can fail to do the job, and pointing out what can be done to change this.

723. Davis, Stanley M. *Managing Corporate Culture.* Cambridge, MA: Ballinger Publishing Co., 1984. 144 p.
Useful mainly in executive briefings and seminars, this book is a how-to, hands-on guide to turning a corporation's visions into effective strategies.

724. Day, William H. *Maximizing Small Business Profits with Precision Management.* Englewood Cliffs, NJ: Prentice-Hall, Inc., 1978. 388 p.
This book deals with the "profit" aspects of managing a small business. It puts into perspective the range of activities needed to manage a business and to manage it profitably.

725. *Developing Executive and Management Talent: A Guide to OPM Courses, Fellowships and Developmental Assignments.* Washington, DC: U.S. Office of Personnel Management, Executive Personnel and Management Development Group, Executive and Management Development Division, 1981. 63 p. (For sale by U.S. Government Printing Office.)

This book contains a checklist of special development programs sponsored by the federal government for improving management. Also included are concise write-ups on fellowships and Office of Personnel Management courses.

726. Edmunds, Stahrl. *Performance Measures for Growing Businesses: A Practical Guide to Small Business Management.* New York: Van Nostrand Reinhold Co., Inc., 1982. 247 p.

This book looks at performance measures that the small business person can take to correct any actions necessary to improve the company's operations.

727. Famularo, Joseph J. *Organization Planning Manual.* Rev. ed. New York: AMACOM, 1979. 372 p.

This discussion on organization planning and organization charts is divided into three major parts: organization and its structure; position descriptions; and policy statements.

728. Foote, Rosslynn F. *Running an Office for Fun and Profit: Business Techniques for Small Design Firms.* Stroudsburg, PA: Dowden, Hutchinson & Ross, 1978. 116 p.

Designed for the small architectural firm, this book gives some basic how-to suggestions on being your own boss, bookkeeping, paperwork, business development, growth, and the future.

729. Francis, Dave, and Woodcock, Mike. *The Unblocked Boss.* San Diego, CA: University Associates, 1981. 274 p.

This book contains well-tested ideas that can help managers do their jobs more effectively.

730. Frantz, Forrest H. *Successful Small Business Management.* Englewood Cliffs, NJ: Prentice-Hall, Inc., 1978. 425 p.

This "how-to book" provides a general view of the basic skills and principles needed to manage a small business. Liberal use is made of examples, figures, and minicases.

731. Fregly, Bert. *How to Be Self-Employed: Introduction to Small Business Management.* Palm Springs, CA: ETC Publications, 1977. 665 p.

This book looks at business and management from a practical point of view and includes suggestions on how to develop solutions to the day-to-day business problems.

732. Friday, Bill. *Successful Management for 1 to 10 Employee Businesses.* San Francisco, CA: Prudential Publishing Co., 1978. 220 p.

This book is aimed at illustrating an ideal management style for ten employees, stating that number to be the most efficient sized group for one manager. It presents a thorough discussion of small businesses, incorporating various facets such as how to organize and finance the business, location, pricing, advertising, and employee relationships, as well as information on insurance and taxes.

733. Glass, Dick. *Service Shop Management Handbook.* Indianapolis, IN: H. W. Sams & Co., Inc., 1979. 280 p.
This reference tool looks at all aspects of the service industry. The author provides detailed information on how to keep company books, what type of records are needed, pricing, inventory management, and insurance.

734. Goldstein, Harvey A. *122 Minutes a Month to Greater Profits.* Los Angeles: Granville Publications, 1985. 174 p.
This book addresses the problems of company management and includes techniques and strategies that will improve management capabilities of owners/managers of small and medium-sized companies.

735. Gordon, Judith R. *A Diagnostic Approach to Organizational Behavior.* Boston: Allyn and Bacon, Inc., 1983. 702 p.
The main theme of this book is the diagnosis of behavior in organizations.

736. Gumpert, David E. *Growing Concerns: Building and Managing the Smaller Business.* New York: John Wiley & Sons, Inc., 1984. 418 p.
This book contains 36 articles on management problems in small companies. The topics covered are acquiring ventures, forming strategies, financial management, how to use outside resources, and how to plan for the future.

737. Gutknecht, Douglas B., ed. *Meeting Organization and Human Resource Challenges: Perspectives, Issues, and Strategies.* Washington, DC: University Press of America, 1984. 463 p.
The readings in this book are intended to provide perspective, as well as strategies and tools for overcoming traditional misconceptions about organizations in an effort to help build more effective and productive company policies.

738. Haimann, Theo, and Hilgert, Raymond. *Supervision: Concepts and Practices of Management.* 3d ed. Cincinnati, OH: South-Western Publishing Co., 1982. 432 p.
Aimed mainly at practicing, newly appointed, or potential supervisors and managers in first-line to middle-level management positions, this book covers such topics as time management, EEO, and union-management relations.

739. Harrigan, Kathryn Rudie. *Strategic Flexibility: A Management Guide for Changing Times.* Lexington, MA: Lexington Books, 1985. 224 p.
This book provides information on what top management needs to know to keep their companies ahead in these changing times.

740. Harris, Philip R. *Management in Transition.* San Francisco, CA: Jossey-Bass Inc., Publishers, 1985. 400 p.
The author of this book describes the various dimensions of the new work culture that is characterized by greater autonomy and teamwork, increased automation and information systems, and describes manage-

ment techniques, organizational guidelines, and team-building skills helpful to operate effectively in this environment.

741. Hazel, Arthur Curwen, and Reid, A. S. *Managing the Survival of Smaller Companies.* London: Business Books, Ltd., 1977. 159 p.
By answering such questions as what causes decline and failure, how to recognize it and how to stop it, the authors set out to help you keep your company on a solid footing.

742. Heller, Robert. *The Pocket Manager.* New York: E. P. Dutton, Inc., 1985. 308 p.
This book contains an alphabetical list of management terms.

743. Heller, Robert. *The Supermanagers: Managing for Success, the Movers and the Doers, the Reasons Why.* New York: E. P. Dutton, Inc., 1984. 400 p.
This book shows how modern "supermanagers" can win by applying strong virtues of American management to the challenges of a changing world.

744. Heyel, Carl, ed. *The Encyclopedia of Management.* New York: Van Nostrand Reinhold Co., Inc., 1982. 1,371 p.
The management definitions included in this book range in length from very brief to over 20 pages.

745. Hodgetts, Richard M. *Effective Small Business Management.* New York: Academic Press, 1982. 496 p.
The basic fundamentals of effective business management are discussed in this book.

746. Hodgetts, Richard M. *Modern Human Relations at Work.* Chicago: Dryden Press, 1984. 513 p.
The author of this book stresses the most up-to-date developments in human relations through the use of exhibits, cases, and self-examination exercises.

747. Hodson, Randy. *Workers' Earnings and Corporate Economic Structure.* New York: Academic Press, Inc., 1983. 242 p.
This book provides an analytic approach that allows systematic investigation of the role that workplace organization plays in setting social inequality.

748. Hogsett, Robert N. *Profit Planning for Small Business.* New York: Van Nostrand Reinhold Co., 1981. 231 p.
The author of this book provides some insight into how to incorporate sophisticated management procedures into small business activities without the help of outside services.

749. Holtz, Herman. *Profit-Line Management: Managing a Growing Business Successfully.* New York: AMACOM, 1981. 337 p.
The author of this book provides information on all levels of management from the chief executive officer who has the responsibility of profit and loss, to the line manager who is responsible for supervising the work for which the customer pays.

750. Hurtubise, Rolland A. *Managing Information Systems: Concepts and Tools.* West Hartford, CT: Kumarian Press, 1984. 168 p.
This book shows how the human being is involved with all aspects of information systems, from their initial design stages to the management of the systems.

751. Huczynski, Andrzej. *Encyclopedia of Management Development Methods.* Aldershot, England: Gower Publishing Co., Ltd., 1983. 339 p.
This book provides a comprehensive compendium of management learning methods for the training specialists.

752. Iaconetti, Joan, and O'Hara, Patrick. *The First-Time Manager.* New York: Macmillan Publishing Co., Inc., 1985. 288 p.
This practical six-point program is designed to help beginning managers and supervisors master the skills they need.

753. Irons, Edward D., and Moore, Gilbert W. *Black Managers: The Case of the Banking Industry.* New York: Praeger Publishers, 1985. 185 p.
This book studies the results of a study of job satisfaction of black managers and creates a "satisfaction index" that shows the intensity of the respondents' feelings.

754. Jacoby, James W. *How to Prepare Managerial Communications.* Rev. ed. Washington, DC: Bureau of National Affairs, 1983. 232 p.
This "how-to" and up-to-date reference source provides the steps required to produce an organization manual, including writing and editing techniques, incorporating material in the manual, review, trial usage, approval, distributing and updating, and instructional materials.

755. Justis, Robert T. *Managing Your Small Business.* Englewood Cliffs, NJ: Prentice-Hall, Inc., 1981. 464 p.
This book shows the day-to-day and long-range activities that are encountered in a small business setting. The four stages of a small business studied are analyzing and buying a business, starting, managing, and expanding or selling the business.

756. Karlins, Marvin. *The Human Use of Human Resources.* New York: McGraw-Hill Book Co., 1981. 173 p.
This book tells how you can be a better manager through the use of psychology and tells how you can develop management skills to make personal and economic growth coexist in your company.

757. Kerzner, Harold, and Thamhain, Hans J. *Project Management for Small and Medium-Size Businesses.* New York: Van Nostrand Reinhold Co., 1984. 367 p.
This book tells how the small company can gain from the use of project management. It looks at the concepts and principles of project managment, organization, planning and control, program management leadership, and team building.

758. Kirkpatrick, Donald L. *How to Manage Change Effectively: Approaches, Methods, and Case Examples.* San Francisco, CA: Jossey-Bass Inc., Publishers, 1985. 250 p.
The author tells why change is a constant element in the successful organization and he shows how to plan, implement, and manage change in the workplace.

759. Kline, John B.; Stegall, Donald P.; and Steinmetz, Lawrence L. *Managing the Small Business.* 3d ed. Homewood, IL: Richard D. Irwin, Inc., 1982. 466 p.
This book attempts to isolate and examine solutions to the problems encountered in managing small businesses. It offers practical approaches to grass roots and real-world problems.

760. Kogut, Kenneth J. *Energy Management for the Community Bank.* Park Ridge, IL: Bank Administration Institute, 1980. 63 p.
This book is designed to help bankers develop and implement an energy management program. In addition, some basic philosophies of management that can be applied to the management of energy are included.

761. Krefetz, Gerald. *More than a Dream: Running Your Own Business.* New York: American Management Association, 1981. 13 p.
This particular book discusses effective management tools and tells how to plan for profitability, how to organize personnel and physical resources, and how to control the operations of a business.

762. Krentzman, Harvey C. *Successful Management Strategies for Small Business.* Englewood Cliffs, NJ: Prentice-Hall, Inc., 1981. 197 p.
This book is designed to help managers of small, growing businesses improve and broaden their administrative and managerial skills.

763. Kuhn, Robert Lawrence. *Mid-Sized Firms: Success Strategies and Methodology.* New York: Praeger Publishers, 1982. 294 p.
This book on strategic management begins by looking at the environment and setting of mid-sized firms. It also includes a model-map formation and data-terrain analysis of matched-pair mid-sized firms and finally a model-map extension that assembles and tests the model-map itself.

764. Kuhn, Robert Lawrence. *To Flourish among Giants: Creative Management for Mid-Sized Firms.* New York: John Wiley & Sons., Inc., 1985. 494 p.
This author shows how the right use of strategies can mean the difference between survival and outstanding profitabilty. Studies the success and failure of mid-sized firms.

765. Lawrie, John. *You Can Lead! Essential Skills for the New or Prospective Manager.* New York: AMACOM, 1985. 219 p.
This book helps you learn and/or teach leadership skills and shows how to put them to work on the job. It also helps you manage group dynamics.

766. Louden, J. Keith. *The Effective Director in Action.* New York: AMACOM, 1975. 190 p.
This book includes a board of directors audit and sample rules and procedures.

767. Louden, J. Keith. *Think Like a President: A Manager's Guide to Making It Happen.* New York: Executive Enterprises Publications Co., Inc.; Englewood Cliffs, NJ: Prentice-Hall, Inc., 1981. 212 p.
This book explains professional management in simple, practical terms.

768. Lundborg, Louis B. *The Art of Being an Executive.* New York: The Free Press, 1981. 270 p.
This book tells how the chief executive and other company executives would manage the company.

769. Lusterman, Seymour. *Managerial Competence: The Public Affairs Aspects.* New York: The Conference Board, Inc., 1981. 42 p.
This book looks at two questions: How are large companies increasing public affairs competence of top executives, and how does this compare with the views of executives responsible for public affairs.

770. Lyles, Richard I. *Practical Management Problem Solving and Decision Making.* New York: Van Nostrand Reinhold Co., Inc., 1982. 198 p.
This book is geared toward managers and presents various strategies which may be used in different situations to improve their performance as problem solvers and decision makers.

771. McConkey, Dale D. *How to Manage by Results.* 4th ed. New York: AMACOM, 1983. 301 p.
Based on *Management by Objectives*, this book shows how to compare actual with expected results and how to eliminate outmoded procedures and move to innovative and successful procedures.

772. Mahin, Philip William. *Entrepreneurial Skills: Cases in Small Business Management.* Plano, TX: Business Publications, 1981. 234 p.
The focus of this book is on the problems of managing a small business.

773. Mali, Paul, ed. *Management Handbook: Operating Guidelines, Techniques and Practices.* New York: John Wiley & Sons, Inc., 1981. 1,522 p.
This book includes the concepts, practices, techniques, and guidelines on management.

774. *Management Aids.* Washington, DC: Small Business Administration, 1960-.
The Small Business Administration provides a series of *Aids* on various aspects of small business management such as borrowing, pricing, cash flow, breakeven analysis, venture capital, recordkeeping, profit pricing, and taxes. Each *Aid* is a four- to eight-page pamphlet.

775. *Manager's Guide for Improving Productivity.* Washington, DC: U.S. Office of Personnel Management, Workforce Effectiveness and Development. Office of Productivity Programs, 1981. 25 p. (For sale by U.S. Government Printing Office.)

A discussion of the various options to raise worker output, including financial incentives and flextime opportunities is included in this book. A "Where to get help" guide is included.

776. Margerison, Charles J. *How to Assess Your Managerial Style.* New York: AMACOM, 1979. 151 p.
This book is aimed at evaluating the self as a manager, from the source of individual motivation to the examination and evaluation of current managerial effectiveness.

777. Margerison, Charles J., and McCann, Dick. *How to Lead a Winning Team.* Bradford, England: MCB University Press, Ltd., 1984.
This book, written for working managers, describes the Team Management Resource approach to management.

778. Marsteller, William A. *Creative Management.* Chicago: Crain Books, 1981. 153 p.
This book is an essential tool to help the manager get the work done through other people.

779. Moreau, James F. *Effective Small Business Management.* Boston: Houghton Mifflin Co., 1984. 362 p.
The author of this book provides information on marketing decisions in small business, planning, organizing, staffing and controlling, as well as a discussion on operational decisions.

780. Morse, H. Clifton. *Cost Reduction Guide for Management.* New York: AMACOM, 1984. 295 p.
Systematically reevaluating work methods, manpower, work layout, equipment utilization, technology and product design can help you achieve cost savings. Included are step-by-step guidelines and audit forms.

781. Morse, Stephen. *Management Skills in Marketing.* London: McGraw-Hill Book Co., 1982. 150 p.
This reference book tells managers facts on many subjects facing the new and untried manager: planning, market research, skills needed in organizing marketing, time measurement, controlled marketing, and decision making.

782. Mumford, Alan. *Making Experience Pay: Management Success Through Effective Learning.* New York: McGraw-Hill Book Co., 1980. 183 p.
This book aids managers in becoming more successful by identifying and meeting their own learning needs.

783. Naumes, William. *The Entrepreneurial Manager in the Small Business: Text, Readings, and Cases.* Reading, MA: Addison-Wesley Publishing Co., 1978. 508 p.
This book emphasizes every aspect of management for the small firm, including information for the entrepreneurial manager who may anticipate direct involvement with new or small businesses through service-oriented functions. The cases are drawn from manufacturing firms, financially-oriented institutions, service organizations, and commercial firms.

784. Nevins, Ellen. *Real Bosses Don't Say "Thank You": A Guide to Being the Perfect Boss.* Somerville, NJ: Pollyanna Press, 1983. 138 p.
This book tells how managers and bosses respond to the numerous challenges facing them in the workplace of today.

785. Odiorne, George S. *How Managers Make Things Happen.* 2d ed. Englewood Cliffs, NJ: Prentice-Hall, Inc., 1982. 288 p.
This clear, easy-to-read book tells how you can become a person who makes things happen.

786. Ogden, Richard W. *Manage Your Plant for Profit and Your Promotion.* New York: AMACOM, 1978. 194 p.
This book tells what to do in various situations as plant manager, i.e., the sharing of real-life experiences common to all plant managers.

787. Persons, Edgar A. *Helping Small Business Make It.* Arlington, VA: American Vocational Association, Inc., 1978. 16 p.
This book covers such topics as how small business can generate and save jobs and the Minnesota model for small business management instruction (a management education program). This program is discussed in detail including the curriculum for the program.

788. Peters, Thomas J., and Waterman, Robert H., Jr. *In Search of Excellence: Lessons from America's Best-Run Companies.* New York: Harper & Row, Publishers, 1982. 360 p.
This book provides some straightforward answers to questions involving successful management techniques.

789. Rausch, Edward N. *Profitable Office Management for the Growing Business.* New York: AMACOM, 1984. 194 p.
This book not only answers questions regarding business profitability but also looks at proper management of a growing business.

790. Ritti, R. Richard, and Funkhouser, G. Ray. *The Ropes to Skip and the Ropes to Know: Studies in Organizational Behavior.* 2d ed. New York: John Wiley & Sons, Inc., 1982. 290 p.
This book looks at striking occasions that demonstrate some fundamental facts of organizational life, i.e., people reacting to situations.

791. *The Roots of the Corporation.* Boston: Inc. Special Reports, 1985. 156 p.
This book brings an update on management techniques of the 80s by investigating the roots of the corporation. It tells how to train and groom an effective management team, how to communicate company values, and more.

792. Rosenberg, Jerry M. *Dictionary of Business and Management.* 2d ed. New York: John Wiley & Sons, Inc., 1983. 631 p.
This book contains terminology of business and management that practitioners need to update their current word usage.

793. *SBIC Digest (Small Business Investment Companies Digest).* Washington, DC: U.S. Small Business Administration, Investment Division. (Semiannual)
Each issue covers a different aspect of small business management. This information includes statistics and addresses.

794. Sargent, Alice G. *The Androgynous Manager.* New York: AMACOM, 1983. 238 p.
This book tells how to unlearn our negative behaviors and learn how to become equally contributing human beings. This theory is applied to management techniques in this book.

795. Scarborough, Norman M., and Zimmerer, Thomas W. *Effective Small Business Management.* Columbus, OH: C. E. Merrill Publishing Co., 1984. 728 p.
The practical aspects of successfully launching and managing a small business are stressed in this book in an easy-to-understand manner.

796. Schulberg, Herbert C., and Jerrell, Jeanette M. *The Evaluator and Management.* Beverly Hills, CA: Sage Publications, 1979. 159 p.
This series of articles covers such topics as promises and pitfalls in organizational effectiveness, an analysis of conflict, metaevaluation in human services, evaluation research, managerial behavior, the management perspective on program evaluation, and the relationship between the evaluator and manager.

797. Schultz, Don E. *Sales Promotion Management.* Chicago: Crain Books, 1982. 487 p.
This book looks at the problems a manager can and cannot solve with sales promotion and provides techniques needed to solve the problems.

798. Schuster, Jay. *Management Compensation in High Technology Companies: Assuring Corporate Excellence.* Lexington, MA: Lexington Books, 1984. 147 p.
The author of this book shows how to set up management reward programs that reflect corporate goals and principles.

799. Simon, Herbert A. *Administrative Behavior: A Study of Decision-Making Processes in Administrative Organization.* 3d ed. New York: Macmillan Publishing Co., Inc., 1985. 364 p.
This book studies the author's theory of human choice in administrative decision making of concrete organizational problems.

800. Sinn, Gerald R. *Cash Operations Management: Profits from Within.* New York: Petrocelli Books, Inc., 1980. 203 p.
The author of this book tells how to improve cash profits and operations management and provides insight into profits lost through the distribution of dollars.

801. *Small Business Management Series.* Washington, DC: U.S. Small Business Administration, Office of Management Assistance, 198-.
The books in this series cover specific management techniques and problems on such topics as profit planning, ratio analysis, financial recordkeeping, franchising, and purchasing management.

802. *Small Business Management Training Guide Series.* Washington, DC: Small Business Administration, Office of Management Assisitance, 198-. (For sale by U.S. Government Printing Office.)
This series of pamphlets is intended to help provide assistance to the small business owner on various aspects of small business management.

803. Sondeno, Stanley R. *Small Business Management Principles.* Dallas, TX: Business Publications, 1985. 505 p.
The basic principles, guidelines, practice methods, and procedures of small business management are included in this text. It is useful as a practical guide for the prospective entrepreneur.

804. Spencer, Anne. *On the Edge of the Organization: The Role of the Outside Director.* New York: John Wiley & Sons Inc., 1983. 137 p.
The various aspects and duties of the nonexecutive director studied in this book include their multiple roles and realities, their notions of competence, their relationships on the board, and issues of power and influence.

805. Sperber, Nathaniel N., and Lerbinger, Otto. *Manager's Public Relations Handbook.* Reading, MA: Addison-Wesley Publishing Co., 1982. 334 p.
This book provides a checklist for anticipating, handling, and following up on events or crises that may confront the general manager or the public relations specialists in order to bring about success and prevent failure in the company.

806. Stanton, William J., and Buskirk, Richard H. *Management of the Sales Force.* 6th ed. Homewood IL: Richard D. Irwin Inc., 1983. 638 p.
This book focuses on the management of an outside sales force and its activities. This edition incorporates the effect of the changing socioeconomic environment on this topic.

807. Stevens, Mark. *How to Run Your Own Business Successfully.* New York: Monarch, 1978. 173 p.
This book provides readers with current and often little-known hints on how to run a profitable small business.

808. Stillman, Richard Joseph. *Small Business Management: How to Start and Stay in Business.* Boston: Little, Brown & Co., 1983. 229 p.
This comprehensive book focuses on all steps the entrepreneur should be aware of when starting a business as well as hints on how to stay in business.

809. Storich, Albert J. *How Accountants Multiply Profits from Small-Clients Services.* Englewood Cliffs, NJ: Executive Reports Corporation, 1980. 250 p.
This book tells how the accountant can provide the small business person with quality management services.

810. Stumm, David A. *The New Sales Manager's Survival Guide.* New York: AMACON, 1985. 234 p.
This book provides the information needed by the successful salesperson who is promoted to sales manager. Some of the areas covered are staffing, recruiting, interviewing, setting objectives, quotas, and budgets.

811. Szonyi, Andrew J., and Steinhoff, Dan. *Small Business Management Fundamentals.* Toronto: McGraw-Hill Ryerson Ltd., 1979. 408 p.
This book offers a simple, concise, how-to-do-it approach to small business management. This edition is slanted toward the Canadian business person with modifications in the areas of taxation, government, legal, and institutional information.

812. *Take a Look at Yourself: Self-in-System Sensitizers.* Boston: Power & Systems Training, Inc., 1978. 41 p.
The exercises in this book are designed to help you become more aware of your patterns of organizational behavior and to recognize potential for yourself and your system.

813. Tate, Curtis E., et al. *Successful Small Business Management.* 4th ed. Dallas, TX: Business Publications, Inc., 1985. 654 p.
In addition to providing a comprehensive coverage of small business management, this book provides material on the acquisition of a business. The author also discusses the type of life-style a small business offers and relates how it can conform to your personal objectives.

814. Thompson, Marilyn Taylor. *Management Information, Where to Find It.* Metuchen, NJ: Scarecrow Press, 1981. 272 p.
The material in this bibliography is divided into three categories: management in general, specific aspects of management, and specific types of management. Materials cited are those published during the 1970s in the English language.

815. Udell, Gerald G. *Managing the Small Service Firm for Growth and Profit.* Washington, DC: U.S. Small Business Administration, 1980. 58 p.
This book can help you obtain a better understanding of how to find business opportunities compatible with your experience and objectives and those that offer a good profit potential.

816. Vazsonyi, Andrew, and Spirer, Herbert F. *Quantitative Analysis for Business.* Englewood Cliffs, NJ: Prentice-Hall, Inc., 1984. 1,072 p.
For those with limited mathematical skills, this book offers an introduction to basic theory and practice and quantitative methods of managerial decision making.

817. Wallace, Marc J., Jr. and Fay, Charles H. *Compensation Theory and Practice.* Boston: Kent Publishing Co., 1983. 282 p.
The major emphasis of this book is to provide the line and compensation manager with the same knowledge base in the area of compensation.

818. Webber, Ross A.; Morgan, Marilyn A.; and Browne, Paul C. *Management: Basic Elements of Managing Organizations.* 3d ed. Homewood, IL: Richard D. Irwin, Inc., 1984. 744 p.
This complete introduction and survey of management bridges the gap between theory and practice.

819. Wellemin, John H. *The Handbook of Professional Service Management.* Brookfield, VT: Brookfield Publishing Co., Inc., 1984. 225 p.
This guide focuses on customer-service management and discusses the interrelations between customer service and other business functions.

820. Welsh, A. N. *The Skills of Management.* New York: AMACOM, 1979. 196 p.
Designed for practicing managers, this book describes practical tips and methods on how to manage people: how to make them do what you want and how to reconcile the objectives of business with the needs and aspirations of the staff.

821. White, Richard M, Jr. *The Entrepreneur's Manual.* Randor, PA: Chilton Book Co., 1977. 419 p.
This step-by-step workbook explains techniques for converting ideas into businesses by using MBO, management-by-exception, and management-by-motivation.

822. Winters, Raymond J. *It's Different When You Manage.* Lexington, MA: Lexington Books, 1983. 256 p.
This book is designed to help the reader gain insight into managerial effectiveness by carefully studying the techniques used by effective managers.

823. Woodcock, Mike, and Francis, Dave. *The Unblocked Manager: A Practical Guide to Self-Development.* Aldershot, Hants, England: Gower Publishing Co., Ltd., 1982. 241 p.
This book tells how managers and supervisors can develop their competence and become better able to cope with difficult organizational situations and make the most of their potential.

824. Woodcock, Mike, and Francis, Dave. *Unblocking Your Organization.* La Jolla, CA: University Associates, 1979. 253 p.
This book points out some ways of identifying aspects of your organization that need changing.

825. Wortman, Leon A. *A Deskbook of Business Management Terms.* New York: AMACOM, 1979. 615 p.
A brief explanation and examples of the practical usage of various management terms are included in this book.

826. Wortman, Leon A. *Successful Small Business Management.* New York: AMACOM, 1976. 262 p.
This reference of what the small business manager needs to know provides the basic organizational management, accounting, and marketing techniques that are needed to launch a small business.

827. Young, Jerrald F. *Decision Making for Small Business Management.* Malabar, FL: Robert E. Krieger Publishing Co., Inc., 1982. 248 p.
This book is designed to help the small business person make successful analyses and decisions. It includes information on legal implementations, planning, communications, records and reports, financial maneuvering, and public policy.

23. MARKETING

828. Adler, Lee, and Mayer, Charles S. *Managing the Marketing Research Function.* Chicago: American Marketing Association, 1977. 172 p.
The two themes in this book are a discussion of and suggestions for the most effective ways to manage the marketing research function and that market research represents an ongoing stream of activity designed to improve the market decision making of a specific division or firm.

829. Baier, Martin. *Elements of Direct Marketing.* New York: McGraw-Hill Book Co., 1983. 389 p.
The author of this book discusses and defines the total marketing concept and distinguishes direct marketing from general marketing.

830. Baker, Michael J., ed. *Macmillan Dictionary of Marketing & Advertising.* New York: Nichols Publishing Co., 1984. 217 p.
This book provides a detailed description of the many terms used in marketing and advertising with cross-references for ease of use.

831. Bencin, Richard L. *The Marketing Revolution: Understanding Major Changes in How Businesses Market.* Philadelphia, PA: Cresheim Publications, 1980. 198 p.
This author offers a look at trends in business-to-business marketing today including the transformation of "junk" mail into "direct" and profitable mail, the computer revolution, and the decline of the field sales force.

832. Betts, Jim. *The Million Dollar Idea.* Pt. Pleasant, NJ: Pt. Pleasant Publishing Co., 1985. 96 p.
This book is a guide to how to generate new product ideas, how to develop them, and how to sell them.

833. Blackwell, Roger D.; Johnston, Wesley J.; and Talarzyk, W. Wayne. *Cases in Marketing Management and Strategy.* Chicago: Dryden Press, 1985. 555 p.
This book includes 36 cases from a variety of industries, such as banks, insurance companies, food processors, and chemical firms.

834. Bloom, Paul N., and Smith, Ruth Belk, eds. *The Future of Consumerism.* Lexington, MA: Lexington Books, 1986. 220 p.
Experts in the field discuss the issues and trends that will confront consumerists regarding the impact of new technologies, health and saftey questions, and the governments as marketers.

835. Bonoma, Thomas V., and Shapiro, Benson P. *Segmenting the Industrial Market.* Lexington, MA: Lexington Books, 1983. 144 p.
This book shows how good marketing segmentation can save the executive time and money by avoiding inefficient marketing programs as well as poor marketing performance.

836. *Bradford's Directory of Marketing Research Agencies and Management Consultants in the U.S. and the World.* Fairfax, VA: Bradford's Directory of Marketing Reserch Agencies. (Biennial)
This directory lists over 500 market-research firms.

837. Bradway, Bruce M.; Frenzel, Mary Anne; and Pritchard, Robert E. *Strategic Marketing: A Handbook for Entrepreneurs and Managers.* Reading, MA: Addison-Wesley Publishing Co., 1982. 283 p.
Written from practical experience, this book focuses on specific marketing expertise in selected areas and includes a detailed business plan outline to aid business managers and owners in improving their efficiency and profits.

838. Brannen, William H. *Practical Marketing for Your Small Retail Business.* Englewood Cliffs, NJ: Prentice-Hall, Inc., 1981. 232 p.
This marketing book for small retailers of consumer goods and services adapts the consumer-oriented marketing concept to fit the needs of the small retailer. An eight-step process on how to build your retail marketing strategy is included.

839. Brannen, William H., comp. *Small Business Marketing: A Selected and Annotated Bibliography.* Chicago: American Marketing Association, 1978. 79 p.
The material annotated in this book was published prior to 1978. It includes books, journal articles, public documents, and other available sources.

840. Brannen, William H. *Successful Marketing for Your Small Business.* Englewood Cliffs, NJ: Prentice-Hall, Inc., 1978. 370 p.
While it is understood that the same principles of marketing apply to both the large firm and the small firm, this book adapts these principles to provide success in the small business.

841. *Business Research: Marketing.* Washington, DC: Research Publishing Co., Inc., 1986. 2 v.
This book provides information on how to apply marketing terms to operations in large and small businesses and tells how to find software and databases.

842. Cannon, Tom. *How to Win Profitable Business.* London: Business Books, Ltd., 1984. 238 p.
The three major sections on promoting your business discussed in this book are marketing and your business, the benefits of obtaining and using information, and putting marketing into action.

843. Chase, Cochrane, et al. *Solving Marketing Problems with VisiCalc.* Radnor, PA: Chilton Book Co., 1984. 286 p.
This book gives the marketing practitioner a background on how to design and implement a range of fundamental marketing analysis charts using VisiCalc.

844. Cheese, John, et al. *Maximising Marketing Effectiveness.* Bradford, England, MCB University Press, Ltd., 1985. 250 p.
This book looks at marketing in an organizational context, showing how it relates to the organization's total activity and objectives.

845. Chisnall, Peter M. *Marketing Research: Analysis and Measurement.* 2d ed. New York: McGraw-Hill Book Co., 1981. 391 p.
This book gives a systematic introduction to marketing research, including sampling methodology, statistical decision theory, advertising research, and scaling techniques.

846. Christopher, Martin, et al. *Effective Marketing Management.* Brookfield, VT: Renouf USA Inc., 1980. 192 p.
This book explains concepts and practices of modern marketing with answers to frequently asked questions at the end of each chapter.

847. Cohen, William A., and Reddick, Marshall E. *Successful Marketing for Small Business.* New York: AMACOM, 1981. 282 p.
The authors of this book have translated marketing theories into practical techniques and processes that the small business person can use to make marketing a successful part of business.

848. Cravens, David W. *The Sales Manager's Book of Marketing Planning.* Homewood, IL: Dow Jones-Irwin, 1983. 244 p.
The two purposes of this book are to provide executives with a basis for evaluating and refining established approaches to marketing planning and to offer a set of guidelines to implement a formal market plan.

849. Davidson, J. P., and Connor, R. A. *Marketing Your Consulting and Professional Services.* New York: John Wiley & Sons, Inc., 1985. 200 p.
This book focuses on the client-centered approach where consultants can target the smallest number of clients and markets in order to produce the greatest profitable revenue.

850. Davies, Anthony Hawes. *The Practice of Marketing Research.* 2d ed. London: William Heinemann, Ltd., 1983. 253 p.
This book explores and explains the basic components of marketing research, from defining the problem to a discussion of techniques and applications.

851. Davis, Robert T., and Smith, F. Gordon. *Marketing in Emerging Companies.* Reading, MA: Addison-Wesley Publishing Co., Inc., 1984. 159 p.
This book discusses the marketing plan and mix, sales management, consumer, industrial, and service marketing and is intended for managers in growth companies who are building a marketing strategy team.

852. Day, George S. *Strategic Market Planning: The Pursuit of Competitive Advantage.* St. Paul, MN: West Publishing Co., 1984. 237 p.
Designed for managers, this book discusses an approach to the problem of adapting businesses to their ever-changing competitive environments.

853. Denney, Robert W. *Marketing Accounting Services.* New York: Van Nostrand Reinhold Co., Inc., 1983. 269 p.
This comprehensive and authoritative reference work on the new and complex subject of marketing of account services covers the subject from both the management and an individual viewpoint.

854. *Departmental Merchandising and Operating Results of Department and Specialty Stores.* New York: National Retail Merchants Association, 1965-. (Kept up to date with supplements.)
This report provides merchants with comprehensively researched information guidelines that reflect the judgment of progressive merchants and gives superior merchandising and marketing information.

855. Dible, Donald M. *Small Business Success Secrets: How to Zap the Competition and Zoom Your Profits with Smart Marketing.* Fairfield, CA: Entrepreneur Press, 1980. 320 p.
This book shows how to spot high-profit products and services, how to identify good customers, how to get quick distribution, and how to promote your business inexpensively. In addition, a directory of national and international retailing, wholesaling, and distribution outlets is included.

856. Dommermuth, William P. *The Use of Sampling in Marketing Research.* Chicago: American Marketing Association, 1975. 37 p.
This book is intended for the marketing executive who relies on research data in making decisions. It includes an overview of sampling as well as some statistical principles on which sampling is based.

857. Dorff, Ralph L. *Marketing for the Small Manufacturer: How to Turn the Disadvantages of Being Small into Big Business Advantage.* Englewood Cliffs, NJ: Prentice-Hall, Inc., 1983. 193 p.
The author of this book shows how to make the marketing function visible and useful from the point of view of management, sales managers, researchers, buyers, advertising people, and salespeople. He includes some methods of adapting marketing strategies to manufacturing situations.

858. Elam, Houston, G., and Paley, Norton. *Marketing for the Non-Marketing Executive.* New York: AMACOM, 1978. 261 p.
Aimed at the nonmarketing manager, this book is divided into three parts: marketing environment, marketing process, and marketing strategy.

859. Ennis, F. Beaven. *Marketing Norms for Product Managers.* New York: Association of National Advertisers, Inc., 1985. 174 p.
This book gives the manager who is new to marketing a sound foundation for a successful marketing program. A useful desk-top guide for preparing marketing plans is included.

860. *Findex: The Directory of Market Research Reports, Studies and Surveys.* 7th ed. New York: Find/SVP, 1985. (With midyear supplements).
This reference tool is for planners, researchers, marketing managers, librarians, and top management. The reports from U.S. and foreign research firms include document title, concise description, publisher,

date, pages, and price on research industries, markets, products, and names of companies vital to your business.

861. Fisk, Raymond R., and Tansuhaj, Patriya S., eds. *Services Marketing: An Annotated Bibliography.* Chicago: AMA Publications, 1985. 256 p.
Over 1,900 references covering a period of 21 years are included in this bibliography. The two major headings included are Conceptual Insights, and Services Fields.

862. Forsyth, Patrick, ed. *Managing Sales & Marketing Training.* Brookfield, VT: Gower Publishing Co., 1984. 328 p.
This guide discusses the training tools, techniques, and organization of the marketing-training function.

863. Foxall, G. R. *Strategic Marketing Management.* New York: John Wiley & Sons, Inc., 1981. 273 p.
This book is intended as an introduction to marketing and attempts to present the basic marketing principles in a concise and stimulating fashion.

864. Gardner, David M., and Belk, Russell W. *A Basic Bibliography on Experimental Design in Marketing.* Chicago: American Marketing Association, 1980. 59 p.
The core around which this bibliography is organized is experimental design. This concept is heavily dependent on the statistical tool of analysis of variance.

865. Gelb, Gabriel M., and Gelb, Betsy D., eds. *Insights for Marketing Management.* 2d ed. Santa Monica, CA: Goodyear Publishing Co., 1977. 303 p.
This book of readings sheds light on the managing of marketing activities in such fields as public relations and government relations.

866. Goetsch, H. W. *How to Prepare and Use Marketing Plans for Profit.* St. Charles, IL: Marketing for Profit, Inc., 1979. 48 p.
The four areas on the market plan discussed in this book are how to analyze the solution, how to develop a blueprint, how to put the plan to work, and how to work with the plan.

867. *A Guide to Marketing New Industrial and Consumer Products.* Englewood Cliffs, NJ: Prentice-Hall, Inc., 1985. 106 p.
This checklist or time-planning aid studies the entire launch program and includes a case study and glossary.

868. Guth, William D., ed. *Handbook of Business Strategy.* Boston: Warren, Gorham & Lamont, 1985. 1 v. various paging.
Each of the 28 chapters in this book are authored by consultants, academics and managers who present a theoretical-oriented approach to marketing and management.

869. Hart, Norman A., and Stapleton, John. *Glossary of Marketing Terms.* 2d ed. London: William Heinemann, Ltd., 1981. 206 p.
A complete range of over 2,000 marketing and associated terms with a short explanation of each is included in this book.

870. Hartley, Robert F. *Marketing Mistakes.* 3d ed. New York: John Wiley & Sons, Inc., 1986. 296 p.
This book provides cases that represent classic marketing mistakes, involving both large and medium-sized firms.

871. Hartley, Robert F. *Marketing Successes: Historical to Present Day; What We Can Learn.* New York: John Wiley & Sons, Inc., 1985. 242 p.
This book describes the lessons that the entrepreneur can learn from marketing success stories and gives case histories on what companies did right and why they did it that way.

872. Hathaway-Bates, John. *How to Organize Your Marketing.* Beverly Hills, CA: Asigan, Ltd., 1981. 152 p.
The author of this book first discusses the marketing team and tells just who they are. He then provides a look at the organization of marketing analysis, growth analysis and sales management contracts and includes a number of forms useful in marketing planning.

873. Hathaway-Bates, John. *How to Promote Your Business.* Beverly Hills, CA: Asigan, Ltd., 1981. 152 p.
Among the topics this author discusses in this book are things to avoid in promoting your business, marketing methods, image marketing, how to consolidate marketing methods, trend marketing, and obtaining information on potential clients.

874. Hayes, R. S., and Elmore, G. B. *Marketing for Your Growing Business.* New York: John Wiley & Sons, Inc., 1985. 283 p.
Geared for the needs of the small business, this hands-on guide to developing a marketing plan features a step-by-step workbook approach.

875. Healy, Denis F. *Increasing Profits Through Better Marketing: The Marketing Productivity Audit.* Washington, DC: Distribution Research and Education Foundation, 1980. 173 p.
Provides an easy-to-use, systematic method that the wholesaler-distributor executive can use to analyze the company's marketing practices.

876. Hughes, G. David. *Marketing Management: A Planning Approach.* Reading, MA: Addison-Wesley Publishing Co., 1978. 576 p.
This text book gives an integrated framework on how to apply marketing concepts, theories, and findings. Planning worksheets are included.

877. Hutt, Michael D., and Speh, Thomas W. *Industrial Marketing Management: A Strategic View of Business Markets.* Chicago: Dryden Press, 1985. 632 p.
This revised version of an earlier book covers the entire spectrum of industrial marketing.

878. Kavis, Kenneth R. *Marketing Management.* 5th ed. New York: John Wiley & Sons, Inc., 1985. 841 p.
This text focuses on problems, decisions, and the decision-making process and covers market strategies and management, consumer behavior analysis, sales forecasting, product policies, advertising, pricing, and sales promotion.

879. Kerin, Roger A., and Peterson, Robert A., ed. *Perspectives on Strategic Marketing Management.* Boston: Allyn & Bacon, Inc., 1983. 483 p.

This book contains 31 articles on an introduction to strategic marketing management, corporate strategic planning and strategic marketing planning, strategic marketing management tasks, and strategic response to change.

880. Kobs, Jim. *Profitable Direct Marketing.* Chicago: Crain Books, 1979. 312 p.

This book provides a wealth of information on how to start and improve a direct marketing program. Includes information on how to select products and services, how to relate the offer to your objective, and how to test and use multimedia for the best results.

881. Kress, George. *Marketing Research.* 2d ed. Reston, VA: Reston Publishing Co., 1982. 427 p.

This book serves as an introduction on how to conduct marketing research, as well as how to evaluate the research of others.

882. Lace, Geoffrey. *Effective Marketing for the Smaller Business: A Practical Guide.* Newbury, Berkshire, England: Scope Books, Ltd., 1982. 221 p.

This book focuses on the practical side of marketing for the small business. A step-by-step approach to the functions of marketing is given.

883. Laczniak, Gene R., and Murphy, Patrick E. *Marketing Ethics: Guidelines for Managers.* Lexington, MA: Lexington Books, 1985. 182 p.

This book provides discussions on the ethics of advertising, sales management, field sales, marketing research, price setting and multinational marketing.

884. Lee, Donald D. *Industrial Marketing Research: Techniques and Practices.* 2d ed. New York: Van Nostrand Reinhold Co., Inc., 1984. 226 p.

This is a "how-to" book aimed at corporate users of marketing research, and is designed for those seeking a pragmatic application of industrial marketing research.

885. Lemmon, Wayne A. *The Owner's and Manager's Market Analysis Workbook for Small to Moderate Retail and Service Establishments.* New York: AMACOM, 1980. 230 p.

This book tells owners or managers of small retail and service establishments how to perform a basic marketing analysis and how to determine the potential probability of opening a specific business in a specific market location.

886. Levinson, Jay Conrad. *Guerrilla Marketing: Secrets for Making Big Profits from Your Small Business.* Boston: Houghton Mifflin Co., 1984. 226 p.

For those businesses that have very little money for marketing, this book provides an alternate to the standard expensive marketing techniques.

887. Luck, David Johnston, and Ferrell, O. C. *Marketing Strategy and Plans.* Englewood Cliffs, NJ: Prentice-Hall, Inc., 1985. 591 p.
This book attempts to integrate the various aspects of marketing into an understandable, cohesive plan.

888. Luther, William M. *The Marketing Plan: How to Prepare & Implement It.* New York: AMACOM, 1982. 182 p.
This book takes you through the development of a marketing plan. When completed the plan is designed to be fewer than ten pages in length and have the approval of management before a penny is spent on marketing.

889. McCarthy, E. Jerome, and Shapiro, Stanley J. *Basic Marketing.* Homewood, IL: Richard D. Irwin, Inc., 1983. 829 p.
This text is a thorough and complete introduction on the topic of marketing.

890. MacDonald, Charles R. *24 Ways to Greater Business Productivity: Master Checklist for Marketing, Advertising, Sales, Distribution, and Customer Service.* Englewood Cliffs, NJ: Institute for Business Planning, 1982. 446 p.
This marketing and self-audit manual can assist the entrepreneur in finding ways to improve marketing performance and functions.

891. *Marketing Planning: How Successful Companies Define & Command Profitable Markets.* Monterey, CA: Small Business Monitoring & Research Co., Inc., 1984. 56 p.
This book offers a step-by-step approach to forming and achieving clear market objectives. In addition, it shows how to conduct a customer analysis, how to establish market objectives, how to determine optimum pricing, and much more.

892. *Marketing-Sales Promotion-Advertising Handbook, 1984.* New York: National Retail Merchants Association, 1983. 84 p.
This book offers direction and help in organizing selling goals and includes plans to help accomplish these goals on schedule.

893. Miller, Mary Lynn. *Increasing Marketing Productivity.* New York: Conference Board, Inc., 1981. 10 p.
This pamphlet discusses ways to increase market productivity including topics on reallocating field resources, revamping the distribution system of the company, stengthening staff planning and support, altering the product mix, improving the information base, and controlling marketing costs.

894. *Minority Marketing.* Chicago: Crain Books, 1980. 88 p.
Focusing on minority marketing, this book includes discussions on minority markets and advertising. The two minorities highlighted here are blacks and Hispanics.

895. Moore, Lois K., and Plung, Daniel L., eds. *Marketing Technical Ideas and Products Successfully!* New York: The Institute of Electrical and Electronics Engineers, Inc., 1985. 390 p.
This book provides the reader with logical solutions to marketing questions and problems. It includes a solid understanding of almost every aspect of the marketing plan.

896. Nash, Edward L., ed. *The Direct Marketing Handbook.* New York: McGraw-Hill Book Co., 1984. 946 p.
This book presents the ideas of more than 60 well-known professionals in the field of direct marketing.

897. Newton, Charlotte, ed. *Helping Small Business Respond to Consumers' Needs.* Washington, DC: U.S. Department of Commerce, Office of Consumer Affairs, 1982. 88 p. (For sale by U.S. Government Printing Office.)
This book describes how four local and state consumer protection agencies produced successful small business workshops to help their communities improve relations with customers.

898. Nykiel, Ronald A. *Marketing in the Hospitality Industry.* Boston: CBI Publishing Co., Inc., 1983. 240 p.
This book discusses such topics as how to understand the hospitality industry, channels of distribution, marketing, public relations, packaging, pricing, and all aspects of marketing as they are used in the hospitality industry.

899. Osborne, G. Scott. *Electronic Direct Marketing.* Englewood Cliffs, NJ: Prentice-Hall, Inc., 1984. 163 p.
This book tells how to take advantage of the many marketing opportunities available through the electronic media.

900. O'Shaughnessy, John. *Competitive Marketing: A Strategic Approach.* Boston: Allen & Unwin, 1984. 372 p.
This book attempts to clarify confusion of the concept of marketing, while dispelling some of the traditional myths on the subject.

901. Pope, Jeffrey L. *Practical Marketing Research.* New York: AMACOM, 1981. 296 p.
This book provides a reference source for what you need to know to be a competent professional researcher. Specific problems and techniques involving product concepts, packaging, advertising, and sales testing are discussed.

902. Rewoldt, Stewart Henry; Scott, James D.; and Warshaw, Martin R. *Introduction to Marketing Management: Text and Cases.* Homewood, IL: Richard D. Irwin, Inc., 1981. 874 p.
This book provides information on the approaches and problems of marketing decision making and provides suggestions for the planning and execution of a complete marketing program.

903. Rexroad, Robert A. *High Technology Marketing Management.* New York: John Wiley & Sons, Inc., 1983. 219 p.
The theme of this book is the marketing management function as it deals with high technology products where the government is the direct or indirect customer.

904. Rexroad, Robert A. *Technical Marketing to the Government.* Chicago: Dartnell Corporation, 1981. (Loose leaf)
This manual is intended to help improve the methods of operation for the managers of government marketing functions, as well as helping to improve their efficiency. It describes how the government system operates and how managers can better operate within that system.

905. Rice, Craig S. *Marketing Planning Strategies.* Chicago: Dartnell Corporation, 1984. 434 p.
This manual develops some guidelines for successful marketing efforts as they affect corporations with limited financial capabilities.

906. Rogers, Leonard Alfred. *Business Analysis for Marketing Managers.* London: William Heinemann, Ltd., 1978. 174 p.
The purpose of this book is to enable the reader to make rational decisions regarding business activities via case analysis.

907. Roman, Murray. *Telemarketing Campaigns that Work!* New York: McGraw-Hill Book Co., 1983. 282 p.
This book includes actual plans, scripts, hard-data results, and step-by-step advice on telemarketing. It provides behind the scenes information on the most successful campaigns in fields ranging from publishing to banking, as well as campaigns in service industries, retailing, and much more.

908. Rushton, Angela M. "Marketing and Small Business." *European Journal of Marketing* 19 (1985).
This special issue looks at small business marketing from several perspectives.

909. Scitovsky, Tibor. *The Joyless Economy: An Inquiry into Human Satisfaction and Consumer Dissatisfaction.* Oxford: Oxford University Press, 1977. 310 p.
This book looks at people's tastes, how they spend their money and how they structure their lives.

910. Seltz, David D. *Food Service Marketing and Promotion.* New York: Lebhar-Friedman Books, 1977. 202 p.
The object of this book is to acquaint the reader with what others are doing in the food service industry and what you can do to help make your business distinctive, popular, and profitable.

911. Seltz, David D. *Handbook of Innovative Marketing Techniques.* Reading, MA: Addison-Wesley Publishing Co., 1981. 329 p.
Aimed at the small business person, this book shows how to achieve maximum market coverage with minimum capital outlay. It also tells how to reach all potential marketplaces as quickly, completely, and economically as possible.

912. Shama, Avraham. *Marketing in a Slow-Growth Economy: The Impact of Stagflation on Consumer Psychology.* New York: Praeger Publishers, 1980. 166 p.
This book discusses the combined impact of inflation, shortages, and recession on life-styles and consumption patterns. It is designed to help business and marketing executives cope with inflation.

913. Shanklin, William L., and Ryans, John K., Jr. *Marketing High Technology.* Lexington, MA: Lexington Books, 1984. 216 p.
This book provides some suggestions on what to do to increase the chances for success in high technology. The experiences of successful high-tech firms with specific concepts, methods, and activities are included.

914. Shapiro, Irving J. *Dictionary of Marketing Terms.* Totowa, NJ: Littlefield, Adams & Co., 1982. 276 p.
Arranged in alphabetical order, this book provides a brief explanation of the many terms used in marketing.

915. Sheth, Jagdish N. *Winning Back Your Market: The Inside Stories of the Companies that Did It.* New York: John Wiley & Sons, Inc., 1985. 225 p.
This book recommends nine generic strategies on how to convert a poor performer into a successful product. These nine strategies can be grouped into four categories: exploiting existing product uses in the markets; finding new markets; developing new uses for the product; and creating new uses in new markets.

916. Skacel, Robert K. *The Marketing Plan: How to Prepare It. . . What Should Be in It.* Chicago: Crain Books, 1985. 64 p.
This manual on how to prepare a marketing plan includes information on the definition of the present marketing situation, the analysis of problems, and how to establish objectives.

917. Smith, Brian R. *Successful Marketing for Small Business.* Brattleboro, VT: The Lewis Publishing Co., 1984. 237 p.
The author of this book first shows where marketing fits into the overall picture of a business. He then discusses marketing research and the marketing plan.

918. Smith, Roger F. *Entrepreneur's Marketing Guide.* Reston, VA: Reston Publishing Co., 1984. 239 p.
This easy-to-read book uses real-world examples on planning and meeting the daily demands of the business, including advertising, sales force development, evaluating the marketing plan, and much more.

919. Stone, Bob. *Successful Direct Marketing Methods.* 3d ed. Chicago: Crain Books, 1984. 496 p.
This updated book includes chapters on selecting and selling merchandise, producing leads, using the broadcast media, and a chapter on segmenting markets by life-style.

920. Strauss, Lawrence. *Electronic Marketing: Emerging TV and Computer Channels for Interactive Home Shopping.* White Plains, NY: Knowledge Industry Publications, Inc., 1983. 141 p.
While electronic marketing may be in the future, this book looks at some key elements that are necessary to its development.

921. Twedt, Dik Warren, ed. *Survey of Marketing Research.* Chicago: American Marketing Association. (Quinquennial)
This pamphlet includes the findings of a survey of more than 3,000 marketing research executives. The information is classified by size and type of company as well as growth and compensation rates.

922. Walters, C. Glenn, and Bergiel, Blaise J. *Marketing Channels.* 2d ed. Glenview, IL: Scott, Foresman & Co., 1982. 547 p.
The authors have attempted to present a book which will help the reader learn the concepts and theories related to the study of distribution channels.

923. Wizenberg, Larry, ed. *The New Products Handbook.* Homewood, IL: Dow Jones-Irwin, 1985. 350 p.
This book offers some insights into ways to stimulate creativity and innovation, how to optimize research and screen new products, how to facilitate technology transfer, and how to improve the chance of success and minimize the risk of failure when launching a new product.

24. OFFICE MANAGEMENT

924. Birchall, David W., and Hammond, V. J. *Tomorrow's Office Today: Managing Technological Change.* New York: John Wiley & Sons Inc., 1981. 202 p.
The goal of this book is to help the practicing manager anticipate and plan to overcome the problems raised by changing technology.

925. Capek, Leslie. *Transforming Your Office.* South Bend, IN: And Books, 1981. 196 p.
By looking at the business, the people, and the office, this author suggests ways to improve the office setting by pointing out changes necessary to meet the business needs of the future.

926. Chorafas, Dimitris N. *Office Automation: The Productivity Challenge.* Englewood Cliffs, NJ: Prentice-Hall, Inc., 1982. 272 p.
Beginning with a thorough discussion of basic concepts regarding office productivity, this book examines office automation, considering the equipment supplier's viewpoint. A step-by-step plan for a word processing package supporting editing and formatting is also included.

927. Cohen, Barbara G. F., ed. *Human Aspects in Office Automation.* New York: Elsevier, 1984. 322 p.
This book examines the workplace from a human health perspective and considers the physical environment as well as the mental health of office workers. It emphasizes safety and stress in the modern office.

928. Curran, Susan, and Mitchell, Horace. *Office Automation: An Essential Management Strategy.* London: Macmillan Publishing Co. Inc., 1982. 193 p.
This book provides an overview of the current state of office automation within the broad managerial context.

929. Keeling, Lewis, and Kallus, Norman F. *Administrative Office Management.* 8th ed. Cincinnati, OH: South-Western Publishing Co., 1984. 392 p.
The majority of this intensive introduction to office management is devoted to the effective use of human resources.

930. Kish, Joseph L. *Office Management Problem Solver.* Radnor, PA: Chilton Book Co., 1983. 363 p.
This book is intended as a reference guide for new office managers looking for a source of techniques for establishing office procedures, systems, and services.

931. Klein, Judy Graf. *The Office Book: Ideas and Designs for Contemporary Work Spaces.* New York: Facts on File, 1982. 288 p.
The physical features of an office and its furniture are discussed in this book, such as the elements of design, the adaptation of space, and office planning.

932. Konkel, Gilbert J., and Peck, Phyllis J. *Word Processing and Office Automation.* Stamford, CT: Office Publications, Inc., 1982. 167 p.
This book discusses hundreds of problems that management faces in developing an effective word processing system.

933. Moore, R. Keith, comp. Revised by Hunt, Susan. *How to Make Big Improvements in the Small PR Shop.* Washington DC: Council for the Advancement and Support of Education, 1985. 116 p.
Samples of guidelines, policies, job descriptions, and objectives for the PR manager are included in this book. Suggestions for better use of time and resources are also discussed.

934. Ruprecht, Mary M., and Wagoner, Kathleen P. *Managing Office Automation.* New York: John Wiley & Sons, Inc., 1984. 680 p.
This book offers suggestions to the manager on how to effectively handle the transition from the traditional to the automated office.

935. Wood, Pauline. *Handbook for a Small Office.* Bryn Mawr, PA: Dorrance & Co., 1982. 93 p.
This handbook is a useful tool for the small office that has a constant turnover of employees. It provides the basics on applying for employment, office equipment, accounts receivable and payable, payroll, and office management.

25. PERSONNEL MANAGEMENT (HIRING, JOB DESCRIPTIONS, MOTIVATION, RECRUITING, TRAINING, STRESS)

936. Abrahamson, Lee. *How to Develop and Administer an Effective Personnel Policy Program.* Barrington, IL: Omega Centre, 1980. (Loose leaf)
This loose-leaf book contains information and sample forms on personnel policy programs.

937. Aft, Lawrence S. *Wage and Salary Administration: A Guide to Job Evaluation.* Reston, VA: Reston Publishing Co., 1985. 264 p.
Intended for those whose job it is to analyze and administer wage and salary programs, this book describes procedures evaluating the work that people perform.

938. Albrecht, Karl G. *Stress and the Manager: Making It Work for You.* Englewood Cliffs, NJ: Prentice-Hall, Inc., 1979. 326 p.
The author emphasizes the importance of understanding stress—what it is, how it affects us physically, and how it affects our performance in the

work place. He also offers suggestions for controlling, redirecting, and managing stress to work to our advantage.

939. Aldag, Ramon J., and Brief, Arthur P. *Task Design and Employee Motivation.* Glenview, IL: Scott, Foresman & Co., 1979. 151 p.
Introducing a source of ideas that can be put to use as human resource management tools is the aim of this book. It includes such topics as essential employee motivation, job redesign, and the changing role of the worker.

940. Anthony, William P. *Managing Incompetence.* New York: AMACOM, 1981. 276 p.
This book tells the manager how to work with incompetent people.

941. Armstrong, Michael. *Be a Better Manager: Improve Performance, Profits, and Productivity.* Rev. ed. Vancouver, BC: International Self-Counsel Press, Ltd., 1984. 255 p.
This book discusses each of the management functions.

942. Arvey, Richard D. *Fairness in Selecting Employees.* Reading, MA: Addison-Wesley Publishing Co., 1979. 273 p.
The author of this book deals with the fairness of the full range of decision-making devices in employee selection including interview and height and weight requirements. and provides a review of the fairness of these selection devices as they affect minorities.

943. Baetz, Mary L. *The Human Imperative: Planning for People in the Electronic Office.* Homewood, IL: Dow Jones-Irwin, 1985. 185 p.
This book provides a new approach for integrating people, technology and the physical environment.

944. Begin, James P., and Beal, Edwin F. *The Practice of Collective Bargaining.* 7th ed. Homewood. IL: Richard D. Irwin, Inc., 1985. 576 p.
This new edition provides information on the basic approach to collective bargaining.

945. Bittel, Lester R. *What Every Supervisor Should Know: The Basics of Supervisory Management.* 5th ed. New York: Gregg Division, McGraw-Hill Book Co., 1985. 658 p.
This book includes studies on human relations, planning and control, staffing, training, how to cope with problem performers, management, and legal aspects of supervision.

946. Blanchard, Kenneth, and Johnson, Spencer. *The One Minute Manager.* New York: William Morrow & Co., Inc., 1982. 111 p.
This book relates how people work best with other people.

947. Blanchard, Kenneth, and Lorber, Robert. *Putting the One Minute Manager to Work.* New York: William Morrow & Co., Inc., 1984. 112 p.
A companion to *The One Minute Manager*, this book is a tool to implement the three secrets brought out in the previous book: set one

minute goals, give one minute praisings, and deliver one minute reprimands.

948. Brief, Arthur P., ed. *Managing Human Resources in Retail Organizations.* Lexington, MA: Lexington Books, 1984. 171 p.
This book discusses some current and important issues on the retail establishment and shows how research methods can be applied to the problems of managing people.

949. Bright, Deborah. *Gearing Up for the Fast Lane: New Tools for Management in a High-Tech World.* New York: Random House, Inc., 1985. 192 p.
New human and organizational skills are offered in this book to help the manager who is challenged by today's intensely competitive environment to come out on the top.

950. Broadwell, Martin M. *The Practice of Supervising: Making Experience Pay.* 2d ed. Reading, MA: Addison-Wesley Publishing Co., 1984. 191 p.
This book offers up-to-date supervisory practices for the experienced supervisor.

951. Brown, Paul L. *Managing Behavior on the Job.* New York: John Wiley & Sons, Inc., 1982. 190 p.
This practical guide for the working manager and executive includes projects and case histories based on actual situations of how to manage human resources.

952. Bullock, Gwendolyn A. *Performance Standards Handbook: A Reference for Managers and Supervisors.* Washington, DC: U.S. Office of Personnel Management, 1981. 56 p. (For sale by U.S. Government Printing Office.)
This self-evaluation tool can also be used to evaluate jobs ranging from secretary to supervisor.

953. Bullock, R. J. *Improving Job Satisfaction.* Elmsford, NY: Pergamon Press, Inc., 1984. 45 p.
This book gives an orientation to the issues of job satisfaction and reviews key areas of recent research.

954. Carlsen, Robert D., and McHugh, James F. *Handbook of Personnel Administration Forms and Formats.* Englewood Cliffs, NJ: Prentice-Hall, Inc., 1978. 549 p.
This catalog contains sample business forms that can actually be used in business, including models on employment, wage and salary administration, industrial relations, organization planning and development, and employee services.

955. Chruden, Herbert J., and Sherman, Arthur W., Jr. *Managing Human Resources.* 7th ed. Cincinnati, OH: South-Western Publishing Co., 1984. 656 p.
This book provides the most current theory, tools, and techniques that are used to improve productivity.

956. Cobb, Norman B. *How to Prepare a Personnel Policy Manual.* Holland, MI: Angus Downs, 1982. 252 p.
This book contains commentaries, analysis work sheets, sample policy statements, and procedural aids, all of which are color-coded, in an effort to make the reader aware of the most current practices and legal changes in the field of personnel management.

957. Cohn, Theodore, and Lindberg, Roy A. *Practical Personnel Policies for Small Business.* New York: Van Nostrand Reinhold Co., Inc., 1984. 216 p.
This book deals with effective personnel management. Topics included range from determining staff needs to coping with unionism.

958. *Create Your Employee Handbook—Fast and Professionally.* Westbury, NY: Caddylack Publishing, 1984. 65 p.
This easy-to-follow manual provides all the forms, guidelines and checklists needed to plan and carry out the writing of an employee handbook.

959. Danner, Jack. *People-Empathy: Key to Painless Supervision.* West Nyack, NY: Parker Publishing Co., Inc., 1976. 214 p.
By managing through empathy, this book shows you how this management technique can lead to job enrichment and growth.

960. Davidson, William Leslie. *How to Develop and Conduct Successful Employee Attitude Surveys.* Chicago: Dartnell Corporation, 1979. 258 p.
Some of the topics discussed in this book include job satisfaction, objections and procedures of attitude surveys, questionnaire development and administration, personal interviews, how to analyze data and draw conclusions, and much more.

961. Day, Janis. *A Working Approach to Human Relations in Organizations.* Monterey, CA: Brooks/Cole Publishing Co., 1980. 382 p.
This workbook provides original and creative ways to teach and learn "people" skills. It includes examples of assertive behavior, behavior modification, dissonance theory, and aggression management.

962. DeReamer, Russell. *Modern Safety and Health Technology.* New York: John Wiley & Sons, Inc., 1980. 615 p.
This book is a current "how-to" handbook on safety, accident prevention, and loss control. It offers details on the organization and administration of safety/health programs that are basic to modern management principles.

963. Dobrish, Cecelia; Wolff, Rick; and Zevnik, Brian. *Hiring the Right Person for the Right Job.* New York: Franklin Watts, 1984. 332 p.
This book serves as a hiring guide for business owners and managers and focuses on the personality traits best suited to various jobs within the organization. Topics include job analysis, employee testing, and the interviewing process.

964. DuBrin, Andrew J. *The Practice of Supervision: Achieving Results Through People.* Dallas TX: Business Publications, Inc., 1980. 493 p.
The author's purpose is to show how to increase productivity at the supervisory level by contributing to employee morale and satisfaction.

965. Eckles, Robert W.; Carmichael, Ronald L.; and Sarchet, Bernard R. *Supervisory Management: A Short Course in Supervision.* 2d ed. New York: John Wiley & Sons, Inc., 1983. 288 p.
Key supervisory skills for managing people, work, and day-to-day activities are discussed in this job-tested short course.

966. Elizur, Dov. *Job Evaluation: A Systematic Approach.* Aldershot, England: Gower Publishing Co., Ltd., 1980. 165 p.
This book presents a new method of job evaluation designed to overcome the limitations of conventional job evaluation methods.

967. Ellman, Edgar S. *Put It in Writing: A Complete Guide for Preparing Employee Policy Handbooks.* New York: Van Nostrand Reinhold Co., Inc., 1983. 144 p.
This handbook serves as a guide to help you produce your own employee policy handbook.

968. Evered, James F. *Shirt-Sleeves Management.* New York: AMACOM, 1981. 180 p.
Aimed at the business manager interested in employee growth and development, this book discusses various aspects of management, from selecting and recruiting employees to performance feedback.

969. Ewing, David W. *"Do It My Way Or You're Fired!" Employee Rights and the Changing Role of Management Prerogatives.* New York: John Wiley & Sons, Inc., 1983. 387 p.
This author addresses various manager-subordinate controversies such as how to motivate workers and handle dissents, finding an effective balance between employee rights and management prerogatives, and much more.

970. Field, Cynthia. *Taking Action on the Problem Employee.* Washington, DC: U.S. Office of Personnel Management, 1983. 20 p. (For sale by U.S. Government Printing Office.)
This book is a guide to how to weigh options and the methods available to fire problem workers.

971. Fisher, Roger, and Ury, William. *Getting to Yes: Negotiation Agreement without Giving in.* New York: Penguin Books, 1981. 161 p.
Some of the ways to negotiate your way through business problems, such as how to focus on interests not positions and how to establish precise goals at the beginning of negotiations, are covered in this book.

972. Fitz-enz, Jac. *How to Measure Human Resources Management.* New York: McGraw-Hill Book Co., 1984. 237 p.
The purpose of this book is to show how the organization can become more successful in running its human resources department.

973. *Flexible Compensation Plans.* New York: Practising Law Institute, 1984. 320 p.
Included in this book are discussions on the historical developements in flexible compensation, participant directed investment in individual account plans, flexible compensation plans, and the effects of flexibility on plan costs.

974. Fraser, T. M. *Human Stress, Work, and Job Satisfaction: A Critical Approach.* Washington, DC: International Labour Office, 1983. 72 p.
This book looks at the interrelationships between job satisfaction and stress.

975. Frew, David R. *Management of Stress: Using TM at Work.* Chicago: Nelson-Hall, Inc., Publishers, 1977. 235 p.
This book relates to the issues of understanding of work, work structure, and the interrelationship between work and nonwork activities.

976. Genua, Robert L. *The Employer's Guide to Interviewing: Strategy and Tactics for Picking a Winner.* Englewood Cliffs, NJ: Prentice-Hall, Inc., 1979. 180 p.
This book provides a systematic approach to help you conduct an effective interview.

977. Gershuny, J. I., and Miles, I. D. *The New Service Economy: The Transformation of Employment in Industrial Societies.* New York: Praeger Publishers, 1983. 281 p.
Dealing with the service industry in England, this book discusses employment in the service industry, the future of the industry, and draws conclusions and projections for the future.

978. Glaser, Rollin O. *Retail Personnel Management.* New York: Lebhar-Friedman Books, 1977. 434 p.
Pointing out the tremendous need for professionalism in the training, management development, and manpower planning areas, this book includes information on how to shape the retail personnel team, laws affecting employment relationships, compensation management, managing employee benefits, health and safety services, and how to keep unions out.

979. Goodworth, Clive T. *How to Be a Super-Effective Manager: A Guide to People Management.* London: Business Books, Ltd., 1984. 158 p.
This book contains practical advice and useful tips on how to be an effective manager.

980. Gorlin, Harriet, and Schein, Lawrence. *Innovations in Managing Human Resources.* New York: Conference Board, Inc., 1984. 38 p.
This book reports on an analysis of the experience of several companies on how they improved organizational effectiveness through the management of human resources.

981. Guest, Robert H. *Innovative Work Practices.* New York: Pergamon Press, 1982. 52 p.
Two aspects necessary to avoid personnel problems discussed in this book are quality of working life and job enlargement and enrichment.

982. Half, Robert. *Robert Half on Hiring.* New York: Crown Publishers, 1985. 241 p.
This leader in the field of personnel selection offers secrets that take the guesswork out of hiring. He shows how to spot phony references, how to establish criteria, and how to negotiate salaries.

983. Hannaford, Earle S. *Supervisors Guide to Human Relations.* 2d ed. Chicago: National Safety Council, 1976. 370 p.
This book provides step-by-step procedures for developing and managing people in on-the-job safety.

984. Harris, O. Jeff, Jr. *How to Manage People at Work: A Short Course for Professionals.* New York: John Wiley & Sons, Inc., 1985. 308 p.
The findings on industrial psychology are explained in this book, showing how to cut through the communication blocks created by employees.

985. Henderson, Richard I., and Clarke, Kitty Lewis. *Job Pay for Job Worth.* Atlanta, GA: Business Publications Division, College of Business Administration, Georgia State University, 1981. 328 p.
This book focuses on the job classification process and studies the pay system in the city of East Point, Georgia, using the Factor Evaluation System.

986. Hess, Karen, ed. *The Positive Manager.* New York: John Wiley & Sons, Inc., 1984. 160 p.
The idea behind this book is learning to manage by motivation. It helps the manager to develop a better understanding of five critical employee motivators: mission, goals, feedback, support, and rewards.

987. Hill, Norman C. *How to Increase Employee Competence.* New York: McGraw-Hill Book Co., 1984. 156 p.
This book focuses on the positive interpersonal development of the employee as a means of organizational effectiveness and improvement.

988. Hollinger, Richard C., and Clark, John P. *Theft by Employees.* Lexington, MA: Lexington Books, 1983. 176 p.
The occupational factors contributing to employee theft are discussed in this book along with other counterproductive forms of behavior.

989. Hunsaker, Phillip L., and Alessandra, Anthony J. *The Art of Managing People.* Englewood Cliffs, NJ: Prentice-Hall, Inc., 1980. 270 p.
This book is based on the premise that people perform best when they are allowed to obtain optimum personality expression while at work.

990. Imundo, Louis V. *The Effective Supervisor's Handbook.* New York: AMACOM, 1980. 239 p.
Many practical tips and workable programs for improving supervisor's performance are included in this book.

991. Jenks, Virginia O. *The Success Triad: Three Keys to Improving Human Relations in Business.* Englewood Cliffs, NJ: Prentice-Hall, Inc., 1983. 158 p.
This book focuses on motivation, communication, and leadership and how to gain a solid foundation in these three areas of human relations.

992. Johnson, Ron. *How to Manage People.* London: Business Books, Ltd., 1984. 228 p.
This book tells the manager how to work better through his or her employees.

993. Keating, Charles J. *Dealing with Difficult People: How You Can Come Out on Top in Personality Conflicts.* New York: Paulist Press, 1984. 212 p.
While discussing how to deal with difficult people in all walks of life, there is one chapter in this book that looks at how to deal with difficult people on the job.

994. King, Patricia. *Performance Planning and Appraisal: A How-To Book for Managers.* New York: McGraw-Hill Book Co., 1984. 160 p.
This guideline on how to evaluate employee performance is written in a clear, conversational style.

995. Kingsley, Daniel T. *How to Fire an Employee.* New York: Facts on File, Inc., 1985. 204 p.
The author explains the psychology behind preparing for, carrying out, and resolving the process of firing an employee, for such reasons as reduction in force, poor performance and attitude problems, age and personality differences.

996. Kirkpatrick, Donald L. *How to Improve Performance Through Appraisal and Coaching.* New York: AMACOM, 1982. 262 p.
This book looks at performance appraisals regarding on-the-job coaching in new areas of work as well as counseling in the employees' weak areas of performance.

997. Levi, L. *Stress in Industry: Causes, Effects and Prevention.* Washington DC: International Labour Office, 1984. 70 p.
This book attempts to answer such common questions about stress such as how does it feel? what does it mean? how common is it? can it be cured or prevented?

998. Levinson, Priscilla. *A Guide for Improving Performance Appraisal: A Handbook.* Washington, DC, U.S. Office of Personnel Management, Workforce Effectiveness and Development Group, 1982. 28 p. (For sale by U.S. Government Printing Office.)
This concise but complete report provides some guidelines on how to analyze the job performance of subordinates.

999. Lindo, David K. *Supervision Can Be Easy!* New York: AMACOM, 1979. 272 p.
This practical, easy-to-read guide gives the reader tips on how to handle supervisory concerns and problems.

1000. Lorentzen, John F. *The Manager's Personnel Problem Solver: A Handbook of Creative Solutions to Human Relations Problems in Your Organization.* Englewood Cliffs, NJ: Prentice-Hall, Inc., 1980. 266 p.
This book attempts to offer new and innovative solutions to some of the age-old problems faced by personnel managers.

1001. McCulloch, Kenneth J. *Selecting Employees Safely under the Law.* Englewood Cliffs, NJ: Prentice-Hall Inc., 1981. 392 p.
This EEO guidebook for personnel practices tells ways to avoid various types of discriminatory practices when hiring, firing, and determining promotion for terms and conditions of employment.

1002. McCurry, Charles M. *Bank Personnel Administration: A Basic Plan.* Rev. ed. Rolling Meadows, IL: Bank Administration Institute, 1979. 229 p.
This manual for those responsible for personnel programs, particularly in community banks, covers the essential principles and practices of good personnel administration.

1003. McDonald, James O. *Management without Tears: A Guide to Coping with Everyday Organizational Problems.* Chicago: Crain Books, 1981. 149 p.
This step-by-step guide covers the secrets of becoming a successful manager. It tells how to delegate, track budgets, prepare flexible schedules, interview, hire, and prepare performance appraisals.

1004. Matteson, Michael T., and Ivancevich, John M. *Managing Job Stress and Health: The Intelligent Person's Guide.* New York: Free Press, 1982. 289 p.
This book discusses the cause of work-related stress and looks at how you respond to stressors as well as the effects stress may have on your health and job performance. It also tells what you can do to prevent or neutralize stress outcomes.

1005. Miller, Edwin L.; Burach, Elmer; and Albrecht, Maryann H., eds. *Management of Human Resources.* Englewood Cliffs, NJ: Prentice-Hall, Inc., 1980. 455 p.
This book includes a series of papers by experts in the field on such topics as changing organizational environment, human resource management planning, maintaining a human resource management system, employee behavior, and how to assess individual qualifications.

1006. Miller, Michael Floyd. *Detecting Training Needs: A Guide for Supervisors and Managers.* Washington, DC: Civil Service Commission, Bureau of Training, 1978. 62 p. (For sale by U.S. Government Printing Office.)
This self-quiz style book helps supervisors to locate and analyze training needs in their staff as well as for themselves.

1007. Miner, John B. *People Problems: The Executive's Answer Book.* New York: Random House, Inc., 1985. 320 p.
An industrial psychologist, the author identifies symptoms and sources of poor on-the-job performance and tells what the employer should and should not do about them.

1008. Mondy, R. Wayne, and Noe, Robert M. *Personnel: The Management of Human Resources?* 2d ed. New York: Allyn & Bacon, Inc., 1984. 672 p.
This combination of strategy and practice shows how human resource management actually works. The book includes cases, incidents, and actual company forms and procedures, and offers practical information about job analysis, cost/benefit analysis, job previews, and criterion-related validity.

1009. Morin, William J., and Yorks, Lyle. *Outplacement Techniques: A Positive Approach to Terminating Employees.* New York: AMACOM, 1982. 200 p.
Intended to appeal to the personnel manager who is concerned with establishing and maintaining effective company practices in the area of firing employees, this book describes policies and skills that should characterize this process.

1010. Mosley, Donald C.; Megginson, Leon C.; and Pietri, Paul H. *Supervisory Management: The Art of Working with and Through People.* Cincinnati, OH: South-Western Publishing Co., 1984. 512 p.
A comprehensive coverage of supervisory management as it applies to the first-line supervisor is the theme of this book.

1011. Olson, Richard F. *Managing the Interview.* New York: John Wiley & Sons, Inc., 1980. 183 p.
This book shows how to use selection and appraisal interviewing to select and promote qualified employees.

1012. Peck, Charles. *Pay & Performance: The Interaction of Compensation & Performance Appraisal.* New York: Conference Board, Inc., 1984. 23 p.
This study focuses on pay for performance for such employees as field sales representatives and top executives.

1013. *Personnel Management Abstracts.* Ann Arbor, MI: Graduate School of Business Administration, University of Michigan. (Quarterly)
This book includes annotated subject listings of articles on management functions, behavior in organizations, decision making, planning, and motivation.

1014. *Problems on the Job: A Supervisor's Guide to Coping.* Washington, DC: Office of Personnel Management, 1981. 8 p. (For sale by U.S. Government Printing Office.)
This book offers some helpful suggestions on how the "new" manager can handle employee problems including drug and alcohol abuse. Also contains a reference guide.

1015. Quick, Thomas L. *The Manager's Motivation Desk Book.* New York: John Wiley & Sons, Inc., 1984. 456 p.
The author offers managers a systematic and practical approach to improving employee motivation. He has included checklists, guidelines, and review quizzes to help managers get immediate results.

1016. Ramey, Ardella R., and Mrozek, Ronald A. *A Company Policy and Personnel Workbook.* Sunnyvale, CA: Oasis Press, 1983. (Loose leaf)
This volume provides model personnel policies for the small business.

1017. Reimold, Cheryl. *Being a Boss.* New York: Dell Publishing Co., Inc., 1984. 60 p.
This book tells how to meet the many challenges for being a good boss such as understanding what it means to be a boss, the techniques needed for hiring the right people, delegating work and staying in control, and how to motivate your people.

1018. Revelle, Jack B. *Safety Training Methods.* New York: John Wiley & Sons, Inc., 1980. 248 p.
This book covers the design, implementation, and monitoring of on-the-job safety training.

1019. Rice, Craig S. *Getting Good People and Keeping Them: A Manager's Guide.* New York: AMACOM, 1982. 312 p.
Part one of this book provides information for managers on how to get the best results from their employee groups, units, teams, or departments. The second part focuses on the managers and how they can become top performers.

1020. Rimler, George W., and Humphreys, Neil J. *Small Business—Developing the Winning Management Team.* New York: AMACOM, 1980. 180 p.
The authors provide information on how to improve the small business manager's ability to develop their personnel within the organization. A workbook at the end contains 12 exercises on management.

1021. Robbins, Stephen P. *Personnel: The Management of Human Resources.* 2d ed. Englewood Cliffs, NJ: Prentice-Hall, Inc., 1982. 520 p.
A full range of topics in human resources management is covered in this book.

1022. Robinson, Pauline K. *Organizational Strategies for Older Workers.* Elmsford, NY: Pergamon Press, Inc., 1983. 32 p.
This book tells how to manage a work force in which age is an important factor. Issues and concerns important to older workers are discussed.

1023. Roseman, Edward. *Managing Employee Turnover: A Positive Approach.* New York: AMACOM, 1981. 260 p.
This book focuses on the average line manager and his or her responsibility in controlling turnover.

1024. Roseman, Edward. *Managing the Problem Employee.* New York: AMACOM, 1982. 262 p.
This book provides managers with ways to help the problem employee. It first offers the manager a way to better understand problem employees, then provides strategies for managing these employees, and finally gives specific strategies for managing 23 common types of problem employees.

1025. Roxe, Linda A. *Personnel Management for the Smaller Company: A Hands-On Manual.* New York: AMACOM, 1979. 246 p.
Since many smaller businesses do not have a personnel director, this book can be used as a "hands-on" guide to establishing sound personnel practices.

1026. Scott, William H. *How to Earn More Profits Through the People Who Work for You.* Englewood Cliffs, NJ: Prentice-Hall, Inc., 1982. 104 p.
The author of this book describes how the small company can gain from a good personnel management program. A step-by-step outline shows how to successfully recruit and select good personnel.

1027. Seppala, John A. *Is That Troubled Employee Still Troubling You? A Strategy for Supervisors.* Center City, MN: Hazeldon Foundation, 1981. 9 p.
This booklet tells how to use employee assistance programs to deal with employee problems. It illustrates both the situations and the solution.

1028. Sethi, Amerjit Singh, and Schuler, Randall S., eds. *Handbook on Organizational Stress Coping Strategies.* Cambridge, MA: Ballinger Publishing Co., 1984. 336 p.
Some of the strategies studied in this book include transaction process models, time management, organizational practices for preventing burnout, use of support groups, and organizational stress auditing.

1029. Shafritz, Jay M. *Dictionary of Personnel Management and Labor Relations.* Oak Park, IL: Moore Publishing Co., Inc., 1980. 429 p.
This dictionary provides detailed descriptions of the terms used on the theory, concepts, practices, and laws in personnel management and labor relations.

1030. Shea, Gordon F. *The New Employee: Developing a Productive Human Resource.* Reading, MA: Addison-Wesley Publishing Co., 1981. 238 p.
This primary reference work for those involved in human resource development covers such topics as motivation, recruitment and selection, the critical first day, probationary period, discovering an individual's potential, career counseling, and much more.

1031. Siegel, William Laird. *People Management for Small Business.* New York: John Wiley & Sons, Inc., 1978. 130 p.
This practical guide to finding the best employees is divided into three major areas: hiring, orientation and training, and people management.

1032. Slyman, Raymond A. *Why Managers Fail.* Cincinnati, OH: National Underwriter Co., 1977. 136 p.
Some of the topics covered in this book are recruiting, training, supervision, upgrading employees, and development.

1033. Stanton, Erwin Schoenfeld. *Successful Personnel Recruiting and Selection.* New York: AMACOM, 1977. 214 p.
This book provides a proven, practical system for recruiting, interviewing, and selecting personnel successfully.

1034. Tjosvold, Dean. *Managing Work Relationships: Cooperation, Conflict and Power.* Lexington, MA: Lexington Books, 1986.
The management techniques useful in helping people work together better are discussed in this book.

1035. Townsend, Robert. *Further up the Organization.* New York: Knopf, 1984. 254 p.
This book studies how people do work together and how they should work together.

1036. Truitt, John. *Executive's Manual of Professional Recruiting.* New York: Facts on File, Inc., 1985. 160 p.
This executive-recruitment handbook is based on the techniques of professional headhunters and is geared for the busy manager. It provides a systematic approach to conducting an independent search for the right candidate.

1037. Ulery, John D. *Job Descriptions in Manufacturing Industries.* New York: AMACOM, 1981. 161 p.
The aim of this book is to assist employers in defining the duties and responsibilities of their employees through detailed job descriptions.

1038. Ullrich, Robert A. *Motivation Methods that Work.* Englewood Cliffs, NJ: Prentice-Hall, Inc., 1981. 149 p.
This book offers suggestions on how to alleviate declining labor productivity and increased rates of absenteeism.

1039. Vough, Clair F. *Productivity, A Practical Program for Improving Efficiency.* Saranac Lake, NY: AMA Book Club Services, 1979. 212 p.
This book provides a field-tested system showing how to get more and better work from employeees in a variety of jobs.

1040. Walker, James W. *Human Resource Planning.* New York: McGraw-Hill Book Co., 1980. 418 p.
The four areas of human resource planning discussed in this book are managerial concerns and staff roles, needs forecasting, performance management, and career management.

1041. Warshaw, Leon J. *Managing Stress.* Reading, MA: Addison-Wesley Publishing Co., Inc., 1979. 212 p.
This book suggests several programs that can be used to alleviate the effects of stress on individuals, groups, and the entire organization.

1042. Williams, J. Clifton. *Human Behavior in Organizations.* Cincinnati, OH: South-Western Publishing Co., 1982. 528 p.
This book tells how to understand, predict, and influence human behavior in organizations through the use of behavioral theory.

1043. Wortman, Max S., Jr., and Sperling, JoAnn. *Defining the Manager's Job: A Manual of Position Descriptions.* 2d ed. New York: AMACOM, 1980. 434 p.
This book looks at managerial position descriptions and shows how to compare a company's present programs with those of similar organizations.

26. PLANT LOCATION (REAL ESTATE)

1044. *A Guide to Industrial Site Selection.* Washington, DC: Society of Industrial Realtors and National Association of Industrial and Office Parks, 1979. 32 p.
This guide directed primarily toward business and corporate real estate personnel includes such topics as facility planning site selection, regional, and community factors, as well as site criteria that are important to those selecting a location of a business.

1045. *Industrial Real Estate.* 4th ed. Washington, DC: S.I.R. Educational Fund of the Society of Industrial Realtors of the National Association of Realtors, 1984. 721 p.
This ready reference tool for real estate practitioners includes information on the rapidly changing economic and regulatory conditions that affect real estate needs of industry. It also offers facts on how real estate transactions are structured and consummated.

1046. Miller, E. Willard, and Miller, Ruby M. *Industrial Location and Planning: Theory, Models and Factors in Localization: A Bibliography.* Monticello, IL: Vance Bibliographies, 1984. 49 p.
This bibliography includes 541 references on books, articles, government bulletins and other publications on the topic of industrial location and planning.

1047. *New Project File and Site Selection Checklist.* Atlanta, GA: Conway Publications, 1979. (Loose leaf)
The purpose of this book is to present the development of a working checklist for location decisions. It provides a logical sequence, beginning with the determination of needs for a facility, establishing criteria for the specific plant to the selection of a site, construction, and disposition of the plant as surplus property after it has served its purpose.

1048. Oakey, Raymond. *High Technology Small Firms: Innovation and Regional Development in Britain and the United States.* New York: St. Martin's Press, 1984. 179 p.
The problems of industrial location and regional development of small high technology instrument and electronics firms in the U.S. and U.K. are discussed in this book.

1049. Rowe, James E. *Industrial Plant Location.* Monticello, IL: Vance Bibliographies, 1980. 52 p.
This bibliography includes material published on the empirical foundation of understanding plant location.

1050. Ryans, John K., Jr. and Shanklin, William L. *Guide to Marketing for Economic Development: Competing in America's Second Civil War.* Columbus, OH: Publishing Horizons, Inc., 1986. 361 p.
This book is designed to help the economic developer, the entrepreneur, or facility locator better market their communities as well as enable corporations to make better location decisions.

1051. Schmenner, Roger W. *Making Business Location Decisions.* Englewood Cliffs, NJ: Prentice-Hall, Inc., 1982. 268 p.
This book is a checklist of things to consider when choosing a new plant location. It not only discusses the factors that can influence a site choice, it also takes a broader view of decision making.

1052. Smith, David M. *Industrial Location: An Economic Geographical Analysis.* 2d ed. New York: John Wiley & Sons, Inc., 1981. 492 p.
This book is aimed at giving the reader an understanding of industrial location selection through the examination of economic and geographic variables.

1053. Stafford, Howard A. *Principles of Industrial Facility Location.* Atlanta, GA: Conway Publications, 1980. 275 p.
This book provides an overview of "state of the art" information on industrial location decisions and gives insight into the essential nature of the location decision process.

1054. Sweet, Morris L. *Industrial Location Policy for Economic Revitalization: National and International Perspectives.* New York: Praeger Publishers, 1981. 184 p.
The government policies and programs that control the location pattern of industry are discussed in this book along with their effects on industrial development and policy.

1055. Webber, Michael J. *Industrial Location.* Beverly Hills, CA: Sage Publications, Inc., 1984. 95 p.
This author analyzes both the strategy and pattern of the location decisions of firms. Some concerns studied here are motivation, profits, transport costs, production costs, and agglomeration.

27. PRODUCTION (QUALITY CONTROL, TIME MANAGEMENT, AUTOMATION)

1056. Baird, John E. *Quality Circles: Leader's Manual.* Prospect Heights, IL: Waveland Press, 1982. 192 p.
This book contains material on the skills needed to participate in quality circle programs. It also includes three chapters on quality circle leader-

ship style, participative leadership, and steps necessary to perform as a quality circle leader.

1057. Barkas, J. L. *Creative Time Management.* Englewood Cliffs, NJ: Prentice-Hall, Inc., 1984. 151 p.
This book provides techniques for productive and efficient time management to help the business person get organized.

1058. Barnes, Ralph M. *Motion and Time Study: Design and Measurement of Work.* 7th ed. New York: John Wiley & Sons, Inc., 1980. 689 p.
This book presents the basic principles that underlie the successful use of motion and time study. Illustrations and practical examples are included.

1059. Carter, C. L. *Quality Assurance, Quality Control and Inspection Handbook: A Guide for Quality, Reliability, Manufacturing, Engineering, Purchasing, Sales, Marketing and All Management & Personnel.* 4th ed, rev. Richardson, TX: C. L. Carter, Jr. and Associates, 1984. 128 p.
This pocket handbook is intended to be used on a day-to-day basis for personal planning, career growth and development, training and motivation, and for the operation of quality, reliability, safety, and inspection functions.

1060. Corbin, Richard H., and Gamache, R. Donald. *Creating Profitable New Products and Markets.* New York: AMACOM, 1980. 53 p.
This book presents an approach to provide workable solutions to the problem of creating new products. The three areas of the approach discussed here are preparation, creation, and evaluation/qualification.

1061. Crocker, Olga; Charney, Cyril; and Chiu, John. *Quality Circles: A Guide to Participation and Productivity.* New York: Facts on File, Inc., 1985. 312 p.
This book explores the theoretical and practical implications of quality circles for American industry.

1062. Dewar, Donald L. *The Quality Circle Guide to Participation Management.* Englewood Cliffs, NJ: Prentice-Hall, Inc., 1980. 414 p.
This book presents basic information on what quality circles are and how they can be used in an organization.

1063. Dewar, Donald L. *Quality Circle Leader Manual and Instruction Guide.* Red Bluff, CA: Quality Circle Institute, 1980. 226 p.
This manual provides step-by-step instructions on employee involvement in quality control.

1064. Dewar, Donald L. *Quality Circle Member Manual.* Red Bluff, CA: Quality Circle Institute, 1984. 165 p.
Step-by-step instructions on employee involvement in quality control are provided in this book.

1065. Dewar, Donald L. *Quality Circles: Answers to 100 Frequently Asked Questions.* Rev. Red Bluff, CA: Quality Circle Institute, 1984. 48 p.
This book is a brief ready reference for those who wish to become more acquainted with quality circles.

1066. Fabrycky, W. J., and Mize, J. H., eds. *Motion and Time Study: Improving Productivity.* 6th ed. Englewood Cliffs, NJ: Prentice-Hall, Inc., 1985. 752 p.
This text describes and analyzes the techniques and applications of motion and time studies for the purpose of improving productivity in the workplace.

1067. Feigenbaum, A. V. *Total Quality Control.* 3d ed. New York: McGraw-Hill Book Co., 1983. 851 p.
This book presents quality control as a body of managerial, technological, behavioral, and economic knowledge and as a means of improving industrial operations for both national and international markets.

1068. Fitzgerald, Laurie, and Murphy, Joseph. *Installing Quality Circles: A Strategic Approach.* San Diego, CA: University Associates, Inc., 1982. 134 p.
This book attempts to answer questions on the installation process of quality circle programs.

1069. Gibson, Price. *Quality Circles: An Approach to Productivity Improvement.* New York: Pergamon Press, Inc., 1982. 79 p.
This annotated bibliography includes material by U.S. practitioners who have been responsible for investigating, initiating, and expanding quality circles in industry, banking, and military.

1070. *Glossary and Tables for Statistical Quality Control.* 2d ed. Milwaukee, WI: American Society for Quality Control, 1983. 160 p.
This book gives a glossary of terms and selected tables useful in statistical quality control applications.

1071. Gregerman, Ira B. *Productivity Improvement: A Guide for Small Business.* New York: Van Nostrand Reinhold Co., Inc., 1984. 239 p.
The author of this book provides true situations as well as developing certain concepts to clarify various aspects of successful productivity for the small business entrepreneur.

1072. Gryna, Frank M. *Quality Circles: A Team Approach to Problem Solving.* New York: AMACOM, 1981. 96 p.
An introduction to the quality circle concept, this book also provides guidance on how to use the quality circle approach to management.

1073. *Guide for Reducing Quality Costs.* Milwaukee, WI: American Society for Quality Control, 1977. 46 p.
This book provides techniques for using quality costs in programs and tells how to reduce costs and improve profits.

1074. Ingle, Sud. *Quality Circles Master Guide: Increasing Productivity with People Power.* Englewood Cliffs, NJ: Prentice-Hall, Inc., 1982. 246 p.
This book develops a systematic approach to quality circles emphasizing the practical implementation of a program as well as providing a model program.

1075. Ingle, Sud, and Ingle, Nima. *Quality Circles in Service Industries: Comprehensive Guidelines for Increased Productivity and Efficiency.* Englewood Cliffs, NJ: Prentice-Hall, Inc., 1983. 353 p.
This book tells how to implement the quality circle process in a systematic and practical way.

1076. Johnson, Ross H., and Weber, Richard T. *Buying Quality.* New York: Franklin Watts, Inc., 1985. 221 p.
This book focuses on total-quality concept, beginning with the procurement of materials and continuing to the finished product.

1077. Kregoski, Ronald, and Scott, Beverly. *Quality Circles: How to Create Them, How to Manage Them, How to Profit from Them.* Chicago: The Dartnell Corporation, 1982. 273 p.
This book covers all aspects of quality circles, first providing a background of employee involvement, explaining quality circles with instructions on how to train quality circle leaders and how to use quality circles in business.

1078. Langevin, Roger G. *Quality Control in the Service Industries.* New York: AMACOM, 1977. 38 p.
In addition to providing an overview of quality control in service industries, this book suggests bases for measuring quality performance.

1079. Lebov, Myrna. *Practical Tools and Techniques for Managing Time.* New York: Executive Enterprises Publications Co., 1980. 79 p.
The theme of this book is time management—making limited time on the job productive.

1080. Lefton, R. E.; Buzzotta, V. R.; and Sherberg, Manuel. *Improving Productivity Through People Skills.* Cambridge, MA: Ballinger Publishing Co., 1980. 504 p.
This book provides ideas on how to increase personal and company productivity.

1081. Mackenzie, R. Alec. *The Time Trap: How to Get More Done in Less Time.* New York: McGraw-Hill Book Co., 1975. 195 p.
Proven ways to cut through major time-wasting problems are included in this book. The author shows you how to focus your energies on priorities, tying time to objectives, and delegating authority.

1082. Niebel, Benjamin W. *Motion and Time Study.* 7th ed. Homewood, IL: Richard D. Irwin, Inc., 1982. 756 p.
This book offers general information on sound time standards and modern techniques for improving worker motivation.

1083. *Quality Circles: A Dynamic Approach to Productivity Improvement.* Waterford, CT: Bureau of Business Practice, 1981. 64 p.
This book provides basic information on quality circles and can be used to determine if quality circles will be effective in your company.

1084. *Quality Circles: Management Fad or Work Force Tool?* New York: Research Institute of America, 1982. 14 p.
The general overview of quality circles is given in this book as well as the steps necessary for setting up such a program. A list of consultants (with addresses) in the quality circle field is included.

1085. *Quality Circles: New Approach to Productivity.* New York: Alexander Hamilton Institute, Inc., 1981. 110 p.
This author explains the philosophy of the importance of quality circles and provides a systematic description on how to start a new program or upgrade an existing one.

1086. *Quality Circles: Participant's Manual.* Prospect Heights, IL: Waveland Press, 1982. 192 p.
This book is a manual designed to teach the skills needed to participate effectively in a quality circle program.

1087. Robson, Mike. *Quality Circles: A Practical Guide.* Aldershot, England: Gower Publishing Co., Ltd., 1982. 204 p.
Information is included in this book on introducing quality circle programs into the organization as well as a discussion of how they work.

1088. Taylor, Harold L. *Making Time Work for You: A Guide to Effective & Productive Time Management.* New York: Beaufort Books, Inc., 1981. 172 p.
This time management book contains a number of techniques that managers can adopt to personal use, such as categorizing income information, a monthly ticker file. Useful for marketing, sales, and advertising managers.

1089. Thompson, Philip C. *Quality Circles: How to Make Them Work in America.* New York: AMACOM, 1982. 198 p.
A clear look at the concept and process and the steps necessary to reach these goals are discussed in this book.

1090. Webber, Ross A. *A Guide to Getting Things Done.* New York: Macmillan Publishing Co., Inc., 1980. 166 p.
The author of this book offers concrete and specific methods on how to overcome procrastination and put plans into action.

1091. Webber, Ross A. *Time Is Money! The Key to Managerial Success.* New York: The Free Press, 1980. 166 p.
This book shows you how to manage time in the short run by describing lists, diaries, logs, and time plans. In addition, the author discusses how to manage time in the long run, through delegating, attacking role stress, and defining goals.

1092. Work in America Institute. *Quality Circles: An Approach to Productivity Improvement.* Elmsford, NY: Pergamon Press, Inc., 1982. 79 p.
This book contains information on issues of interest to organizations considering the implementation of the quality circles process.

28. PURCHASING

1093. *Aljian's Purchasing Handbook.* 4th ed. New York: McGraw-Hill Book Co., 1982. 1 v. various paging.
This handbook can help the purchasing manager ensure delivery of the right commodity or service at the right time. Topics discussed are purchasing responsibilities, legal considerations, training, sources of supply, budgeting, and management.

1094. Dollar, William E. *Effective Purchasing and Inventory Control for Small Business.* Boston: INC/CBI Publishing Co., 1983. 143 p.
This book gives the small business owner/manager the necessary working tools to manage purchasing and inventory dollars effectively and to create an awareness of their profit potential.

1095. Dollar, William E. *Purchasing Management and Inventory Control for Small Business.* Washington, DC: U.S. Small Business Adminstration, Office of Management Information and Training, 1980. 66 p. (For sale by U.S. Government Printing Office.)
This book provides ways to evaluate existing purchasing policies and improve on them.

1096. Messner, William A. *Profitable Purchasing Management: A Guide for Small Business Owners/Managers.* New York: AMA-COM, 1982. 309 p.
Aimed at the rising buyer or young purchasing executive in the small firm, this book looks at some of the functions and responsibilities of this position, information on vendor relations and negotiations, and the ethics of purchasing.

29. RESEARCH AND DEVELOPMENT

1097. Balachandra, R. *Early Warning Systems for R&D Projects.* Lexington, MA: Lexington Books, 1986.
The information in this book is useful in showing managers how to identify troubled research projects and tells them how to make the decision on whether or not to continue the projects.

1098. Breen, George E., and Blankenship, A. B. *Do-It-Yourself Marketing Research.* 2d ed. New York: McGraw-Hill Book Co., 1982. 303 p.
This book shows the business person in the small to medium-sized firm how to do marketing research simply and inexpensively.

1099. Brown, James K., and Elvers, Lita M., eds. *Research & Development: Key Issues for Management.* New York: Conference Board, Inc., 1983. 102 p.

This book reports on the experiences and ideas of leading experts in R&D management regarding using R&D to restore U.S. preeminance in the world marketplace.

1100. Gibson, John E. *Managing Research and Development.* New York: John Wiley & Sons, Inc., 1981. 367 p.

Aimed primarily toward engineers, this book provides the basic aspects of managing R&D in two areas: personnel-oriented and technical-oriented activities.

1101. Gill, Kay, ed. *Government Research Directory.* 3d ed. Detroit, MI: Gale Research Co., 1985. 675 p.

More than 2,300 entries describing U.S. government research centers are listed in this book. Descriptions of appropriate R&D installations, institutes, centers, laboratories, bureaus, test stations, and data collection and analysis centers are also included.

1102. Gorton, Keith, and Carr, Isobel. *Low Cost Marketing Research; A Guide for Small Business.* New York: John Wiley & Sons, Inc., 1983. 111 p.

This book is intended for organizations which do research on a small budget. It includes chapters on information collection, desk research and field research, sampling methods, the questionnaire, and international marketing research.

1103. Haller, Terry. *Danger, Marketing Researcher at Work.* Westport, CT: Quorum Books, 1983. 200 p.

This book looks at the many dangers in marketing research that can be hidden in a research report and tells how to avoid these dangers. It examines such areas as product research, advertising research and pretests, and production aspects.

1104. Rawnsley, Allan, ed. *Manual of Industrial Marketing Research.* New York: John Wiley & Sons, Inc, 1978. 196 p.

Some of the areas of marketing research studied in this book include how to plan industrial marketing research, the use of published information sources, surveys, forecasting, new techniques on research, and some views on the topic by the Industrial Marketing Research Association.

1105. Tijunelis, D., and Clausen, N. *R&D on a Minimum Budget.* New York: AMACOM, 1979. 37 p.

This study is mainly directed toward product development in a small firm and short-range R&D projects in the large organization.

1106. Worcester, Robert M., and Downham, John, eds. *Consumer Market Research Handbook.* New York: Van Nostrand Reinhold & Co., Inc., 1978. 739 p.

All facets of marketing research are studied in this book which deals with both the techniques and applications of market research.

30. SALARIES/BENEFITS (INSURANCE, PENSION PLANS, HEALTH PROGRAMS)

1107. Beam, Burton T., Jr., and McFadden, John J. *Employee Benefits.* Homewood, IL: Richard D. Irwin, Inc., 1985. 528 p.
This book studies the relationship of current law through the Tax Reform Act and the Retirement Equity Act of 1984 on varous aspects of employee benefits.

1108. Burgess, Leonard R. *Wage and Salary Administration: Pay and Benefits.* Columbus, OH: C. E. Merrill Publishing Co. 1984. 434 p.
This book stresses the "hands-on" approach to wage and salary administration, featuring five areas: pay and benefits projects; job descriptions; pay rates for selected jobs; employee benefits tables; and end-of-chapter summaries, discussion questions, case studies, and references.

1109. Clark, Robert Louis. *Cost-Effective Pension Planning.* New York: Pergamon Press, Inc., 1982. 38 p.
This bibliography focuses on pension plans and provides annotations for the sources cited.

1110. Cohn, Theodore, and Lindberg, Roy A. *Compensating Key Executives in the Smaller Company.* New York: AMACOM, 1979. 224 p.
The authors of this book show how to use compensation for key executives as a productive force in the small company.

1111. *The Complete Portfolio of Time Management Forms.* Westbury, NY: Caddylak Publishing, 1985. 184 p.
This book contains 180 professionally designed planners to fit all time management needs in ready-to-photocopy form.

1112. *Controlling Employee Health Care Costs: Management Actions to Contain Expense and Define Employee Responsibility.* Monterey, CA: Management Information Studies, 1985. 104 p.
This book offers a thorough understanding of the many health care costs such as establishing a cost-sharing structure, creating financial incentives to reward employees and avoid expensive treatment, selecting benefits that will be best for your company, dental plan options, direct reimbursement plans, and wellness/fitness programs.

1113. *Employee Benefits in Medium and Large Firms, 1984.* Washington, DC: U.S. Department of Labor, Bureau of Labor Statistics, 1985. 69 p. (For sale by U.S. Government Printing Office.)
This bulletin gives data from a survey of private-industry firms in the U.S. and provides information on the incidence and provisions of 11 employee benefits that are paid for in part by the employer.

1114. *Employment and Earnings.* Washington, DC: U.S. Government Printing Office. (Monthly with annual supplements)
This publication provides current data on employment, hours, and earnings in the U.S. for more than 200 local areas.

1115. Gaunt, Larry D.; Williams, Numan A.; and Randall, Everett D. *Commercial Liability Underwriting.* 2d ed. Malvern, PA: Insurance Institute of America, 1982. 672 p.
How the fundamental concepts of underwriting are applied to commercial liability insurance are discussed in this book.

1116. *How to Make the Right Business Insurance Choices for Your Closely Held Corporation.* Englewood Cliffs, NJ: Prentice-Hall, Inc., 1981. 32 p.
This booklet provides information on how to make intelligent decisions on the use of business insurance and estate planning.

1117. Kamerman, S. B. *Meeting Family Needs: The Corporate Response.* Elmsford, NY: Pergamon Press, Inc., 1983. 45 p.
This book points out what employers are doing to meet the family needs of their employees. These include basic benefits, vacation policies, services, maternity/paternity leaves, child care, and flextime.

1118. Milkovich, George T., and Newman, Jerry M. *Compensation.* Plano, TX: Business Publications, Inc., 1984. 549 p.
This text is intended to give awareness to the reader of the various factors and potential outcomes of compensation decisions made within a business organization. It consists of three main sections dealing with equity, employee benefits, and administrative issues of compensation.

1119. Peck, Charles A. *Compensating Salaried Employees during Inflation: General vs. Merit Increases.* New York: Conference Board, 1981. 20 p.
This book looks at corporate salary increase policies in relation to high inflation, slow growth, and government pay standards during 1977 through 1979.

1120. Rosen, Corey; Klein, Katherine J.; and Young, Karen M. *Employee Ownership in America.* Lexington, MA: Lexington Books, 1985. 75 p.
This book gives a comprehensive and practical analysis of the variety of employee ownership plans and studies how and why they work.

1121. Rosenbloom, Jerry S., and Hallman, G. Victor. *Employee Benefit Planning.* Englewood Cliffs, NJ: Prentice-Hall, Inc., 1981. 480 p.
This book follows the functional approach toward employee benefit planning and discusses considerations and techniques that employers and their consultants can use in planning a well-conceived and efficient employee benefit program.

1122. Siegel, Mayer, and Buckman, Carol. *Executive's Guide to Pension and Retirement Benefits.* New York: Law & Business, Inc., 1981. 286 p.
The authors of this book show you how to manage your most significant assets intelligently and tell the reader how to get the most from your company's retirement plan. In addition, the role of the federal agencies responsible for regulating private pension plans and your rights as a plan participant are also covered.

1123. Slimmon, Robert F. *Successful Pension Design for Small-to-Medium Sized Businesses.* Reston, VA: Reston Publishing Co., 1985. 461 p.
This book provides an in-depth study of the alternate types of pension plans for small and medium-sized businesses in an effort to enable the small business operator to choose the most appropriate plan for his or her organization. Various types of pension and profit-sharing plans are discussed as well as the information needed to choose a plan wisely.

1124. Wolfson, Jay, and Levin, Peter J. *Managing Employee Health Benefits: A Guide to Cost Control.* Homewood, IL: Dow Jones-Irwin, 1985. 195 p.
The authors look at health care and health cost control from the employers' perspective and offer insights into the management of health benefits.

31. SALES

1125. Bethards, H. Gordan. *Selling Is a Personal Affair.* Skokie, IL: Century Communications Inc., 1984. 185 p.
The 29 essays in this book discuss selling demonstrations, benefit description, underselling, and pricing.

1126. Bolt, Gordan J. *Market and Sales Forecasting Manual.* Englewood Cliffs, NJ: Prentice-Hall, Inc., 1982. 342 p.
The majority of this book covers forecasting methods, both predictions and projections as well as conclusions.

1127. Brewer, James H.; Ainsworth, J. Michael; and Wynne, George E. *Power Selling: A Three-Step Program for Successful Selling.* Englewood Cliffs, NJ: Prentice-Hall Inc., 1985. 129 p.
This book tells how to assess a prospects personality type and create the proper sales strategy. The focus here is on power rather than motivation.

1128. Brownstone, David M. *Successful Selling Skills for Small Business.* New York: John Wiley & Sons, Inc., 1978. 112 p.
Some of the selling skills discussed in this book include how to identify customer benefits, getting product knowledge, the salesperson appearance, communication, listening, and the first contact through all the sales stages to finally making the sale.

1129. Buzzotta, V. Ralph; Lefton, R. E.; and Sherberg, Manuel. *Effective Selling Through Psychology: Dimensional Sales and Sales Management Strategies.* New ed. Cambridge, MA: Ballinger Publishing Co., 1982. 338 p.
This book provides insight into how to exercise interactional skills in selling.

1130. Cohen, W. A. *Building a Mail Order Business.* 2d ed. New York: John Wiley & Sons, Inc., 1985. 565 p.
This book covers every area of selling through the mail, including how to avoid legal problems due to recent government regulations, new forms of copyright, and information on list selection.

1131. Cohen, William A. *Direct Response Marketing: An Entrepreneurial Approach.* New York: John Wiley & Sons, Inc., 1984. 496 p.
Using the small company entrepreneurial approach, this book offers a comprehensive easy-to-read look at major techniques and concepts needed for a successful mail order business.

1132. Dawson, Clint. *Hourly Selling: Your Fast Track to Sales Success.* Englewood, Cliffs, NJ: Prentice-Hall Inc., 1985. 147 p.
This book tells how to increase sales while still retaining time for your personal life.

1133. Delmar, Ken. *Winning Moves: The Body Language of Selling.* New York: Warner Books, 1984. 229 p.
This book teaches you the body language of America's top salespeople.

1134. Ford, Neil M.; Churchill, Gilbert A., Jr.; and Walker, Orville C., Jr., eds. *Sales Force Performance.* Lexington, MA: Lexington Books, 1985. 306 p.
This book provides a model of motivation and performance of industrial salespeople. The five factors analyzed are motivation, skill level, aptitude, role perceptions, and personal-organizational-environmental variables.

1135. Frankel, Bud, and Phillips, H. W. *Your Advertising's Great...How's Business? The Revolution in Sales Promotion.* Homewood, IL: Dow Jones-Irwin, 1985. 250 p.
The entire strategy of sales promotions and how they are best used in today's business climate is discussed in this book.

1136. Goodman, Gary S. *60-Second Salesperson.* Englewood Cliffs, NJ: Prentice-Hall Inc., 1985. 100 p.
This book tells how to psych yourself up to build rapport, how to effectively describe your products and services, make an offer, create commitment and close the sale, each within a ten-second period.

1137. Haas, Kenneth B., and Ernest, John W. *Principles of Creative Selling.* 3d ed. Encino, CA: Glencoe Publishing Co., Inc., 1978. 486 p.
Primarily a textbook, this book is divided into four parts: the nature of selling, getting ready to sell, basic sales techniques, and special sales situations.

1138. Healy, James T. *Winning the High Tech Sales Game.* Reston, VA: Reston Publishing Co., Inc., 1985. 373 p.
This book is a "how to" primer on selling, mainly dealing with high-tech industries.

1139. *How to Create Successful Catalogs.* Colorado Springs, CO: Maxwell Sproge Publishing, 1985. 480 p.
This how-to guide on creating successful catalogs gives hints by 39 industry experts. It tells how to control costs, get more orders, and create the right theme.

1140. *Industrial Telephone Marketing & Territory Management.* Laguna Niguel, CA: Intempo Communications, Inc., 1982. (Loose leaf)
The telephone programs practiced today by leading corporate marketers are included in this book: how to plan, structure, and document a presentation; the forms needed; and a presentation design package.

1141. Issel, Carl K. *How to Promote Your Territory and Yourself.* Wallingford, CT: Industry Book Publishing, Inc., 1981. 166 p.
The author of this book provides the reader with practical marketing savvy and communications tools necessary for success in applying promotional ideas in your territory.

1142. Johnson, H. Webster, and Faria, Anthony. *Creative Selling.* 3d ed. Cincinnati, OH: South-Western Publishing Co., 1981. 393 p.
This book includes information on basic selling techniques, customer behavior, and the necessity of knowing about your product.

1143. Jordan, Alan. *The Only Telemarketing Book You'll Ever Need.* Wayne, PA: Add-Effect Associates, Inc., 1982. (Loose leaf)
Written for salespeople who want to enhance their sales efforts, this book provides information on data collection, the scheduling of appointments, and tells how to convert phone inquiries and complaints into sales.

1144. Kirkpatrick, C. A., and Russ, Frederick A. *Effective Selling.* 7th ed. Cincinnati, OH: South-Western Publishing Co., 1981. 441 p.
This book offers the principles and techniques of successful selling as it is practiced by leading business firms that lead to a profitable relationship between the salesperson and the customer.

1145. Konikow, Robert B. *How to Participate Profitably in Trade Shows.* Chicago: Dartnell Corporation, 1983. 286 p.
In addition to showing the reader how to determine which of the 8,000 trade shows to participate in, this book helps you integrate your exhibit into the marketing plan for maximum sales success.

1146. Kordahl, Eugene B. *Telemarketing for Business: A Guide to Building Your Own Telemarketing Operation.* Englewood Cliffs, NJ: Prentice-Hall, Inc., 1984. 324 p.
This book includes material for businesses that wish to sell products and services to other businesses in the commercial/industrial market. In loose-leaf format, it includes sections on how to develop a telemarketing plan, your work habitat, how to select equipment, personnel requirements, training, promotion, management, and maintaining your telemarketing program.

1147. Kozubska, Joanna, et al. *Maximising Industrial Sales.* Bradford, England: MCB University Press, Ltd., 1985. 116 p.
This book, directly relevant to sales managers, training officers, and senior managers is designed to help with selling skills and know-how.

1148. Kuswa, Webster. *The Sales Rep's Letter Book.* New York: AMACOM, 1984. 216 p.
The author of this book shows salespeople how to put their best foot forward in their correspondence, as well as providing advice that can extend to all business correspondence.

1149. Lancaster, Geoff; Seekings, David; and Wills, Gordon. *Maximising Industrial Sales.* Bradford, England: MCB University Press, Ltd., 1984. 120 p.
Part one of this book is written for the practicing salesperson and sales manager, examining a distinct aspect of selling, and showing how it relates to marketing. Part two includes case studies.

1150. Lebell, Frank. *Fine Point Techniques of Successful Independent Marketing/Selling.* San Mateo, CA: Hills-Bay Press, 1977. 284 p.
The main theme of this book concerns how to handle the sales agents growth problems, the need for new ideas, and ways sales managers can establish a more productive rapport with salespeople.

1151. Martin, Thomas John, and Trabue, Bruce. *Sell More and Spend Less: A Sourcebook of Profit-Building Ideas for Owners and Managers of Smaller Businesses.* New York: Holt, Rinehart, & Winston, 1980. 159 p.
This book discusses modern sales tactics that are based on examples from 60 (mostly small) successful companies.

1152. Masser, Barry Z., and Leeds, William M. *Telemarketing: The Corporate-Caller Skills Programs.* New York: Macmillan Publishing Co., 1984. 210 p.
This training and reference tool is for field sales reps and the professional business-to-business telemarketer. It tells how to profile a market, how to design a formula for building components of a presentation manual, includes a section on how to diagnose problems, and tells how to use your voice and vocabulary to the best advantage. Two cassette tapes are included.

1153. Miller, Robert B.; Heinman, Stephen E.; and Tuleja, Tad. *Strategic Selling: The Unique Sales System Proven Successful by America's Best Companies.* New York: William Morrow & Co., Inc., 1985. 319 p.
This sales guide is based on customer-needs analysis and satisfaction.

1154. Moffett, Carol Willis, and Hawkins, O. Rebecca. *The Receiving, Checking, Marking, Stocking Clerk.* 2d ed. New York: McGraw-Hill Book Co., 1980. 156 p.
This text-workbook is a self-pacing guide designed to prepare qualified workers for jobs in the areas mentioned in the title.

1155. *1985 Directory of Texas Manufacturers.* Austin TX: Bureau of Business Research, 1985. 2 v.
This directory provides information needed to buy, sell, and plan sales territories and to find out who makes what. In two volumes, it is updated monthly.

1156. Nirenberg, Jesse S. *How to Sell Your Ideas.* New York: McGraw-Hill Book Co., 1984. 252 p.
This book tells how to convince others of the merits of your ideas by using gentle assertiveness, constructive reasoning, and supportive fundamental courtesy.

1157. Okhuereigbe, Andy. *How to Promote Your Business & Increase Sales.* Providence RI: Unlimited Marketing Publications, 1983. 120 p.
All aspects of sales promotion are examined in this book in an easily understandable format.

1158. Ortland, Gerald I. *Telemarketing: High-Profit Telephone Selling Techniques.* New York: John Wiley & Sons, Inc., 1982. 171 p.
This self-paced guide starts with how to set up and manage a telephone selling program and shows how to integrate it with other marketing efforts. Explains how to take full advantage of this profitable, efficient sales technique.

1159. Piper, Julia, ed. *Managing Sales Promotion.* Brookfield, VT: Renouf USA Inc., 1980. 280 p.
Contributions from leading specialists showing how the various sales promotion techniques can be applied to maximum effect are included in this book. Emphasis is on planning, evaluation of activities, and management.

1160. Pope, Jeffery. *Business-to-Business Telemarketing.* New York: AMACOM, 1983. 185 p.
The author of this book tells how to prospect, qualify, service, and sell business accounts by telephone. In addition, he tells how to increase market penetration, cover more territory, zero in on home offices, and much more.

1161. Porterfield, James D. *Selling on the Phone: A Self-Teaching Guide.* New York: John Wiley & Sons, Inc., 1985. 146 p.
This five-step system on basic selling skills includes self-assessment exercises, application activities, and sample call-flow plans.

1162. Roman, Murray. *Telemarketing Campaigns that Work!* New York: McGraw-Hill Book Co., 1983. 267 p.
This casebook gives readers the facts needed to use telemarketing successfully. Eighteen classic telemarketing campaigns that work are described in detail.

1163. Schultz, Don, and Robinson, William A. *Sales Promotion Essentials.* Chicago: Crain Books, 1982. 234 p.
The 12 basic techniques essential to every successful sales promotion program are presented in this book.

1164. Sheehan, Don, and O'Toole, John. *Becoming a Superstar Seller.* New York: AMACOM, 1985. 159 p.
By looking at the traits of supersalespeople, this book tells how you can develop these traits. Such topics as sales-promotion ideas, treatment of customers, attitude, and family and leisure are also discussed.

1165. Sujan, Harish, and Weitz, Barton A. *The Amount and Direction of Effort: An Attributional Study of Salesperson Motivation.* Cambridge, MA: Marketing Science Institute, 1985. 30 p.
This paper reports on the results of a two-stage mail survey to identify what factors motivate changes in the direction and effort expended by salespeople.

1166. Taylor, Robert F. *Back to Basic Selling.* Englewood Cliffs, NJ: Prentice-Hall Inc., 1985. 187 p.
Over 100 basic sales tips on 14 areas of selling are included in this book along with some sample forms, charts, and checklists.

1167. Young, Rodney. *Five-Minute Lessons in Successful Selling: Increase Your Sales Skills without Going Back to School.* Englewood Cliffs, NJ: Prentice-Hall, Inc., 1985. 181 p.
The 100 short lessons in this book cover the basics including getting attention, arousing interest, creating desire, impelling action, and closing a sale.

32. SECURITY

1168. Berger, David L. *Security for Small Business.* Boston: Butterworth Publishers, Inc., 1981. 193 p.
Security measures that are discussed in this book include security equipment and methods, crime control, and fire and accident prevention.

1169. Keogh, James Edward. *The Small Business Security Handbook.* Englewood Cliffs, NJ: Prentice-Hall, Inc., 1981. 258 p.
This book offers technical knowledge necessary to make the right decisions regarding business security, i.e., how to select the most secure business location and how to conduct security surveys in your business.

33. SMALL BUSINESS ADMINISTRATION

1170. *Catalog of Completed Research Studies.* Washington, DC: U.S. Small Business Administration, Office of Advocacy, 1984. 24 p.
This pamphlet lists (in chronological order) the contracted research of the Office of Advocacy between 1978 and 1983. Over 140 studies are included on such topics as finance, credit, taxes, government competition and procurement, and women and minority business ownership.

1171. *Facts about Small Business and the U.S. Small Business Administration.* Washington, DC: U.S. Small Business Administration, 1981. 31 p.
This pamphlet provides some general information on small business, minority-owned and women-owned small business, finance, investment, procurement and technology, management assistance, and assistance to members of minority groups and women.

1172. Hayes, Rick Stephan, and Howell, John Cotton. *How to Finance Your Small Business with Government Money: SBA and Other Loans.* 2d ed. New York: John Wiley & Sons, Inc., 1983. 258 p.
This book explains in detail the various programs and services available to the small business person and tells how to take advantage of them. In addition, it tells how to apply for a SBA loan.

1173. *Management Training: Key to Small Business Success.* Washington, DC: Small Business Administration, Office of Management Information and Training, 1979. 26 p.
This book covers such topics as why a small business entrepreneur needs management skill training, how is this need being met by the SBA, and what kinds of training are available from the SBA to help the small business entrepreneur.

1174. *SBA: What It Does.* Washington, DC: U.S. Small Business Administration, 1976. 20 p.
This pamphlet gives some general information on the Small Business Administration and what it can do for the small business owner.

1175. *SBA Financing—Existing Business.* Santa Monica, CA: International Entrepreneurs' Association, 1978. 101 p.
This book looks at the types of SBA loans available and the requirements for getting a loan. Some hints on how to avoid rejection and examples of application forms are included as well as other helpful forms.

1176. *Secondary Participation in SBA Guaranteed Loans Through SBA Guaranteed Interest Certificates: Investor Information Manual.* Washington, DC: U.S. Small Business Administration, 1979. 66 p.
This book includes documents, forms, and a discussion on a Guaranteed Interest Certificate made by a lending institution to a small business.

1177. *Your Business and the U.S. Small Business Administration.* Washington, DC: Public Communications Division, U.S. Small Business Administration, 1983. 22 p. (For sale by U.S. Government Printing Office.)
This book tells who is eligible for SBA assistance, how the SBA helps women get into business, how they can financially assist the small business person, and how they assist minority-owned small business and veterans. A list of SBA field offices is included.

34. STARTING A BUSINESS

1178. Albert, Kenneth J. *How to Pick the Right Small Business Opportunity: The Key to Success in Your Own Business.* New York: McGraw-Hill Book Co., 1980. 239 p.
This book provides a step-by-step plan to help you pick a business opportunity best suited for your talents.

1179. Albert, Kenneth J. *Straight Talk about Small Business: What Other Books Don't Tell You about the Pitfalls and Profits of Starting and Managing Your Own Business.* New York: McGraw-Hill Book Co., 1981. 242 p.

This book tells about the risks and the rewards, the disadvantages and advantages of starting a business.

1180. Allen, Louis L. *Starting and Succeeding in Your Own Small Business.* New York: Grosset & Dunlap, 1977. 157 p.

The author of this book includes such information as ways to raise money for your business, how to get customers and select products, and tips on management and venture capital.

1181. Barrientos, Lawless J. *Ohio Business Kit: For Starting and Existing Businesses.* New York: Simon & Schuster, Inc., 1983. 175 p.

The basic information and forms needed to start a business in Ohio are included in this book, including those needed for beginning registration and reporting requirements for state and federal government agencies.

1182. Baumback, Clifford M. *Baumback's Guide to Entrepreneurship.* Englewood Cliffs, NJ: Prentice-Hall, Inc., 1981. 235 p.

This book discusses what it takes to be an entrepreneur, including the risks involved, how to start a business, market potential, location, physical facilities, inventory, staffing, financing, and recordkeeping.

1183. Belkin, Gary S. *How to Start and Run Your Own Word-Processing Business.* New York: John Wiley & Sons, Inc., 1984. 206 p.

This book serves as a "how-to" guide for starting your own business in word processing. Topics include choosing the right equipment, getting started, and managing your business. Word processing terms are defined and software systems are recommended.

1184. Birley, Sue. *New Enterprises: A Start-Up Case Book.* London: Croom Helm, 1982. 215 p.

This case book provides information for people who want to learn about the process and problems they may encounter when starting a business.

1185. Blagrove, Luanna C. *Untapped Profits by Professionals in the Business Field.* Manchester, CT: Blagrove Publications, 1980. 169 p.

This book offers some insight into the problems one encounters and the understanding of why these problems occur when starting a business. The author also discusses the need for a professional advisor and includes various aspects concerning the client.

1186. Breen, James J., and Sanderson, William D. *How to Start a Successful Restaurant: An Entrepreneur's Guide.* New York: Lebhar-Friedman Books, 1981. 117 p.

This book provides some critical competitive advantages on starting a restaurant and highlights the necessary ingredients of a successful operation including how to find a good location, menu planning, and financial management.

1187. Buchanan, Laurie. *Pages to Go!! How to Start and Maintain a Successful Free-Lance Typing Service.* Escondido, CA: Pages to Go!!, 1982. 73 p.
This easy-to-follow book provides guidelines and instant information on starting a typing service. Included are sections on establishing goals, selecting your clientele, advertising, necessary equipment and supplies, determining rates, and bookkeeping.

1188. Burstiner, Irving. *Run Your Own Store: From Raising the Money to Counting the Profits.* Englewood Cliffs, NJ: Prentice-Hall, Inc., 1981. 321 p.
The specifics of opening a retail store are covered in this book. A "how-to" format contains the nuts and bolts of running a store.

1189. Burstiner, Irving. *The Small Business Handbook: A Comprehensive Guide to Starting and Running Your Own Business.* Englewood Cliffs, NJ: Prentice-Hall, Inc., 1979. 342 p.
This book is an informative, comprehensive, and balanced guide to the management of a small business. While narrowing in on certain areas, the author still provides the comprehensiveness of the entire subject of running a business.

1190. Church, Olive D. *Small Business: Management and Entrepreneurship.* Chicago: Science Research Associates, Inc., 1984. 514 p.
The author of this book has organized the material needed (law, accounting, communications, human relations, marketing, personnel) to run a successful business, in the way they would be needed to get ready for "opening day."

1191. Clark, Douglas L. *Starting a Successful Business on the West Coast: California, Oregon, Washington.* Vancouver, BC: Self-Counsel Press Inc., 1982. 194 p.
Many tried and true business techniques are included in this book, including how to set goals, what kind of business to start and where to locate it, how start a business, personnel, franchising, record keeping, financing, and taxes.

1192. Cohen, William A. *The Entrepreneur and Small Business Problem Solver: An Encyclopedic Reference and Guide.* New York: John Wiley & Sons, Inc., 1983. 655 p.
This book answers questions often asked on starting or expanding a small business. Includes information on how to get a loan, insurance, laws, recruiting, advertising, and pricing.

1193. Coleman, Bob. *The Small Business Survival Guide: A Handbook.* New York: W. W. Norton & Co., Inc., 1984. 350 p.
Approximately 60 common trouble spots that people going into business are faced with are discussed in this book.

1194. Creedy, Richard F. *Time Is Money: A Guide to Selling Your Professional Services.* New York: E. P. Dutton, Inc., 1980. 170 p.
This book tells how to start and run a consulting or freelancing service.

1195. Delaney, William A. *So You Want to Start a Business!* Englewood Cliffs, NJ: Prentice-Hall, Inc., 1984. 240 p.
This book offers a blueprint for starting a business including where to get working capital, how to increase profits, information on lawyers, how to motivate your employees, and how to increase profits.

1196. Dible, Donald, ed. *Business Startup Basics.* Reston, VA: Reston Publishing Co., Inc., 1978. 263 p.
This book tells you what you need to know when starting a new business. It includes information on how to understand the problems you will meet in business and how to work these problems out.

1197. Dorland, Gilbert N., and Van Der Wal, John. *The Business Idea: From Birth to Profitable Company.* New York: Van Nostrand Reinhold Co., Inc., 1978. 196 p.
This practical step-by-step study of the realization of business development covers such topics as the business plan, forms of organization, start-up financing, franchising-partnerships, venture capital, and mergers.

1198. Feinman, Jeffrey. *100 Surefire Businesses You Can Start with Little or No Investment.* New York: The Berkeley Publishing Group, 1984. 262 p.
This book lists and discusses 100 business opportunities. It offers information on how to start a business with little or no investment. Many of the businesses listed here can be started part time.

1199. Fierro, Robert Daniel. *The New American Entrepreneur: How to Get Off the Fast Track into a Business of Your Own.* New York: William Morrow and Co., Inc., 1982. 286 p.
This author gives basic information on organization, management, budget, products, taxes, cash flow, and other facts you need to know when starting a business of your own.

1200. Fox, Philip J., and Mancuso, Joseph R. *402 Things You Must Know Before Starting a New Business.* Englewood Cliffs, NJ: Prentice-Hall, Inc., 1980. 240 p.
This book breaks down into 12 areas of information you must know before starting a business. Some of these are development, financing, investments, personnel, importing/exporting, and marketing.

1201. Gaedeke, Ralph M., and Tootelian, Dennis H. *Small-Business Management.* 2d ed. Glenview, IL: Scott, Foresman & Co., 1985. 426 p.
This book discusses preoperations decisions, operations, and other information on why go into business. A checklist, cases, and source lists are included along with explanations of loan packages and credit laws.

1202. Goldstein, A. S. *Starting on a Shoestring: Building a Business without a Bank Roll.* New York: John Wiley & Sons, Inc., 1984. 286 p.
This step-by-step guide to success in start-up enterprise is aimed at those who are low on cash but have the skills necessary to become successful entrepreneurs.

1203. Goldstein, Jerome. *How to Start a Family Business & Make It Work.* New York: M. Evans and Co., Inc., 1984. 156 p.
While not a one-step encyclopedic text on all you need to know about managing a small business, this book does offer many helpful hints on the subject. Some of these are spouses as partners, early testing and planning, family business life-cycles, staying healthy, choosing a successor, and outside help.

1204. Goldstein, Jerome. *In Business for Yourself: A Guide to Starting a Small Business and Running It Your Way.* New York: Charles Scribner's Sons, 1982. 176 p.
This book looks at the discoveries regarding America's new small business movement and the people behind it. It includes discussions on the successful new small business, sideline enterprises, traditional business with a twist, and how to build a business.

1205. Goodrich, Donna Clark. *How to Set Up and Run a Tax Preparation Service.* New York: John Wiley & Sons, Inc., 1985. 145 p.
This book features details on the supplies needed to set up a tax preparation service, the formats to use, and file keeping tips.

1206. Goodrich, Donna Clark. *How to Set Up and Run a Typing Service.* New York: John Wiley & Sons, Inc., 1983. 176 p.
In addition to pointers on determining if this type of business is for you, this book tells how to start a typing business, the equipment needed, what is needed as the business grows, and how to run it successfully.

1207. Grayson, Fred N. *Getting Independent! A Proven Entrepreneur's Guide to Starting Your Own Successful Business.* Piscataway, NJ: New Century Publishers, Inc., 1981. 228 p.
Divided into two major sections, the first section of this book looks at six basic areas of business with specific businesses singled out such as technical, service, creative, and sales while the second section contains the business basics.

1208. Greene, Gardiner G. *How to Start and Manage Your Own Business.* New York: New American Library, 1983. 243 p.
Designed to help the small business person, this book is divided into five parts: financial strategies, selection of professional services, tips on management functions, and constructive and cautionary thinking.

1209. Gross, Len, and Stirling, John T. *How to Build a Small Advertising Agency and Run It at a Profit.* Alameda, CA: Kentwood Publications, 1984. 103 p.
This guide discusses how to start a business and includes information on public relations for clients and yourself, how to keep clients, advertising law, market research, agency financial plans, billing, taxes, and income statements.

1210. Gupta, Brijen K., and Lopatin, Arthur D. *Starting and Succeeding in Small Business. A Guide for the Inner City Businessman.* New York: Council on International and Public Affairs, 1978. 105 p.

This book answers the basic questions of existing and prospective minority small business people in the city of Rochester, New York.

1211. Hasley, David. *Starting Up: The Complete Guide to Starting and Maintaining Your Own Business.* Westlake Village, CA: Coltrane and Beach, Book Publishers, 1984. 328 p.
This self-help guide for the entrepreneur is designed to help improve management skills and avoid common operating pitfalls.

1212. Hodgetts, Richard M., and Keel, Pamela. *Topics in Small Business Management.* 2d ed. Dubuque, IA: Kendall/Hunt Publishing Co., 1982. 2 v.
This two-volume set contains materials needed to start and operate a small business. The topics relate to real-life situations.

1213. Hoelscher, Russ von, and Sterne, George. *How to Start Making Money in a Business of Your Own: The Best Business Opportunities for the 1980's.* San Diego, CA: Sterne Profits Ideas, 1985. 420 p.
This book offers step-by-step start-up and operating information.

1214. Hollingsworth, Abner Thomas, and Hand, Herbert H. *A Guide to Small Business Management: Text and Cases.* Philadelphia, PA: W. B. Saunders Co., 1979. 446 p.
This book serves as a guide for those opening or operating a small business. It focuses on those aspects likely to lead to success and improvement in business performance.

1215. Holt, Nancy; Shuchat, Jo; and Regal, Mary Lewis. *Small Business Management and Ownership.* Belmont, MA: CRC Education and Human Development, Inc., 1979. 4 v. (For sale by U.S. Government Printing Office.)
This four-volume set provides materials for introductory and advanced training on starting a small business. Vol. 1: Minding Your Own Small Business; vol. 2: Something Ventured, Something Gained; vol. 3: Location Decision: A Simulation; and vol. 4: Mind-Problems in Entrepreneurship.

1216. Holtz, Herman. *Profit from Your Money-Making Ideas: How to Build a New Business or Expand an Existing One.* New York: AMACOM, 1980. 370 p.
The author begins by explaining how you know if you have a money-making idea and follows with suggestions to market the idea.

1217. *How to Buy & Sell a Small Business.* Rev. ed. New York: Sterling Publishing Co., Inc., 1982. 122 p.
Guidelines on how to buy or sell a small business including sources of markets, financial and legal information, value of business, and how to negotiate a contract are included in this book.

1218. *How to Run a Small Business.* 5th ed. New York: McGraw-Hill Book Co., 1982. 298 p.
Some areas on operating a small business included in this book are financing, buying a business, location, tax management franchise operations, government management, and personnel.

1219. *How to Start Your Own Small Business.* Expanded ed. New York: Sterling Publishing Co., Inc., 1982. 320 p.
For the person starting a small business this book provides information on financing the business, how to buy a business location, various types of business ownership, business records, and advertising.

1220. Jenkins, Michael D. *Starting and Operating a Business in California.* Sunnyvale, CA: Oasis Press, 1985. 1 v. various paging.
This book is a self-help book for the business owner who wants a current guide to basic financial, legal, and tax ground rules that apply to the business. The information can be applied to states other than California.

1221. Jenkins, Michael D.; Harrold, Thomas J., Jr., and Kilberg, Lori E. *Starting and Operating a Business in Georgia.* Sunnyvale, CA: Oasis Press, 1984. (Loose leaf)
This book draws together in a readable, usable, and nontechnical format the facts that you need to know when establishing a business in Georgia. There is information explaining in layman's language many key financial, tax, and legal pitfalls and planning opportunities.

1222. Johnson, Mary Pat. *Everything You Need to Know to Start a Housecleaning Service.* 2d ed. Seattle, WA: Cleaning Consultant Services, Inc., 1980. 108 p.
This book contains detailed information on how to start a housecleaning service including the amount of capital required, the type of equipment to use, what to charge, and how to find customers.

1223. Kahm, H. S. *50 Big Money Businesses You Can Start and Run with $250 to $5,000.* Garden City, NY: Doubleday & Co., Inc., 1983. 225 p.
In addition to a brief discussion on the various aspects of running a small business, this book provides a look at 50 big-money businesses you can run.

1224. Kishel, Gregory F., and Kishel, Patricia Gunter. *How to Start, Run and Stay in Business.* New York: John Wiley & Sons, Inc., 1981. 200 p.
This book covers each stage of business operations in a handbook format beginning with selection of financing and including insuring and promoting the business. Checklists are included throughout to help measure your progress and point out areas that need improvement.

1225. Kryszak, Wayne D. *The Small Business Index.* Metuchen, NJ: Scarecrow Press, 1978. 210 p.
This bibliography to American and Canadian material on the various aspects of starting a small business lists books, pamphlets, and periodicals.

1226. Kuriloff, Arthur, and Hemphill, John M., Jr. *How to Start Your Own Business. . .and Succeed.* Rev. ed. New York: McGraw-Hill Book Co., 1981. 367 p.
This guide/workbook contains many sample forms on various aspects of managing the small businesss.

1227. Kuriloff, Arthur H., and Hamphill, John M., Jr. *Starting and Managing the Small Business.* New York: McGraw-Hill Book Co., 1983. 592 p.
The five sections included in this book on developing a plan for a new business include: what is necessary to bring to the business, how to understand marketing, how to buy a business opportunity, financial management information, and some management pointers for the small business.

1228. Lane, Byron. *How to Free Yourself in a Business of Your Own.* Englewood Cliffs, NJ: Prentice-Hall, Inc., 1980. 174 p.
Step-by-step procedures on how to start your own small business that will earn good money and bring satisfaction and personal fulfillment at the same time are included in this book. It describes how to move into your own business without leaving the security of your present job.

1229. Lipper, Arthur. *Venture's Guide to Investing in Private Companies.* Homewood, IL: Dow Jones-Irwin, 1984. 279 p.
The risks as well as the rewards of investing in private companies are discussed in this book. Special emphasis is given to start-up and early stage costs.

1230. Lowry, Albert J. *How to Become Financially Successful by Owning Your Own Business.* New York: Simon & Schuster, Inc., 1981. 407 p.
This book gives step-by-step information on how to take advantage of business opportunities, avoid pitfalls, and make a success in your own business.

1231. Lundberg, Terence. *Starting in Business.* Cambridge: Woodhead-Faulkner, 1985. 200 p.
This book offers a broad outline of the problems that can be incurred when acquiring or setting up a small business and tells of the many pitfalls that can be avoided.

1232. Mancuso, Joseph R. *Checklist for Starting a Successful Business.* Worcester, MA: Center for Entrepreneurial Management, 1979. 40 p.
Three separate checklists useful in covering all aspects of starting a business are included in this book.

1233. Mancuso, Joseph R. *Have You Got What It Takes? How to Tell If You Should Start Your Own Business.* Englewood Cliffs, NJ: Prentice-Hall, Inc., 1982. 230 p.
While providing an outline of a basic approach to starting and managing a business, the author emphasizes the business plan and tells how to raise capital. The names and addresses of organizations useful in small business planning and management are included in the appendix.

1234. Mancuso, Joseph R. *How to Name a Business.* Worcester, MA: Center for Entrepreneurial Management, 1979. 32 p.
This pamphlet tells how 100 companies were named.

1235. Mancuso, Joseph R. *How to Start, Finance, and Manage Your Own Small Business.* Rev. ed. Englewood Cliffs, NJ: Prentice-Hall, Inc., 1984. 392 p.
This book on starting your own business contains sample questionnaires and business plans in addition to current bibliographies and sources of entrepreneurial aid.

1236. Metcalf, Wendell O. *Starting and Managing a Small Business of Your Own.* Washington, DC: U.S. Small Business Administration, Management Assistance Division, Support Services Branch, 1982. 84 p. (For sale by U.S. Government Printing Office.)
This "how-to" book provides guidelines on the benefits and disadvantages of owning your own business, including choice of business, chances of success, purchasing a going business, and investing in a franchise.

1237. Metcalf, Wendell O., Bunn, Verne A.; and Stigelman, C. Richard. *How to Make Money in Your Own Small Business.* Vacaville, CA: The Entrepreneur Press, 1977. 201 p.
The value of other people's experience is the focus of this book. The four main sections are starting and managing your business, selling and buying a going business, buying a franchise, and a venture capital directory.

1238. Mitchell, Linda S. *For Women, Managing Your Business: A Resource and Information Handbook.* Washington, DC: U.S. Small Business Administration, Office of Women's Business Ownership, 1983. 230 p. (For sale by U.S. Government Printing Office.)
This book focuses on how you go about starting a business and how you can improve and professionalize your operations.

1239. Nichols, Donald R. *Starting Small, Investing Smart: What to Do with $5 to $5,000.* Homewood, IL: Dow Jones-Irwin, 1984. 174 p.
Explanations of investment alternatives for the first-time investor are included in this book, with an emphasis on preserving capital and earning stable returns.

1240. Nicholas, Ted. *Opportunities Unlimited: Step-by-Step Guide for a Small Business.* Wilmington, DE: Enterprise Publishing Co., 1979. 506 p.
This workbook provides a step-by-step guide to make the road to starting a successful business much easier. Some chapters include self-test questions.

1241. Nicholas, Ted. *The Ted Nicholas Small Business Course: A Step-by-Step Guide.* Wilmington, DE: Enterprise Publishing Co., 1981. 234 p.
Based on many years experience in starting and building successful businesses, this author provides a short-cut on this topic. Worksheets are included.

1242. Packard, Sidney, and Carron, Alan J. *Start Your Own Store: Managing, Merchandising, and Evaluating.* Englewood Cliffs, NJ: Prentice-Hall, Inc., 1982. 238 p.
A case approach to owning and operating a business is provided in this book. The authors walk the reader through a women's apparel store from the initial planning stage to the end of its first year. Each chapter contains a practical assignment, and information on government regulations, insurance requirements, SBA loans and publications.

1243. Park, William R., and Chapin-Park, Sue. *How to Succeed in Your Own Business.* New York: John Wiley & Sons, Inc., 1978. 346 p.
This book tells how to successfully establish and operate a small independent retail or service business. It looks at the personnel, market, environmental, and financial requirements for the business.

1244. Petteruto, Ray. *How to Open and Operate a Restaurant.* New York: Van Nostrand Reinhold Co., Inc., 1979. 269 p.
This step-by-step guide is geared to people who want to open a restaurant. It does not provide theory, charts, questions or statistical data but rather information on location, menues, purchasing, profit, management, merchandising, sanitation, and safety.

1245. Phillips, Michael, and Rasberry, Salli. *Honest Business: A Superior Strategy for Starting and Managing Your Own Business.* New York: Random House, 1981. 209 p.
This book emphasizes openness, community, and extensive access to information in business.

1246. Pineles, Dean. *Checklist for Starting a Small Business.* Montpelier, VT: Secretary of State's Office, 198?. 9 p.
While aimed at starting a business in Vermont, this pamphlet provides important facts such as seeking competent advice, legal structure of the business, arranging for adequate financing and insurance coverage, tax requirements, and licenses and permits.

1247. Pogue, Paul. *Start and Run a Profitable Beauty Salon: A Step-by-Step Business Plan.* Seattle, WA: Self-Counsel Press Inc., 1983. 158 p.
This book is prepared by a businessman on the management side of operating a beauty salon. Many of the ideas on management discussed here have been tested in actual business situations.

1248. Redinbaugh, Larry D., and Neu, Clyde W. *Small Business Management: A Planning Approach.* St. Paul, MN: West Publishing Co., 1980. 475 p.
These two business consultants present the necessary steps for planning a new business venture as well as for strengthening an existing business. The authors stress planning, market opportunities, and financial management.

1249. Revel, Chase. *168 More Businesses Anyone Can Start and Make a Lot of Money.* New York: Bantam Books, 1984. 296 p.
This book lists 168 types of small businesses that have been successful. A brief discussion of the business is given along with pointers on how to get started.

1250. Rich, Andrew M. *How to Survive and Succeed in a Small Financial Planning Practice.* Reston, VA: Reston Publishing Co., Inc., 1984. 315 p.
This book tells how to set up and conduct a successful financial planning practice.

1251. Rohrlich, Chester A. *Organizing Corporate and Other Business Enterprises.* Albany, NY: Matthew Bender & Co., Inc., 1985. 1 v. various paging. (Kept up to date by annual supplements.)
This comprehensive work leads the attorney through the organization of a new business. It compares all the legal and tax considerations that arise when forming a business with the provisions for future operation and possible liquidation.

1252. Sandberg, William. *New Venture Performance.* Lexington, MA: Lexington Books, 1986. 224 p.
This book presents a conceptual model of new venture performance. The results indicate the types of industries most receptive to newcomers, the most effective strategies within different types of industries, the impact of the entrepreneurs on performance within the new venture, and the effect of industry structure on the strategy-performance relationship.

1253. Scase, Richard, and Goffee, Robert. *The Real World of the Small Business Owner.* London: Croom Helm, 1980. 166 p.
The authors of this book looks at some of the reasons why people start their own businesses and some of the problems they face as they expand.

1254. Schaefer, Robert A. *Starting and Managing a Small Service Business.* Washington, DC: U.S. Small Business Administration, Management Assistance Division, Support Services Section, 1981. 58 p. (For sale by U.S. Government Printing Office.)
This book is designed to assist in sorting out personal capabilities and weaknesses, evaluate ideas, and set priorities before starting a business.

1255. Schollhammer, Hans, and Kuriloff, Arthur H. *Entrepreneurship and Small Business Management.* New York: John Wiley & Sons, Inc., 1979. 608 p.
The theory, general principles, and practice that is required to start and manage a small business successfully is covered in this book. Entrepreneurship as it applies to starting a small business and how to run the business is emphasized.

1256. Seigel, David, and Goldman, Harold L. *Successful Small Business Management: It's Your Business—Mind It!* New York: Fairchild Publications, 1982. 346 p.
These authors have designed this book in the logical order useful in starting a business: first know the preliminaries to starting the business; know what the possibilities for your business are; know the marketing

function; know how to manage the business; and finally a section is included on business opportunities for women and minorities.

1257. Seltz, David. *A Treasury of Business Opportunities.* Rockville Centre, NY: Farnsworth Publishing Co., Inc., 1984. 319 p.
This author begins by describing how you can use the "gold mine" within you to help you to succeed. In addition he has given a brief description of over 1,000 businesses a person can start. In the Franchise section, he has included addresses to write to for more information.

1258. Silvester, James L. *How to Start, Finance, and Operate Your Own Business.* Secaucus, NJ: L. Stuart, 1984. 448 p.
The author of this book stresses the importance of self-evaluation and proper business investigation. He also points out some details of the legal structure in business and some often overlooked sources of assistance.

1259. Simon, Arthur C. *How to Start a Business and Make It Grow.* Hollywood, CA: Future Shop, 1978. 139 p.
Some of the basic information on starting a business is provided in this book including how to choose the right business for you, management techniques, advertising, public relations, and how to calculate your risks.

1260. Singh, Daljit. *Small Business and Public Policy in America.* Bloomington, IN: Publications Press, 1981. 205 p.
This collection of readings can be helpful to those who are already in business or who are starting a business in finding useful information on major issues and challenges that confront the small business person. Some topics covered are Social Security, business trends, SBA programs, hiring, wages, and taxation.

1261. Small, Samuel. *Starting a Business after Fifty.* New York: Pilot Books, 1977. 46 p.
This book is aimed at the "older person" who has saved a little capital but does not want to run a business requiring strenuous activities. Rather, a business is preferred where lifetime experience can be used and little capital investment and adjustable hours are required.

1262. Smilor, Raymond W., and Gill, Michael. *The New Business Incubator: Linking Talent, Technology, Capital, and Know-How.* Lexington, MA: Lexington Books, 1986. 192 p.
The authors of this book show how incubators can serve and support new businesses as a source of seed money or to provide access to venture capital. They show how incubators can also offer secretarial, office, and computer services and provide access to university research facilities and faculty consultations.

1263. Smith, Brian R. *How to Prosper in Your Own Business: Getting Started and Staying on Course.* Brattleboro, VT: Stephen Greene Press, 1981. 323 p.
This easy-to-read book offers information on how to prepare for business ownership, how to develop a business plan, and includes discussions of the various facets of running a business such as marketing, finance, personnel management, and administration.

1264. Smith, Brian R. *Raising Seed Money for Your Own Business.* Lexington, MA: Lewis Publishing Co., 1984. 133 p.
This book shows how to go about getting money for a business by first developing a business plan and how to approach sources with this plan.

1265. Smith, Randy Baca. *Setting Up Shop: The Do's and Don'ts of Starting a Small Business.* New York: McGraw-Hill Book Co., 1982. 274 p.
This book provides some ideas on what questions you should ask when starting a business and whom you should ask. Some areas discussed here are law, banking, insurance, advertising, government, and accounting.

1266. Smith, Richard D. *Getting Started: A Practical Guide to Your Small Business Success in Canada.* Vancouver, BC: International Self-Counsel Press, 1982. 84 p.
In addition to helping the reader set up a part-time or full-time business or improving the success of your present business, the author also includes some information on Canadian business income tax deductions, cash and credit information, and how to sell your product or service.

1267. *Starting Out Series.* Washington, DC: U.S. Small Business Administration, 1983. (Irregular)
This series of pamphlets includes material on how to start specific businesses such as a dry cleaning business, a sporting goods store, interior design services, and many more.

1268. Sterne, George. *How to Start Making Money in a Business of Your Own: The Best Opportunities for the 1980's.* Rev. ed. San Diego, CA: Sterne Profit Ideas, 1984. 420 p.
This manual contains over 100 businesses that you can start with limited investment, about 100 franchise opportunities, tricks for advertising and promoting a business on a shoestring, how to buy and sell a business, and much more.

1269. Stevens, Mark. *How to Pyramid Small Business Ventures into a Personal Fortune.* West Nyack, NY: Parker Publishing Co., 1977. 202 p.
This book provides some lucrative ideas for starting a business and information on the technique of pyramiding. Rather than dealing with theories, this book contains case histories showing how the average business person has used these principles to their advantage.

1270. Stevenson, Howard H.; Roberts, Michael J.; and Grousbeck, H. Irving. *New Business Ventures and the Entrepreneur.* 2d ed. Homewood, IL: Richard D. Irwin, Inc., 1985. 750 p.
This book provides information for those who wish to start a business or purchase one. Included are actual documents such as prospectuses, leases, and business plans.

1271. Stoner, J. A. F., and Dolan, Edwin G. *Introduction to Business.* Glenview, IL: Scott Foresman & Co., 1985. 684 p.
This basic book discusses the organizations, economics, marketing, management, information automation, production, operations, finance, ethics, and international business practices that the entrepreneur needs to know when starting a business.

1272. Taetzsch, Lyn. *Opening Your Own Retail Store.* Chicago: H. Regnery Co., 1977. 204 p.

The basics of retail store management are examined in this book including location, selection, type of store to open, employee selection, customer relations, and a variety of related management topics. It offers a comprehensive look at all phases of retailing.

1273. Tarrant, John J. *Making It Big on Your Own: How to Start, Finance, and Manage a New Business in the '80s.* New York: Playboy Press, 1981. 248 p.

This book provides some general information on going into business for yourself, along with information on how to get organized, where to get money, developing a business plan, and legal and tax angles of the start-up.

1274. Taylor, Frederick John. *How to Be Your Own Boss: A Complete Guide to Starting and Running Your Own Business.* London: Business Books, Ltd., 1975. 171 p.

This book tells how to take advantage of your assets to make a success in running a small business.

1275. Taylor, John R. *How to Start and Succeed in a Business of Your Own.* Reston, VA: Reston Publishing Co., Inc., 1978. 325 p.

This author uses personal experiences to illustrate potential pitfalls for new small businesses and provides first-hand information to small business initiation and management.

1276. Tetreault, Wilfred, and Clements, Robert W. *Starting Right in Your New Business.* Reading, MA: Addison-Wesley Publishing Co., 1982. 242 p.

The various problems and alternatives that are involved in starting a new business are examined in succinct detail in this book. Includes an evaluation test to determine whether or not a person is qualified to start a business.

1277. Thompson, James M. *The Handbook of Small Business Organization and Management: Including Information for the Small Manufacturer.* Huntsville, AL: Akens-Morgan Press, 1979. 242 p.

This book helps you to prepare yourself for going into business by discussing such topics as location, study of the competition, technical know-how, crimes against business, family problems, conflict with business partners, planning, partnerships, how to incorporate, how to prepare the business proposal, franchising, finance, cost analysis, and taxes.

1278. Timmons, Jeffrey; Smollen, Leonard E.; and Dingee, Alexander L. M. *New Venture Creation: A Guide to Small Business Development.* Homewood, IL: Richard D. Irwin, Inc., 1977. 606 p.

This book brings together the experiences that entrepreneurs encounter when starting a business.

1279. Walton, John B. *Small Business Start Up Manual: A Professional Manual for Entrepreneurs Who Want to Buy or Start a Small Business.* Dallas, TX: Waybridge Publishing Co., 1981. 220 p.

Designed to help the new business person avoid costly start-up costs, this book tells how to make successful business acquisitions, how to evaluate the business operation, where to find financial data, and much more.

1280. Webb, Terry; Quince, Thelma; and Watkins, David. *Small Business Research: The Development of Entrepreneurs.* Aldershot, Hampshire, England: Gower Publishing Co., Ltd., 1984. 218 p.
This series of papers is divided into three parts: those that describe programs designed to develop interest in entrepreneurship; those that discuss who starts a business; and those that tell how to develop an ongoing business.

1281. Welsh, John A., and White, Jerry F. *The Entrepreneur's Master Planning Guide: How to Launch a Successful Business.* Englewood Cliffs, NJ: Prentice-Hall, Inc., 1983. 408 p.
Divided into six parts, this book first answers questions about the business plan; Part 2 looks at the profile of a successful entrepreneur; Part 3 studies the product or service offered for sale; Part 4 looks at venture capital; Part 5 covers critical management skills and Part 6 studies specific businesses, i.e., a retail/service business, a contracting business, and a manufacturing business.

1282. Will, Mimi, and Weber, Nancy. *How to Create a Successful Word Processing Business.* Mountain View, CA: TPW Publishing Co., 1983. 1 v. various paging.
This manual includes information on the opportunities in the word processing business, strategies for success, how to set up a word processing service business, equipment selection, operating procedures, cash flow, marketing, and learning and growing with your business.

1283. Woy, Patricia A. *Small Businesses that Grow and Grow and Grow.* White Hall, VA: Betterway Publications, 1983. 216 p.
Step-by-step instructions for setting up and successfully operating a number of different businesses is covered in this book. These businesses range from the $100 investment through the $10,000 investment.

35. STRATEGIC PLANNING

1284. Abell, Derek F. *Defining the Business: The Starting Point of Strategic Planning.* Englewood Cliffs, NJ: Prentice-Hall, Inc., 1980. 257 p.
This book includes some organizing concepts to use when determining how to define businesses and markets.

1285. Brandt, Steven C. *Strategic Planning in Emerging Companies.* Reading, MA: Addison-Wesley Publishing Co., 1981. 187 p.
The key for any growing company is strategic planning. This author gives concise, professional advice on how to select strategies for pursuing company objectives, how to anticipate organizational problems, and how to use strategic planning to build the corporation.

1286. Curtis, David A. *Strategic Planning for Smaller Businesses.* Lexington, MA: Lexington Books, 1983. 224 p.
This book provides a practical set of tools for strategic planning specifically designed for use by small businesses. These are derived from the best practices that are currently used by major corporations.

1287. Harrigan, Kathryn Rudie. *Strategies for Declining Businesses.* Lexington, MA: Lexington Books, 1980. 448 p.
A comprehensive empirical study of declining demand, this book isolates key strategic factors that influence the firms' performances in coping with declining demand.

1288. Henderson, Bruce D. *The Logic of Business Strategy.* Cambridge, MA: Ballinger Publishing Co., 1984. 128 p.
This author analyzes the underlying logic of business strategies and presents models for the implementation of the relationships between the components of successful planning.

1289. Kastens, Merritt L. *Long-Range Planning for Your Business: An Operating Manual.* New York: AMACOM, 1976. 160 p.
This "operating manual" provides information on operating a planning procedure by discussing a single sequence of critical planning steps that together make up a complete planning cycle.

1290. Lauenstein, Milton C. *What's Your Game Plan? Creating Business Strategies that Work.* Homewood, IL: Dow Jones-Irwin, 1985. 225 p.
This book shows how to define promising business segments, how to find key resources for these segments, how to develop long-range plans to cultivate these resources, and much more.

1291. Linneman, Robert E. *Shirt Sleeve Approach to Long-Range Planning for the Smaller, Growing Corporation.* Englewood Cliffs, NJ: Prentice-Hall, Inc., 1980. 290 p.
This practical how-to book presents a general step-by-step approach for adapting comprehensive planning into the corporate structure. Emphasis is on long-range strategic planning.

1292. Pritchard, Robert E., and Bardway, Bruce M. *Strategic Planning and Control Techniques for Profit: A Handbook for Small Business Owners.* Englewood Cliffs, NJ: Prentice-Hall, Inc., 1981. 260 p.
This book, written for the established business, provides basic information on the methods and vocabulary of professional management. The main focus is on strategic planning.

1293. Rothschild, William. *How to Gain (and Maintain) the Competitive Advantage in Business.* New York: McGraw-Hill Book Co., 1984. 227 p.
This book contains guidelines for developing strategic plans for gaining and keeping the competitive edge.

1294. Shanklin, William L., and Ryans, John K., Jr. *Thinking Strategically: Planning for Your Company's Future.* New York: Random House, Inc., 1985. 332 p.
The authors of this book provide real meaning to the concepts and techniques necessary for coping with the uncertainties of the increasingly turbulent environment. The book covers such topics as how to analyze your business environment and prepare alternate "scenarios" dealing with future environments. In addition, the book analyzes competitors' market positions and discusses the strengths of your board of directors.

1295. Stevens, Robert E. *Strategic Marketing Plan Master Guide.* Englewood Cliffs, NJ: Prentice-Hall, Inc., 1982. 209 p.
The author of this book gives a systematic approach to strategic marketing planning. This approach is both philosophically sound and practically oriented.

1296. Stonich, Paul J. *Implementing Strategy: Making Strategy Happen.* Cambridge, MA: Ballinger Publishing, 1982. 177 p.
This operating charter for the consultants at the Management Analysis Center in Cambridge stresses planning to make strategy happen.

1297. *Strategic Planning: A Structured Approach to Company Success.* Monterey, CA: Small Business Monitoring & Research Co., Inc., 1984. 55 p.
This book combines short-range planning and long-range planning to show how to achieve success in your company. It studies outside events, competitors, business cycles, market shifts, and the company's own evolution.

1298. Tregoe, Benjamin B., and Zimmerman, John W. *Top Management Strategy: What It Is and How to Make It Work.* New York: Simon & Schuster, 1980. 128 p.
Aimed at senior managers, this book is about strategy formulation. It defines strategy, analyzes the concept of the "Driving Force," describes how organizations can integrate strategy in its operations, and encourages top management to improve their strategic thinking.

36. VENTURE CAPITAL

1299. *Capital Formation: Private and Public Financings 1984.* New York: Practising Law Institute, 1984. 440 p.
This reference manual contains numerous sections on venture capital written by experts in the field.

1300. *Getting Money for Your Business.* Phoenix, AZ: Business Financial Consultants, Inc., 1982. 195, 24 p.
Some of the various ways of obtaining money for your business that are discussed in this book are from a bank, leasing, private investors, Small Business Administration, trade financing, factoring, selling equity, partnerships, corporations, going private, going public, and direct sale.

1301. Gladstone, David J. *Venture Capital Handbook.* Reston, VA: Reston Publishing Co., Inc., 1983. 402 p.
The entire process of raising venture capital is covered in this book.

1302. *Guide to Innovation Resources and Planning for the Smaller Business.* Springfield, VA: National Technical Information Service, U.S. Department of Commerce, 1984. 85 p.
The first part of this book discusses the innovation process and the second part lists the resources available to those involved in innovation, including federal, state and local, and private sector resources.

1303. Kieschnick, Michael. *Venture Capital and Urban Development.* Washington, DC: Council of State Planning Agencies, 1979. 59 p.
This book provides an overview of the role of small business in the U.S. economy and provides new evidence about individual small firms and the entrepreneurs who start them.

1304. Kozmetsky, George; Gill, Michael D., Jr.; and Smilor, Raymond W. *Financing and Managing Fast-Growth Companies: The Venture Capital Process.* Lexington, MA: Lexington Books, 1985. 144 p.
This book provides an in-depth look at the venture capital industry.

1305. Kravitt, Gregory I., et al. *How to Raise Capital: Preparing and Presenting the Business Plan.* Homewood, IL: Dow Jones-Irwin, 1984. 187 p.
This book offers a complete guide to writing a financing proposal effective in attracting potential investors and lenders.

1306. Krefetz, Gerald. *More than a Dream: Raising the Money.* New York: American Management Associations, 1981. 11 p.
This booklet discusses such topics as capital needs for your business, how to prepare a set of projections, legal forms of business, sources of capital, and some hints on buying a franchise or existing business.

1307 Mancuso, Joseph R. *How to Read and Write a Business Plan.* Worcester, MA: Center for Entrepreneurial Management, 1979. 84 p.
This how-to-do-it book includes information and specific examples on venture capital.

1308. Nicholas, Ted. *How and Where to Raise Venture Capital to Finance a Business.* Wilmington, DE: Enterprise Publishing Co., 1978. 66 p.
Aimed at both a new enterprise and an established business, this book lists over 200 sources of capital and classifies them by name, address, telephone number, and the individual to contact.

1309. Pratt, Stanley E., ed. *Guide to Venture Capital Sources.* 7th ed. Wellesley Hills, MA: Capital Publishing Corp., 1983. 489 p.
This book lists the various venture capital sources.

1310. Pratt, Stanley E. *How to Raise Venture Capital.* New York: Charles Scribner's Sons, 1982. 254 p.
This guide to the venture capital market tells how to decide what kind of financing you need, where to locate it, and other essentials for the new venture company.

1311. Rubel, Stanley M. *Guide to Venture Capital Sources.* 4th ed. Chicago: Capital Publishing Corp., 1977. 393 p.
This reference tool, a series of information articles written by professionals in the field, includes basic information for entrepreneurs, information on how to raise and utilize venture capital, articles on when to go public, and a list of directories on U.S. venture capital companies and underwriters as well as international venture capital companies.

1312. Silver, David A. *Venture Capital: The Complete Guide for Investors.* New York: John Wiley & Sons, Inc., 1985. 259 p.
This book gives information on the steps in the venture capital investment process. These include forming a venture capital fund, generating a deal flow, facts on the due diligence process, valuation, terms and conditions, monitoring and adding value and selling, liquidating, and portfolio management.

1313. Silver, David A.. *Who's Who in Venture Capital.* New York: John Wiley & Sons, Inc., 1984. 378 p.
In addition to some general information on venture capital, this book contains a biographical directory of venture capitalists, a directory of venture capital funds and small business investment companies, and a list of asset-based lenders.

1314. Vesper, Karl H. *New Venture Statistics.* Englewood Cliffs, NJ: Prentice-Hall, Inc., 1980. 303 p.
Some of the topics discussed in this book are career departure points, evaluating your venture ideas, how to obtain venture capital, and some hints on success and failure in venture capital.

1315. Weissman, Rudolph Leo. *Small Business and Venture Capital.* New York: Arno Press, 1979. 174 p.
This book analyzes some major problems that face the small to medium-sized business in the national economy. It looks at some proposals for providing equity capital economically.

1316. Wilson, John W. *The New Venturers: Inside the High-Stakes World of Venture Capital.* Reading, MA: Addison-Wesley Publishing Co., 1985. 237 p.
Based largely on personal interviews with venture capitalists, entrepreneurs, attorneys, academics, and consultants, this book takes a look at how a venture capital deal works.

37. WAREHOUSING/SHIPPING AND PACKING

1317. *The ABC's of Warehousing.* Washington, DC: Marketing Publications Inc., 1978. 103 p.
Written for the manager or supervisor of a warehouse, this book includes 501 ways you can cut costs and increase productivity in handling, storage, and shipping.

1318. Ackerman, Kenneth B. *Practical Handbook of Warehousing.* Washington, DC: Traffic Service Corp., 1983. 516 p.
This book describes the present status of the warehousing industry, with special emphasis on dry storage of packaged products. It is designed for use by warehouse operators and those who use public or contract warehouses.

1319. Compton, H. K. *Storehouse and Stockyard Management.* 2d ed. Eastover, Plymouth, England: Macdonald & Evans, 1981. 530 p. (Distributed by International Ideas, Philadelphia, PA.)
The chapters in this book are arranged in sequence of operations starting with principle stock levels, covering such areas as storage in a smaller firm, basic forms of stack, counting and weighing, special storage bins, types of racking, terms used for coding, and finally waste reduction.

1320. Cornwell, Richard E., and Victor, Buzz. *Self-Service Storage: The Handbook for Investors and Managers.* Chicago: Institute of Real Estate Management, 1983. 185 p.
This handbook is a useful hands-on reference for every stage of development and operation of a miniwarehouse. Chapter 10 discusses the changes taking place in the self-service storage business.

1321. Frey, Stephen L. *Management's Guide to Efficient, Money-Saving Warehousing.* Chicago: Dartnell Corp., 1982. 359 p.
This loose-leaf book is an aid in managing warehouse operations. It includes an outline of the fundamental principles and practices of good warehousing.

1322. Frey, Stephen L. *Warehouse Operations: A Handbook.* Beaverton, OR: M/A Press, 1983. 295 p.
This handbook on warehousing and distribution management provides help in warehouse operations by outlining the fundamental principles and accepted practices of good warehousing.

1323. Leonard, Edmund A. *Managing the Packaging Side of the Business.* New York: AMACOM, 1977. 50 p.
This book traces the packaging involvement in a company, beginning with the packaging functions and their individual management, followed by considerations affecting their coordination.

38. WOMEN IN BUSINESS

1324. Brown, Linda Keller. *The Woman Manager in the United States: Research Analysis and Bibliography.* Washington, DC: Business and Professional Women's Foundation, 1981. 87 p.
This book discusses the historical contributions of women in management, the social forces that have contributed to finding more women in business, the current status of women managers, affirmative action, career development, the profile of a woman executive, and the social and business impact of a dual-career lifestyle.

1325. Danco, Katy. *From the Other Side of the Bed: A Woman Looks at Life in the Family Business.* Englewood Cliffs, NJ: Prentice-Hall, Inc., 1981. 163 p.
The author points out in this book ways to understand the various problems facing women in the family-owned business.

1326. Hisrich, Robert D., and Brush, Candida G. *The Woman Entrepreneur: Starting, Financing, and Managing a Successful New Business.* Lexington, MA: Lexington Books, 1986. 216 p.
This book begins by describing the background and characteristics of a woman entrepreneur and continues by discussing the factors that are involved in starting and managing a new business.

1327. Hunsaker, Phillip, and Hunsaker, Johanna S. *Strategies and Skills for Managerial Women.* Cincinnati, OH: South-Western Publishing Co., 1986. 224 p.
The underlying premise brought out in this book is the possibility for women with ability and ambition to earn recognition and advancement in the business world.

1328. Jessup, Claudia, and Chipps, Genie. *The Woman's Guide to Starting a Business.* Rev. ed. New York: Holt, Rinehart & Winston, 1979. 335 p.
This guide tells how to turn an idea into a profit-making business with an emphasis on women-owned businesses. It includes new tax, legal, credit, and insurance information.

1329. Leslie, Mary, and Seltz, David D. *New Businesses Women Can Start and Successfully Operate: The Woman's Guide to Financial Independence.* New York: Barnes & Noble, 1979. 244 p.
This book lists the many businesses that women can start and includes a brief description of what is needed to make a success of the business.

1330. Lester, Mary. *A Woman's Guide to Starting a Small Business.* New York: Pilot Books, 1981. 32 p.
This book tells what some women have accomplished and provides pointers on how you can start a business. Lists of agencies and private organizations that can help in this venture are provided.

1331. Lynch, Edith M. *The Woman's Guide to Management.* Rev. ed. New York: Cornerstone Library, 1978. 272 p.
This book examines the roles women play in the management process, from supervisory roles to corporate presidents, and discusses topics rang-

ing from the traditional roles for women to the characteristics of the successful corporate woman.

1332. McCaslin, Barbara S., and McNamara, Patricia P. *Be Your Own Boss: A Woman's Guide to Planning & Running Her Business.* Englewood Cliffs, NJ: Prentice-Hall, Inc., 1980. 351 p.
Based on the experience and advice of more than 300 women business owners and experts, this book discusses such topics as marketing research, developing a marketing plan, choosing a legal structure, and starting and financing your business.

1333. McVicar, Marjorie, and Craig, Julia F. *Minding My Own Business.* New York: Playboy Paperbacks, 1982. 348 p.
This book is intended for women going into business. It begins by discussing what you do when you get the idea, how to plan the business, and then the action: actually setting up the business, choosing the location, and preparing your taxes. Examples for starting various types of businesses are discussed.

1334. Moran, Peg. *Invest in Yourself: A Woman's Guide to Starting Her Own Business.* Garden City, NY: Doubleday and Co., Inc., 1983. 193 p.
This book takes the woman's view to starting a business and examines such topics as "who am I," "what do I have," "where do I want to go," and stresses the importance of consulting the experts.

1335. Oana, Katherine. *Women in Their Own Business.* Skokie, IL: VGM Career Horizons, 1982. 147 p.
This book talks about the types of businesses that women have recently entered and tells how they planned their enterprises. It tells about the women themselves, their stories and successes, and gives some encouraging words for would-be women entrepreneurs.

1336. Rogalin, Wilma C., and Pell, Arthur R. *Women's Guide to Management Positions.* New York: Simon & Schuster, Inc., 1975. 149 p.
The areas studied in this book include how to evaluate your career potential, the attitudes of business toward women, laws affecting women in industry, affirmative action, how to advance within your own company and how to change jobs, and the opportunities available to women in the business world.

1337. Scollard, Jeannette Reddish. *The Entrepreneurial Female.* New York: Simon & Schuster, Inc., 1985. 256 p.
This book, written specifically for women, explains the steps necessary to become a successful entrepreneur, including starting, running, and selling a business.

1338. Stead, Bette Ann. *Women in Management.* Englewood Cliffs, NJ: Prentice-Hall, Inc., 1978. 362 p.
This book is a compilation of over 40 articles dealing with problems, solutions, and achievements of women in responsible managerial positions.

1339. Tepper, Terri P., and Tepper, Nona Dawe. *The New Entrepreneurs: Women Working from Home.* New York: Universe Books, 1980. 238 p.

This book contains 40 personal narratives on women who operate businesses from their own homes. They discuss their frustrations, their objectives, and tell how these businesses mesh with their goals.

1340. Winter, Maridee Allen. *Mind Your Own Business, Be Your Own Boss: Every Woman's Guide to Starting a Business and Succeeding.* Englewood Cliffs, NJ: Prentice-Hall, Inc., 1980. 229 p.

The author interviewed 150 women throughout North America and the United Kingdom to obtain the information for this book. She discusses such topics as how to get started in business, capital intensive businesses, the business plan, how to get money, the future of the business, and much more.

1341. *Women Business Owners: Selling to the Federal Government.* Washington, DC: U.S. Small Business Administration, Office of Women's Business Ownership, Interagency Committee on Women's Business Enterprise, 1984. 65 p.

This book provides women with information about how to market their goods and services to the federal government.

Core Library Collection

1. ALMANACS

1342. *Commodity Year Book.* New York: Commodity Research Bureau. (Annual)
Information useful in making decisions in the futures market is provided in this book. Also included are long-range price charts and current key supply/demand statistical tables.

1343. *Information Please Almanac Atlas & Yearbook.* Boston: Houghton Mifflin Co. (Annual)
This comprehensive guide provides information on various aspects of business and economics such as consumer price indexes, incomes, consumer credit, freight and passenger traffic, and other business topics as well as facts on many general topics of interest to the business person.

1344. *International Year Book and Statemen's Who's Who.* East Grinstead, England: Thomas Skinner Directories, Ltd., 1984. 643 p.
This directory of international, national, and regional organizations contains current facts and figures on all countries.

1345. Levine, Sumner N., ed. *The Dow Jones-Irwin Business and Investment Almanac, 1986.* Homewood, IL: Dow Jones-Irwin. (Annual)
Some of the features in this new edition include sources of venture capital, price-earnings ratio, comparative returns of different investment vehicles, discount-brokerage rates, selected online business/financial databases, employee benefits, and a business information directory.

1346. *World Almanac & Book of Facts.* New York: Newspaper Enterprise Association. (Annual)
This publication contains a "compendium of universal knowledge," including statistics, dates, information on foreign countries, and much more.

1347. Wright, John W. *American Almanac of Job Salaries.* New York: Avon Books, 1984. 824 p.
This standard reference book is a good starting place to look for an overall view of salary range on a particular job.

2. BIBLIOGRAPHIES AND INDEXES

1348. *Associations' Publications in Print 1984–1985.* New York: R. R. Bowker, Co., 1984. 3 v.
These sourcebooks include an annual list of titles of interest to public, academic and special library users as well as all corporate libraries with research and R&D programs. A list of names and addresses of associations and publishers/distributors is also included.

1349. Brownstone, David M., and Carruth, Gorton. *Where to Find Business Information.* 2d ed. New York: John Wiley & Sons, Inc., 1982. 632 p.
More than 5,000 publications are listed in this book on all subjects of interest to the business person. The material is categorized by subject and listed alphabetically by title within subjects. Each entry contains a publisher, address, telephone number, and a brief description.

1350. *Commerce Publications Update.* Washington, DC: U.S. Department of Commerce. (Biweekly) (For sale by U.S. Government Printing Office.)
A biweekly newsletter, this publication provides recent publications of the Department of Commerce including titles, prices, ordering instructions, and some annotations.

1351. Daniells, Lorna M. *Business Information Sources.* Rev. ed. Berkeley, CA: University of California Press, 1985. 673 p.
This book "is a selected, annotated list of business books and reference sources, with an emphasis on recent material in the English language."

1352. Gumpert, David E., and Timmons, Jeffrey A. *The Insider's Guide to Small Business Resources.* New York: Harper & Row, Publishers, 1984. 407 p.
Information on necessary resources for the small business person are included in this book. Some of the topics covered are management training, venture capital, consulting services, loans, franchising, and overseas business opportunities.

1353. Johnson, H. Webster; Maier, Ernie L.; and Faria, Anthony J. *How to Use the Business Library: With Sources of Business Information.* 5th ed. Cincinnati, OH: South-Western Publishing Co., 1984. 256 p.
Current information on the use of handbooks, directories, periodicals, government, and trade publications are included in this book along with a section on using the business library.

1354. *Monthly Catalog of United States Government Publications.* Washington, DC: U.S. Government Printing Office. (Monthly)
This serial contains a list of publications sold by the Superintendent of Documents during each month.

1355. Mossman, Jennifer, and Wood, Donna. *Business Firms Master Index.* Detroit, MI: Gale Research Co., 1985. 1,124 p.
Arranged by company name, this index provides information on a wide range of business information sources such as directories, encyclopedias, buying guides, and special issues of leading periodicals.

1356. Ryans, Cynthia C. *International Business Reference Sources: Developing a Corporate Library.* Lexington, MA: Lexington Books, 1983. 195 p.
This book provides a single source of representative holdings of international business sources. Sections on government publications, journals, annuals, loose-leaf services, directories, almanacs, handbooks, and international business books contain annotations for each entry.

1357. Schlessinger, Bernard. *The Basic Business Library: Core Resources.* Phoenix, AZ: Oryx Press, 1983. 232 p.
Full bibliographic data are given in this book for basic business references that business libraries should have. In addition, the author has included an annotated bibliography of additional reference material.

1358. Thompson, Marilyn Taylor. *Management Information, Where to Find It.* Metuchen, NJ: Scarecrow Press, 1981. 272 p.
The material in this bibliography is divided into three categories: management in general, specific aspects of management, and specific types of management. Materials cited are those published during the 1970s in the English language.

1359. U.S. Small Business Administration. *Small Business Bibliography Series.* Washington, DC: U.S. Small Business Administration. (Irregular)
These short, annotated bibliographies list books, government publications, directors, journals and associations of interest to the small business entrepreneur.

3. DATABASES

1360. Byerly, Greg. *Online Searching: A Dictionary and Bibliographic Guide.* Littleton, CO: Libraries Unlimited, 1983. 288 p.
This book provides concise and understandable definitions of online search terminology along with a selective annotated bibliography of journal articles, books, directories, bibliographies, annuals, and proceedings on the topic.

1361. Hall, James L., and Brown, Marjorie J. *Online Bibliographic Databases.* 3d ed. Detroit, MI: Gale Research Co., 1983. 383 p.
Essential details on 200 online bibliographic databases are listed in this book. Included is the name and acronym of the database, supplier's name and address, subject, etc.

1362. Hoover, Ryan E. *Executive's Guide to Online Information Services.* White Plains, NY: Knowledge Industry Publications, Inc., 1984. 296 p.
This book tells you what some of the many online services are, how they can be used and their cost, and what they can mean for you. Illustrations are included that show specific kinds of information available and data as they actually will appear on the terminal.

1363. Kruzas, Anthony T., and Schmittroth, John, Jr., eds. *Encyclopedia of Information Systems and Services.* 4th ed. Detroit, MI: Gale Research Company, 1981. 933 p.
Descriptions of more than 2,000 organizations that produce, process, store, and use bibliographic and nonbibliographic information are given in this book. In addition, there are over 1,500 databases listed here.

1364. *Predicast Basebook.* Cleveland, OH: Predicast, Inc. (Annual)
Statistical information from several hundred business press and government sources are included in this *Basebook.* Includes information on specific product markets, supply, demand, and price statistics on the construction industries, agriculture, durable and nondurable goods, transportation, communications, and utilities.

1365. Schmittroth, John, Jr., and Maxfield, Doris Morris, eds. *Online Database Search Services Directory.* Detroit, MI: Gale Research Co., 1984. 2 v.
This directory on organizations that provide computerized information retrieval services includes the systems accessed, subject, database specializations, staff size, and fee structure.

1366. Sears, Jean L., and Moody, Marilyn K. *Using Government Publications.* Phoenix, AZ: Oryx Press, 1985. 2 v.
Volume one of this two-volume set covers searches by subject and agency. Volume two includes statistical searches and discusses the use of special techniques.

4. DICTIONARIES AND ENCYCLOPEDIAS

1367. Akew, Denise, ed. *Encyclopedia of Associations: A Guide to National and International Organizations.* 18th ed. Detroit, MI: Gale Research Co., 1984. 3 v.
This three-volume set lists over 16,000 active organizations and provides a geographic and executive index as well as lists of new associations and projects.

1368. Baker, Michael J., ed. *Macmillan Dictionary of Marketing & Advertising.* New York: Nichols Publishing Co., 1984. 217 p.
This book provides a detailed description of the many terms used in marketing and advertising with cross-references for ease of use.

1369. *Exporters' Encyclopaedia.* New York: Dun and Bradstreet International. (Annual)
Some of the indexes included in this book are the export-order index, export markets index, and export know-how index. Each section contains detailed information on these topics for countries throughout the world and definitions of terms, statistical information, and important names and addresses.

1370. Garcia, F. L. *Encyclopedia of Banking and Finance.* 8th ed. Boston: Bankers Publishing Co., 1983. 1,024 p.
Not only does this book cover the entire area of banking and finance, this new edition includes information on the rapid changes in this area.

1371. Hart, Norman A., and Stapleton, John. *Glossary of Marketing Terms.* 2d ed. London: William Heinemann, Ltd., 1981. 206 p.
A complete range of over 2,000 marketing and associated terms with a short explanation of each is included in this book.

1372. Heyel, Carl, ed. *The Encyclopedia of Management.* New York: Van Nostrand Reinhold Co., Inc., 1982. 1,371 p.
The management definitions included in this book range in length from very brief to over 20 pages.

1373. Huczynski, Andrzej. *Encyclopedia of Management Development Methods.* Aldershot, Hants, England: Gower Publishing Co., Ltd., 1983. 339 p.
This book provides a comprehensive compendium of management learning methods for the training specialists. In addition to a variety of different techniques and methods, it also provides detailed readings in this area.

1374. Johannsen, Hano, and Page, G. Terry. *The International Dictionary of Business.* Englewood Cliffs, NJ: Prentice-Hall, Inc., 1981. 376 p.
Covering the whole area of business and management, this book includes over 5,000 entries on international usage. Also includes information on nongovernment agencies, associations, trade unions, and stock exchanges.

1375. Pugh, Eric, comp. *Pugh's Dictionary of Acronyms and Abbreviations: Abbreviations in Management, Technology and Information Science.* Phoenix, AZ: Oryx Press, 1981. 344 p.
Aimed at supplying information to both business professionals and lay persons, this book contains acronyms and abbreviations for those acronyms relating to management, technology, and information systems.

1376. Rice, Michael Downey. *Prentice-Hall Dictionary of Business, Finance, and Law.* Englewood Cliffs, NJ: Prentice-Hall, Inc., 1983. 362 p.
This dictionary includes information in the field of business law, including federal legislation, administrative law, environmental law, pensions and profit sharing plans, bank and transportation regulations, and corporate law.

1377. Rosenberg, Jerry M. *Dictionary of Business and Management.* 2d ed. New York: John Wiley & Sons, Inc., 1983. 631 p.
This book contains terminology of business and management that practitioners need to up-date their current word usage.

1378. Shafritz, Jay M. *Dictionary of Personnel Management and Labor Relations.* Oak Park, IL: Moore Publishing Co., Inc., 1980. 429 p.
This dictionary provides detailed descriptions of the terms used on the theory, concepts, practices, and laws. in personnel management and labor relations.

1379. Shapiro, Irving J. *Dictionary of Marketing Terms.* Totowa, NJ: Littlefield, Adams & Co., 1982. 276 p.
Arranged in alphabetical order, this book provides a brief explanation of the many terms used in marketing.

1380. *Trade Names Dictionary: Company Index.* Detroit, MI: Gale Research Co., 1984. 2 v.
An alphabetical list of over 36,000 companies that manufacture, distribute, import or market consumer-oriented products is included in this book.

1381. Urdang, Lawrence, ed. *Dictionary of Advertising Terms.* Chicago: Crain Books, 1985. 209 p.
This miniencyclopedia includes the working vocabulary of all areas of the advertising and marketing world. It contains over 4,000 terms.

1382. Wasserman, Paul. *Encyclopedia of Geographic Information Sources.* 3d ed. Detroit, MI: Gale Research Co., 1978. 167 p.
Directories, almanacs, periodicals, and bibliographies. are listed in this guide for states, cities, and some foreign countries.

1383. Wasserman, Paul; Georgi, Charlotte; and Way, James, eds. *Encyclopedia of Business Information Sources.* 5th ed. Detroit, MI: Gale Research Co., 1983. 728 p.
Over 20,000 entries are given on such subjects as statistical sources, directories, almanacs, periodicals, associations, dictionaries, and handbooks.

5. DIRECTORIES

1384. *American International Trade and Project Directory.* Washington, DC: North American Communications, Inc., 1985.
More than 3,000 listings of U.S. organizations that finance foreign projects are included in this reference guide.

1385. Angel, Juvenal Londono. *Multinational Marketing and Employment Directory.* New York: Uniworld Business Publications, 1982. 939 p.
This book is divided into two sections. The first section is an alphabetical listing of over 7,500 U.S. corporations which operate both here and overseas. Products and services rendered by these companies are given, as well as names of the executives. The second section discusses, in

length, employment opportunities, hints on how to compile resumes, and compensation systems associated with international firms.

1386. Ash, Francesca, ed. *The International Licensing Directory 1985.* Southport, CT: Expocon Management Associates Inc., 1985. 224 p.
This book lists over 1,000 licensing companies worldwide offering over 3,000 properties. Each entry includes address, phone, contact name, and list of properties.

1387. *Business Traveler's City Guide 1986.* Chicago: Rand McNally & Co., 1986. 440 p.
This book features selected hotels and restaurants from 76 leading cities in the U.S. and includes color maps, frequent-flyer club charts, 800 numbers for hotel-motel chains and car rental agencies.

1388. Campbell, Malcolm J., comp. *Financial Directories of the World: A Guide to Information Sources in Finance, Economics, Employment, Property and the Law.* Guernsey, British Isles: Vallancey Reference Books, Ltd., 1982. 338 p.
This book contains a record of directory materials on financing economic activities and financial information on specific organizations. Each entry contains the title of the directory, the name and address of the organization, number of pages in the directory, and a brief description of each book.

1389. *Chain Store Guide: 1985 Directory of Department Stores.* New York: Lebhar-Friedman Inc., 1985. 970 p.
This book includes more than 1,330 department store companies that represent over 10,300 stores, and 1,000 upscale general merchandise and apparel mail-order firms in the U.S. The listings include ownership, locations, key personnel, square footage, and some financial data.

1390. *Developing Executive and Management Talent: A Guide to OPM Courses, Fellowships and Developmental Assignments.* Washington, DC: U.S. Office of Personnel Management, Executive Personnel and Management Development Group, Executive and Management Development Division, 1981. 63 p. (For sale by U.S. Government Printing Office.)
This book contains a checklist of special development programs sponsored by the federal government for improving management. Also included are concise write-ups on fellowship and Office of Personnel Management courses.

1391. *Directory of Business, Trade, and Public Policy Organizations.* Washington, DC: U.S. Small Business Administration, Office of Advocacy. (Annual)
This book lists the names and addresses of over 1,000 trade and business organizations that assist in the communications between the small business community and the federal government. The information is divided by type of industry.

1392. *Directory of Corporate Affiliation 1985: Who Owns Whom.* Skokie, IL: National Register Publishing Co., 1985. 2,465 p.
This publication gives an in-depth look at major U.S. corporations and their subsidiaries and affiliates.

1393. Ethridge, James, ed. *Directory of Directories.* 3d ed. Detroit, MI: Gale Research Co., 1984. 1,322 p.
This book describes over 7,000 directories with an index listing topics such as education, foreign directories, public affairs, business, and government.

1394. *Directory of Management Consultants.* 3d ed. Fitzwilliam, NH: Consultants News, 1983. 392 p.
The types of services offered, name of president, size of staff, branches, and geographical area served are all listed for management consultant firms.

1395. *Directory of Operating Small Business Investment Companies.* Washington, DC: U.S. Small Business Administration. (Irregular)
Divided into two parts, this directory lists small business investment companies alphabetically by state. The second part contains licensees listed alphabetical by state. These licensees are limited to those assisting small businesses owned by socially or economically disadvantaged people.

1396. *Directory of Personal Image Consultants.* New York: Fairchild Books, 1982. 94 p.
This book contains over 200 listings of information on the services provided by image consultants located in 74 cities in 35 states and 4 foreign countries. Each consultant's specialty, credentials, number of staff, fees, and principal corporate clients are listed.

1397. *Directory of State Small Business Programs.* Washington, DC: U.S. Small Business Administration, Office of Advocacy. (Annual)
The first part of this book provides a survey of state small business programs. This is followed by a listing (alphabetical by state) of small business programs and summaries.

1398. *Directory of U.S. and Canadian Marketing Surveys and Services.* Bridgewater, NJ: Rauch Associates, 1985. 402 p.
This book describes 250 research firms offering over 3,000 studies, surveys, and services. Information includes prices, age of information, and people to contact.

1399. Elster, Robert J., ed. *Trade Shows and Professional Exhibits Directory.* Detroit, MI: Gale Research Co., 1985. 549 p.
Detailed information on over 2,100 scheduled exhibitions, trade shows, association conventions, and other sales events are listed in this book. Focus is on the U.S. but some international events are listed.

1400. *Export Directory/U.S. Buying Guide.* New York: Journal of Commerce. (Biennial)
This book profiles the business activities of over 37,000 exporters who sell products and commodities in world markets.

1401. *Findex: The Directory of Market Research Reports, Studies and Surveys.* 7th ed. New York: Find/SVP, 1985. (With midyear supplements.)
This reference tool is for planners, researchers, marketing managers, librarians, and top management. The reports from U.S. and foreign research firms include document title, concise description, publisher,

date, pages, and price on research industries, markets, products, and companies vital to your business.

1402. Frankenstein, Diane Waxer. *Brandnames: Who Owns What.* New York: Facts on File, Inc., 1981. 559 p.

This book gives company information on manufacturers that produce over 15,000 brand-name products including addresses, telephone number, chief executive, and brief description of the corporation.

1403. Gill, Kay, ed. *Government Research Directory.* 3d ed. Detroit, MI: Gale Research Co., 1985. 675 p.

More than 2,300 entries describing U.S. government research centers are listed in this book. Descriptions of appropriate R&D installations, institutes, centers, laboratories, bureaus, test stations, and data collection and analysis centers are also included.

1404. Grant, Mary McNierney, and Berleant-Schiller, Riva, eds. *Directory of Business and Financial Services.* 8th ed. New York: Special Libraries Association, 1984. 189 p.

This book contains an alphabetical listing of services, both business and financial, which should help the user determine its applicability to various needs. Listings include printed sources and online databases, as well as a listing of investment consultants.

1405. *The Great 800 Toll Free Directory.* Jackson, MS: The Great 800 Directory Company. (Annual)

This comprehensive directory provides toll-free numbers for more than 50,000 numbers nationwide. They include over 2,000 product and service classifications. Arranged by state within classifications, the book also contains an alphabetical index.

1406. Holtz, Herman. *2001 Sources of Financing for Small Business.* New York: Arco Publishing, Inc., 1983. 173 p.

This book provides names and addresses of agencies available to small business people who need money for the business. It includes lists of federal agencies and programs, state agencies, venture capitalists, and organizations funded by Minority Business Development Agency.

1407. *International Business Travel and Relocation Directory.* 3d ed. Detroit, MI: Gale Research Co., 1984. 978 p.

For personnel in companies doing business overseas, this book contains background information for employees going abroad and resources and reference materials for the five major areas of the world.

1408. Kruzas, Anthony T.; Thomas, Robert C.; and Gill, Kay, eds. *Business Organizations and Agencies Directory.* 2d ed. Detroit, MI: Gale Research Co., 1984. 1,371 p.

This book lists 16,000 organizations that promote, regulate, or coordinate business in the United States, including government agencies, franchise firms, and convention bureaus.

1409. *Membership Directory.* Washington, DC: National Association of Small Business Investment Companies. (Annual)

Over 300 Small Business Investment Companies (SBICs) and Minority Enterprise Small Business Investment Companies (MESBICs) are listed in this book which is arranged alphabetically by state. Preferred limit for loans or investments as well as industry preferences is given for each entry.

1410. *Million Dollar Directory.* Parsippany, NJ: Dun & Bradstreet Inc. (Annual)
This book lists pertinent information on the top 50,000 companies. The entries are listed alphabetically, geographically, and by industry and contain addresses, telephone numbers, sales, and officers in the company.

1411. Mossman, Jennifer, and Wood, Donna, eds. *Business Firms Master Index.* Detroit, MI: Gale Research Co., 1985. 1,124 p.
Over 110,000 firms, associations, individuals, and others are listed in this book. The focus is mainly on the communications field.

1412. *National Trade and Professional Associations of the United States.* Washington, DC: Columbia Books, Inc. (Annual)
This book lists approximately 5,800 national trade associations, professional, scientific and technical societies, and labor unions. It includes the chief officer, membership, budget, history, publications, and date of annual meeting for each entry.

1413. Office of the Under Secretary of Defense for Research and Engineering. *Small and Disadvantaged Business Utilization Specialists.* Washington, DC: U.S. Government Printing Office, 1983. 57 p.
This book lists the locations for the Department of Defense procurement offices and gives the names and addresses of their small and disadvantaged business specialists.

1414. Pratt, Stanley E., ed. *Guide to Venture Capital Sources.* 7th ed. Wellesley Hills, MA: Capital Publishing Corp., 1983. 489 p.
This book lists the various venture capital sources.

1415. *Principal International Business; The World Marketing Directory.* New York: Dun & Bradstreet, Inc. (Annual)
Over 50,000 businesses are listed in this book with information on their legal name, parent company, address, cable, sales volume, chief executives, and SIC number.

1416. *Profiles of 23 Retail Markets Worldwide.* London: Newman Books, Ltd., 1982. 96 p.
Addresses, telephone numbers, names of chief executives and buyers are listed in this book for over 7,000 department stores, supermarkets, and chains worldwide.

1417. Silver, David A. *Who's Who in Venture Capital.* New York: John Wiley & Sons, Inc., 1984. 378 p.
In addition to some general information on venture capital, this book contains a biographical directory of venture capitalists, a directory of venture capital funds and small business investment companies, and a list of asset-based lenders.

1418. *The Small Business Answer Desk Directory.* Washington, DC: Office of the Chief Counsel for Advocacy, U.S. Small Business Administration, 1985. 123 p.
This directory tells you where to get quick answers to your small busi-

ness inquiries. In addition to a glossary of small business terms, it includes phone numbers of state small business offices, regional small business administration divisions, and other government agencies.

1419. *Small Business Guide to Federal R&D.* Washington, DC: National Science Foundation, 1980. 265 p.
This guide gives information on business opportunities to small firms working in the area of R&D. Names, addresses, and phone numbers of people to contact regarding the programs are also included.

1420. *Small Business Sourcebook.* Detroit, MI: Gale Research Co. (Biennial with supplements)
This publication contains profiles on a wide range of small businesses, listing pertinent professional or trade associations, educational resources, and trade shows. The first edition supplement updates this material and includes a cumulative index of all listings in the main sourcebook.

1421. *The States and Small Business: Programs and Activities.* Washington, DC: U.S. Small Business Administration, Office of Advocacy. (Annual)
This book provides a list of state support structures, programs, and activities. The small business activities are listed in alphabetical order by state.

1422. Stopford, John M.; Dunning, John H.; and Haberich, Klaus O. *World Directory of Multinational Enterprises, 1982–1983.* 2d ed. Detroit, MI: Gale Research Co., 1983. 3 v.
Corporate profiles and five-year financial summaries of approximately 550 multinational corporations are given in this book, along with an overview of MNCs surveys, their history, growth, and development.

1423. *Thomas Register of American Manufacturers and Thomas Register Catalog File.* New York: Thomas Publishing Co. (Annual)
This set of books gives information on the name of U.S. manufacturing firms and tells who makes each specific product.

1424. Wasserman, Paul, ed. *Statistics Sources: A Subject Guide to Data on Industrial Business, Social, Educational, Financial, and Other Topics for the United States and Internationally.* 9th ed. Detroit, MI: Gale Research Co., 1984. 2 v.
This subject guide contains information on industrial, business, social, financial, and other aspects of interest to the business person. Entries are under the name of the country as well as the subject.

1425. Wasserman, Paul, and Wasserman, Steven, eds. *Law and Legal Information Directory.* 3d ed. Detroit, MI: Gale Research Co., 1984. 902 p.
This volume provides comprehensive coverage of both live and print sources of legal information.

1426. Wasserman, Paul, and McLean, Janice. *Training and Development Organizations Directory.* 3d ed. Detroit, MI: Gale Research Co., 1983. 1,198 p.
This sourcebook provides details and extensive profiles on the activities and specialties of businesses, institutes, and consulting groups that offer

managerial and supervisory training courses for business firms and government agencies.

1427. *Who Owns Whom: North America.* London: Dun & Bradstreet, Ltd., Directories Division. (Annual)
The ownership of subsidiary and associate companies is listed in this book.

6. GENERAL

1428. Baldrige, Letitia. *Complete Guide to Executive Manners.* New York: Rawson Associates, 1985. 519 p.
This book details the rules of etiquette in the business world, reflecting the author's view that "good manners are cost effective."

1429. *A Basic Guide to Exporting.* Washington, DC: United States Department of Commerce, International Trade Administration, 1981. 133 p. (For sale by U.S. Government Printing Office.)
This book contains information on what is needed by the small to medium-sized firm to be successful in international trade. Also ways to get assistance to reach these goals are discussed.

1430. Block, Julian. *Julian Block's Guide to Year-Round Tax Savings, 1985.* 5th ed. Homewood, IL: Dow Jones-Irwin, 1985. 343 p.
This book provides practical, effective, and legal tax angles that can reduce your tax bill.

1431. Butler, Robert, and Rappaport, Donald. *Money and Your Business: How to Get It, How to Manage It, How to Keep It.* New York: New York Institute of Finance, 1982. 6 v. in 2.
This series of guides is designed to assist the entrepreneur through the entire life cycle of the business.

1432. Buttress, F. A. *World Guide to Abbreviations of Organizations.* 7th ed. Glasgow, Scotland: L. Hill, 1984. 731 p. (Distributed by Grand River Books, Detroit, MI.)
The complete names are given for companies worldwide that are usually identified by initials or abbreviations.

1433. *Capital Formation: Private and Public Financings 1984.* New York: Practising Law Institute, 1984. 440 p.
This reference manual contains numerous sections on venture capital written by experts in the field.

1434. Colby, Barnard L. *How to Write Like a Pro: Errors Too Often Seen in Print or Heard on the Air.* New London, CT: The Day, 1984. 69 p.
This book contains a list of words and pairs of words that are mistaken for one another or are misused. By using examples, it explains their proper usage.

1435. *Controlling Employee Health Care Costs: Management Actions to Contain Expense and Define Employee Responsibility.* Monterey, CA: Management Information Studies, 1985. 104 p.
This book offers a thorough understanding of the many health care costs such as establishing a cost-sharing structure, creating financial incentives to reward employees and avoid expensive treatment, explaining how to select benefits that will be best for your company, dental plan options, direct reimbursement plans, and wellness/fitness programs.

1436. Croner, Ulrich H. E. *Reference Book for World Traders: A Guide for Exporters and Importers.* Queens Village, NY: Croner Publications, Inc., 1985. 3 v.
This book contains information for the business planning of exporting or importing as well as information on market research.

1437. *Economic Indicators.* Washington, DC: U.S. Government Printing Office. (Monthly)
This publication contains economic information on prices, production, purchasing power, credit, wages, money, and federal finance.

1438. Ennis, F. Beaven. *Marketing Norms for Product Managers.* New York: Association of National Advertisers, Inc., 1985. 174 p.
This book gives the manager who is new to marketing a sound foundation for a successful marketing program. A useful desk-top guide for preparing marketing plans is included.

1439. Faber, Peter L., and Holbrook, Martin E. *Subchapter S Manual: A Special Tax Break for Small Business Corporations.* Englewood Cliffs, NJ: Prentice-Hall, Inc., 1983. 221 p.
Some of the topics covered in this book include how to handle income, deductions and credits, retirement plans, distributions, and special tax savings, all involving S Corporations.

1440. *Financial Studies of the Small Business.* Washington, DC: Financial Research Association. (Annual)
The financial and operations of approximately 50 types of businesses are included in this book. They are based on 25,000 financial statements of firms with capital under $250,000.

1441. *Futures Market Service.* New York: Commodity Research Bureau. (Weekly)
Known as the "blue sheet," this publication reports on the factors that influence commodity prices.

1442. Goldstein, Arnold S. *Basic Book of Business Agreements.* Wilmington, DE: Enterprise Publishing, Inc., 1983. 923 p.
This book offers a complete collection of ready-to-use agreement forms for most any personal or business situation. In a loose-leaf binder, each form can be photocopied and filled in with your information.

1443. *A Guide to Doing Business with the Department of State.* Washington, DC: Bureau of Mangement, Office of Small and Disadvantage Business Utilization, 1984. 1 v. various paging. (For sale by U.S. Government Printing Office.)
This book is designed to help the small, minority, and female-owned

firms who are seeking to do business with the Department of State to identify procurement opportunities within the department. Names and telephone numbers of contacts within the department, other agencies within the Washington, DC, area, and overseas contacts are included.

1444. Hayes, Rick Stephan, and Howell, John Cotton. *How to Finance Your Small Business with Government Money: SBA and Other Loans.* 2d ed. New York: John Wiley & Sons, Inc., 1983. 258 p.
This book explains in detail the various programs and services available to the small business person and tells how to take advantage of them. In addition, it tells how to apply for a SBA loan.

1445. Hoffman, Roger. *The Complete Software Marketplace, 1984–1985.* New York: Warner Software/Warner Books, 1985. 236 p.
This guide to developing and marketing software covers case studies on how to name the company, structuring the business, getting insurance, legal matters, venture capital, advertising, promotions, and PR. In addition, lists of computer industry lawyers, agents, and brokers are included as well as trade shows, consultants, market research firms, distributors, and trade publications.

1446. *The INC. Executive Compensation Study.* Boston: INC. Executive Compensation Study. (Annual)
Important trends in executive compensation are covered in this book including salary, bonus, benefits, and perks for CEOs, CFOs, and Chief Operating and Marketing Officers for small to mid-sized companies.

1447. *International Financial Statistics.* Washington, DC: International Monetary Fund. (Monthly)
This publication arranges all aspects of international and domestic finance by country.

1448. Kess, Sidneyand Weslin, Bertil. *Business Strategies.* Chicago: Commerce Clearing House, Inc., 1984. 4 v. (Loose leaf)
This loose-leaf reporting service is an excellent working tool for the person who works with the accounting, tax or legal problems of small, medium, or large businesses.

1449. *Management Aids.* Washington, DC: Small Business Administration, 1960. (Irregular)
The Small Business Administration provides a series of aids on various aspects of small business management such as borrowing, pricing, cash flow, breakeven analysis, venture capital, recordkeeping, profit pricing, taxes, etc. Each aid is a four- to eight-page pamphlet.

1450. Nicholas, Ted. *The Complete Book of Corporate Forms.* Wilmington, DE: Enterprise Publishing, Inc., 1985. (Loose leaf)
This loose-leaf book contains virtually all the forms you need for your corporation: minutes of stockholder meetings, directors meetings, special meetings, negotiation of contracts, directors fees, forms for tax savings, fringe benefits, and mergers.

1451. *Overseas Business Reports.* Washington, DC: U.S. Government Printing Office. (Quarterly)
Current detailed marketing information for the export business is contained in this book as well as economic and commercial profiles of many countries.

1452. Poe, Roy W. *The McGraw-Hill Guide to Effective Business Reports.* New York: McGraw-Hill Book Co., 1982. 208 p.
This author shows how to analyze other people's reports and tells how to become involved in an editorial process that ensures effective writing.

1453. *SBIC Digest.* (Small Business Investment Companies Digest). Washington, DC: U.S. Small Business Administration Investment Division. (Semiannual)
Each issue covers a different aspect of small business management. This information includes statistics and addresses.

1454. *Small Business Market Is the World.* Washington, DC: U.S. Small Business Administration, Office of International Trade, [n.d.].
This publication lists programs designed to help small businesses enter into or expand in international markets.

1455. *Sole Proprietorship Returns.* Washington, DC: Department of the Treasury, Internal Revenue Service. (Annual) (For sale by U.S. Government Printing Office.)
This publication provides annual statistics on sole proprietorships, including receipts, cost of sales and operations, deductions, and net income or deficit.

1456. *Subchapter S Revision Act of 1982: Law and Explanation.* Chicago: Commerce Clearing House, Inc., 1982. 136 p.
This book provides coverage of the Subchapter S Revision Act of 1982 along with the texts of the amended Internal Revenue Code provisions. A list of effective dates along with a topical index are also included.

1457. *Survey of Current Business.* Washington, DC: Department of Commerce. Bureau of Economic Analysis. (Monthly) (For sale by U.S. Government Printing Office.)
This publication includes statistical information on foreign and domestic investments, and trade information.

1458. U.S. Bureau of the Census. *Statistical Abstract of the United States.* Washington, DC: U.S. Government Printing Office. (Annual)
This publication is a prime source for industrial, social, political, and economic statistics of the U.S.

1459. Woodwell, Donald R. *Using and Applying the Dow Jones Information Services.* Homewood, IL: Dow Jones-Irwin, 1985. 200 p.
This book shows how databases can be used in investing, corporate planning, education and communications, and how these data can be analyzed and interpreted.

1460. *Words that Sell.* Westbury, NY: Caddylack Publishing, 1984. 128 p.
This thesaurus lists more than 2,500 words, slogans, and phrases that are used by professional copywriters to sell an audience.

7. HANDBOOKS AND MANUALS

1461. *AMA Management Handbook.* 2d ed. New York: AMACOM, 1983. 1 v. various paging.
This complete business library offers proven profit-making information on every conceivable business topic. It contains the expertise of more than 200 outstanding authorities.

1462. Blair, Frank E., ed. *International Marketing Handbook.* 2d ed. Detroit, MI: Gale Research Co., 1985. 3 v.
In-depth marketing and trade profiles for 142 nations are provided in this handbook. The data include foreign trade outlook, industry trends, transportation and utilities, distribution and sales channels, credit, trade regulations, and much more.

1463. Bullock, Gwendolyn A. *Performance Standards Handbook: A Reference for Managers and Supervisors.* Washington, DC: U.S. Office of Personnel Management, 1981. 56 p. (For sale by U.S. Government Printing Office.)
This self-evaluation tool can also be used to evaluate jobs ranging from secretary to supervisor.

1464. Cohen, William A. *The Entrepreneur and Small Business Problem Solver.* New York: John Wiley & Sons, Inc., 1983. 655 p.
This book answers questions often asked when starting or expanding a small business. Included is information on how to get a loan, insurance, laws, recruiting, advertising, and pricing.

1465. *The Complete Portfolio of Time Management Forms.* Westbury, NY: Caddylak Publishing, 1985. 184 p.
This book contains 180 professionally designed planners to fit all time management needs in ready-to-photocopy form.

1466. Gladstone, David J. *Venture Capital Handbook.* Reston, VA: Reston Publishing Co., Inc., 1983. 402 p.
The entire process of raising venture capital is covered in this book.

1467. Gourgues, Harold W., Jr. *Financial Planning Handbook: A Portfolio of Strategies and Applications.* New York: New York Institute of Finance, 1983. 443 p.
Beginning with a definition of financial planning as an ongoing process, this book presents a segmented approach on how to use the financial planning process to achieve the accumulation, preservation, and distribution of wealth.

1468. *Handbook for Small Business: A Survey of Small Business Programs of the Federal Government.* 5th ed. Washington, DC: U.S. Government Printing Office, 1984. 228 p.
Information on programs and services offered to small businesses by 25 federal agencies is included in this book.

1469. Heller, Robert. *The Pocket Manager.* New York: E. P. Dutton, Inc., 1985. 308 p.
An alphabetic list of management terms, the author gives a brief description of each term.

1470. *International Postal Handbook.* Richmond, CA: New Harbinger Publications, 1980. 54 p.
This guide to international correspondence explains all classes of outgoing and incoming mail, rates, regulations, and restrictions for every country in the world.

1471. Jacoby, James W. *How to Prepare Managerial Communications.* Rev. ed. Washington, DC: Bureau of National Affairs, 1983. 232 p.
This "how-to" and up-to-date reference source provides the steps required to produce an organization manual, including writing and editing techniques, incorporating material in the manual, review, trial usage, approval, distributing and updating, and instructional materials.

1472. Keithley, Erwin M., and Schreiner, Philip J. *A Manual of Style for the Preparation of Papers and Reports—Business and Management Applications.* 3d ed. Cincinnati, OH: South-Western Publishing Co., 1980. 118 p.
The two basic parts in this manual, designed as a reference and guide to written reports are: an explanation of report style and a complete model report.

1473. Kish, Joseph L. *Office Management Problem Solver.* Radnor, PA: Chilton Book Co., 1983. 363 p.
This book is intended as a reference guide for new office managers looking for a source of techniques for establishing office procedures, systems, and services.

1474. Lane, Marc J. *Legal Handbook for Small Business.* New York: AMACOM, 1977. 181 p.
This book includes checklists on trademarks, patents, copyrights, and contractual agreements.

1475. Lazare, Linda, ed. *The Financial Desk Book: Your Complete Guide to Financial Planning, Investments, Taxation, and Estate Planning.* New York: Simon & Schuster, Inc., 1985. 600 p.
This reference tool offers financial information for investors and financial professionals on tax tables, interest tables, tax law summaries, key dates, and historical charts.

1476. *Marketing-Sales Promotion-Advertising Handbook, 1984.* New York: National Retail Merchants Association, 1983. 84 p.
This book offers direction and help in organizing selling goals and plans to help accomplish these goals on schedule.

1477. Moffat, Donald W. *Concise Desk Book of Business Finance.* 2d ed. Englewood Cliffs, NJ: Prentice-Hall, Inc., 1984. 382 p.
This book is intended as a time-saving reference guide and contains an alphabetical listing of terms associated with business finance. Definitions of the terms are given, along with examples and illustrations to further clarify meanings.

1478. *Moody's Industrial Manual: American and Foreign.* New York: Moody's Investor's Service. (Annual)
This manual includes financial and business information on more than 5,000 major corporations, both national and international, including company history, descriptions of businesses and property, financial statements, management, debt, capital, and other important data.

1479. Poe, Roy W. *The McGraw-Hill Handbook of Business Letters.* New York: McGraw-Hill Book Co., 1983. 286 p.
This book includes model letters for more than 160 business situations including requests, transmittals, confirmations, and credit and collections.

1480. Quick, Thomas L. *The Manager's Motivation Desk Book.* New York: John Wiley & Sons, Inc., 1984. 456 p.
The author offers managers a systematic and practical approach to improving employee motivation. He has included checklists, guidelines, and review quizzes to help managers get immediate results.

1481. Rao, Dileep. *Handbook of Business Finance and Capital Sources.* 3d ed. Minneapolis, MN: InterFinance Corp., 1982. 662 p.
This book provides names and phone numbers of people to contact in many financial institutions plus their lending terms and limits. It tells you where the money is, how to get it, and how to raise the cash you need from over 2,000 private, state, federal, and local sources of capital.

1482. Silver, David A. *Venture Capital: The Complete Guide for Investors.* New York: John Wiley & Sons, Inc., 1985. 259 p.
This book gives information on the steps in the venture capital investment process. These include forming a venture capital fund, generating a deal flow, facts on the due diligence process, valuation, terms and conditions, monitoring and adding value and selling, liquidating, and portfolio management.

1483. *Small Business Guide to Government.* Washington, DC: U.S. Small Business Administration, Office of Advocacy, 1980. 72 p.
In addition to a brief description of the Office of Advocacy, this booklet lists various SBA programs, small business investment companies and organizations, selected executive departments, and agencies of interest to small business.

1484. *Tax Desk Book for the Small Business.* 3d ed. Englewood Cliffs, NJ: Institute for Business Planning, 1979. 511 p.
This book is one of the few tax reference books available for the small business entrepreneur. Some areas covered are Subchapter S, benefits, partnerships, fringe benefits, tax breaks, and depreciation.

8. PERIODICALS

1485. *Across the Board.* New York: The Conference Board, Inc. (Monthly)
This publication provides information that is of interest to managers in both business and industry.

1486. *Advertising Age.* Chicago: Crain Communications Inc. (Irregular)
This national periodical covers advertising campaigns, agency appointments, and government actions affecting advertising and marketing, data on television, newspapers, radio, and other media.

1487. *American Journal of Small Businesses.* Baltimore, MD: University of Baltimore. (Quarterly)
Theoretical and practical research articles on all phases of small business are included in this journal.

1488. *Business.* Atlanta, GA: Georgia State University, College of Business Administration. (Quarterly)
The articles in this jounal cover aspects of business on the national and international level and are aimed at upper- and middle-level managers.

1489. *Business America.* Washington, DC: U.S. Department of Commerce. (Biweekly) (For sale by U.S. Government Printing Office.)
This journal on international trade and business includes information on international business opportunities and commerce.

1490. *Business Marketing.* Chicago: Business Marketing. (Monthly)
This journal includes information on business-to-business marketing news.

1491. *Business Week.* New York: McGraw-Hill Book Co. (Weekly)
This periodical contains articles covering new business trends and developments.

1492. *Credit & Financial Management.* New York: National Association of Credit Management. (Monthly)
Along with special issues on factoring, construction, legislation, and insurance, the articles in this journal are directed toward managers who are involved with extending credit.

1493. *Direct Marketing.* Garden City, NY: Hoke Communications. (Monthly)
This journal contains information on business communications in selected markets.

1494. *Dun's Business Month.* New York: Dun & Bradstreet, Inc. (Monthly)
The short articles included in this publication cover such topics as management, money and markets, industries, and communications.

1495. *The Economist.* Farmingdale, NY: The Economist. (Weekly)
The articles in this journal cover various aspects of world politics, current affairs, business, finance and science.

1496. *Entrepreneur Magazine.* Santa Monica, CA: Chase Revel, Inc. (Monthly)
This business opportunity journal includes new business ideas for the self-employed.

1497. *Exporter Directory/U.S. Buying Guide.* Phillipsburg, NJ: The Journal of Commerce. (Biennial)
This publication lists by state (U.S. & Puerto Rico) more than 37,000 exporters including when established, type of business handled, officers, bank reference, port of entry, telex and cable address, and custom house broker.

1498. *Financial World.* New York: Macro Communications. (Semimonthly)
This financial investment journal is directed at both private investors and managers and covers individual companies as well as industrial development, dividends, and corporate earnings.

1499. *Fortune.* New York: Time, Inc. (Biweekly)
Articles on every aspect of management and business are included in this journal.

1500. *Governmental Finance.* Chicago: Municipal Finance Officers Association. (Quarterly)
Articles on all areas of governmental finance are included in this journal. Each issue focuses on a specific theme.

1501. *Harvard Business Review.* Boston: Graduate School of Business Administration, Harvard University. (Bimonthly)
This journal includes articles on every aspect of general management and policy by experts in their fields.

1502. *Inc.* Boston: Inc. Publishing Co. (Monthly)
Covering all aspects of business, some special sections included in this journal are a table of "Smaller Company Initial Public Offerings," profiles of companies, stories on successful entrepreneurs, news, trends, taxes, and books. Annual list of the 100 fastest growing small companies is included once a year, as well as the Inc. 500.

1503. *Industry Week.* Cleveland, OH: Penton Publishing Co. (Biweekly)
This publication contains many short articles on new business and management ideas.

1504. *Journal of Business.* Chicago: University of Chicago Press. (Quarterly)
The articles in this publication are original research on business and economic theory, with many studies using quantitative techniques.

1505. *Journal of Commerce and Commercial.* New York: Twin Coast Newspapers, Inc. (5/week)
The main areas featured in this publication include world trade, maritime industry, railroads, aviation, trucking, air cargo, coal industry, as well as general news articles.

1506. *Journal of Purchasing and Materials Management.* Albany, NY: National Association of Purchasing Agents. (Quarterly)
This journal includes articles in the fields of business, statistics, economics, engineering, and behavioral science that relate to purchasing and management.

1507. *Journal of Retailing.* New York: NYU Institute of Retail Management. (Quarterly)
This periodical looks at the retail trade from consumer demand to distribution channels.

1508. *Journal of Small Business Management.* Morgantown, WV, Bureau of Business Research, West Virginia University. (Quarterly)
This journal provides current articles on many aspects of small business. Each issue covers one specific topic.

1509. *Management World.* Willow Grove, PA: Administrative Management Society. (Monthly)
This journal contains four to five articles per issue on administration problems.

1510. *Marketing News.* Chicago: American Marketing Association. (Biweekly)
This publication contains articles on all aspects of marketing, news articles in this area and information on the American Marketing Association.

1511. *The National Business Employment Weekly.* New York: Dow Jones-Irwin. (Weekly)
This weekly publication includes career-advancement positions from the four regional editions of the Wall Street Journal.

1512. *Nation's Business.* Washington, DC: Chamber of Commerce of the United States. (Monthly)
Popular articles on business, economics, and political topics are contained in this journal.

1513. *Personnel.* New York: American Management Association. (Bimonthly)
The articles in this journal cover the technical and practical aspects of personnel with special emphasis on business.

1514. *Personnel Administrator.* Alexandria, VA: American Society for Personnel Administration. (9 times/year)
All aspects of personnel work in business, government, and education are covered in this journal. It also includes an opinion and comment section on current problems.

1515. *Personnel Journal.* Costa Mesa, CA: The Personnel Journal, Inc. (Monthly)
All aspects of personnel management are covered in the articles in this publication. It is mainly directed toward the individual charged with personnel supervision.

1516. *Purchasing.* Denver, CO: Cahners Publishing Co. (Semi-monthly)
A news magazine for industrial buyers, this periodical covers information on distributors, transportation, purchasing ideas, and market trends.

1517. *Purchasing World.* Solon, OH: Huebner Publications. (Monthly)
Current news on purchasing, materials, and related topics are included in this journal as well as current raw material prices and industrial prices.

1518. *SBR Update.* Monterey, CA: SBR Update. (Monthly)
This newsletter updates the monthly issues of *Small Business Report.*

1519. *Sales & Marketing Management.* New York: Sales Management, Inc. (16 times/year)
Articles on the strategies and tactics of marketing that lead to effective sales teams are the focus of the articles in this journal. The annual service issue, *Survey of Buying Power,* contains current estimated figures in buying power.

1520. *Small Business Report.* Monterey, CA: Business Research & Communications. (12 times/year)
This journal contains articles on numerous subjects of interest to decision makers in small and mid-size companies.

1521. *Supervisory Management.* New York: American Management Association. (Monthly)
Practical articles aimed at helping the office or industrial manager make better decisions is the focus of this journal.

1522. *Tax Promoter.* Washington, DC: Capitol Publications, Inc. (Monthly)
This monthly bulletin helps you with your use of small business tax control.

1523. U.S. Bureau of Economic Analysis. Department of Commerce. *Business Conditions Digest.* Washington, DC: U.S. Government Printing Office. (Monthly)
This publication includes charts and statistical tables useful to business analysts and forecasters on leading economic time series.

1524. *United States Department of Commerce Publications Catalog.* Washington, DC: U.S. Government Printing Office. (Annual)
This publication contains a bibliography of the listings of Department of Commerce entries in GPO monthly catalogs.

1525. *Venture.* New York: Venture Magazine. (Monthly)
The short articles for entrepreneurs in this journal include profiles of new businesses, individual entrepreneurs, articles on venture capital, and franchising.

1526. *Voice of Small Business.* Washington, DC: National Small Business Association. (Bimonthly)
This is a free publication on small business matters.

1527. *Wall Street Journal.* West Middlesex, PA: Wall Street Journal. (5/week)
Besides current national business and investment information, this publication includes a weekly column on various topics of interest to small business people.

Appendices

Appendix A:
Directory of Publishers

AICPA. *See* American Institute of Certified Public Accountants

AMA Book Club Services
P.O. Box 319
Saranac Lake, NY 12983

AMA Publications
American Management Association
135 W. 50th St.
New York, NY 10020

AMACOM
135 W. 50th St.
New York, NY 10020

Arco Publishing, Inc.
219 Park Ave. South
New York, NY 10003

Academic Press, Inc.
111 Fifth Ave.
New York, NY 10003

Add-Effect Associates, Inc.
P.O. Box 401
Wayne, PA 19087

Addison-Wesley Publishing Co.
Reading, MA 01867

Administrative Management Society
World Headquarters
2360 Maryland Rd.
Willow Grove, PA 19090

Advertising Age
Crain Communications, Inc.
740 Rush St.
Chicago, IL 60611

Agency for International Development
Washington, DC 20523

Akens-Morgan Press, Inc.
720 Church St., N.W.
Huntsville, AL 35801

Alexander Hamilton Institute, Inc.
1633 Broadway
New York, NY 10019

Alfred A. Knopf, Inc.
201 E. 50th St.
New York, NY 10022

Allen & Unwin. *See* George Allen & Unwin Publishers, Ltd.

Allyn & Bacon, Inc.
Customer Services
Rockleigh, NJ 07647

American Accounting Association
5717 Bessie Dr.
Sarasota, FL 33583

American Association of MESBIC
915 15th St., N.W.
Washington, DC 20005

American Bankers Association
1120 Connecticut Ave., N.W.
Washington, DC 20036

American Bankers Association
Economic and Financial
Research Division
1120 Connecticut Ave., N.W.
Washington, DC 20036

American Bankers Association
Small Business Credit Committee
1120 Connecticut Ave., N.W.
Washington, DC 20036

American Bar Association
750 N. Lake Shore Dr.
Chicago, IL 60611

American Business Communication
Association
100 English Bldg.
608 S. Wright St.
Urbana, IL 61801

The American Business Press, Inc.
205 E. 42nd St.
New York, NY 10017

American Council of Voluntary
Agencies for Foreign Service
200 Park Ave., South
New York, NY 10003

American Entrepreneurs
Association
2311 Pontius Ave.
Los Angeles, CA 90064

American Enterprise Institute for
Public Policy Research
1150 17th St., N.W.
Washington, DC 20036

American Institute of Banking
1213 Bankers Way
Manhattan, KS 66502

American Institute of Certified
Public Accountants
1211 Ave. of the Americas
New York, NY 10036–8775

American Institute of Certified
Public Accountants
Federal Tax Division
1211 Ave. of the Americas
New York, NY 10036

American Institute of Real Estate
Appraisers
430 N. Michigan Ave.
Chicago, IL 60611

American Journal of Small Business
University of Baltimore
School of Business
1420 N. Charles St.
Baltimore, MD 21201

American Law Institute-American
Bar Association
4025 Chestnut St.
Philadelphia, PA 19104

American Management Association
135 W. 50th St.
New York, NY 10020

American Marketing Association
Central Services Office, Suite 200
250 S. Wacker Dr.
Chicago, IL 60606

American Patent Law Association
2001 Jefferson Davis Hwy.
Room 203
Arlington, VA 22202

American Personnel and Guidance
Association
Two Skyline Place, Suite 400
5203 Leesburg Pike
Falls Church, VA 22041

American Society for Personnel
Administration
606 N. Washington St.
Alexandria, VA 22314

American Society for Quality
Control
161 W. Wisconsin Ave.
Milwaukee, WI 53203

American University Press Services,
Inc.
One Park Ave.
New York, NY 10016

American Vocational Association,
Inc.
2020 N. 14th St.
Arlington, VA 22201

And Books
702 S. Michigan, Suite 836
South Bend, IN 46618

Angus Downs, Ltd.
4101 Lake Ridge Dr.
Holland, MI 49423

Arno Press. *See* Ayer Co., Inc.

Ashley Books
30 Main St.
Port Washington, NY 11050

Ashton-Tate
10150 W. Jefferson Blvd.
Culver City, CA 90230

Asigan, Ltd.
P.O. Box 10688
Beverly Hills, CA 90213

Association for Systems
Management
24587 Bagley Rd.
Cleveland, OH 44138

Association of National Advertisers,
Inc.
Publications Department
155 E. 44th St.
New York, NY 10017

Association of Records Managers
and Administrators
4200 Somerset Dr., Suite 215
Prairie Village, KS 66208

Austin Press
P.O. Drawer 9774
Austin, TX 78766

Avon Books
959 Eighth Ave.
New York, NY 10019

Ayer Co., Inc.
382 Main St.
P.O. Box 958
Salem, NH 03079

Baen Enterprises
8–10 W. 36th St.
New York, NY 10018

Ballantine Books, Inc.
201 E. 50th St.
New York, NY 10022

Ballinger Publishing Co.
54 Church St.
Cambridge, MA 02138

Banbury Books
353 W. Lancaster Ave.
Wayne, PA 19087

Bank Administration Institute
60 Gould Ctr.
Rolling Meadows, IL 60008

Bank Marketing Association
309 W. Washington St.
Chicago, IL 60606

Bank of America
Dept. 3120
P.O. Box 37000
San Francisco, CA 94137

Bankers Publishing Co.
210 South St.
Boston, MA 02111

Bantam Books
Dept. WP2
666 Fifth Ave.
New York, NY 10019

Barnes & Noble
10 E. 53rd St.
New York, NY 10022

Barron's Educational Series
113 Crossways Park Dr.
Woodbury, NY 11797

Barry Jones Advertising
2725 Mary St.
Easton, PA 18042

Basic Books, Inc.
10 E. 53rd St.
New York, NY 10022

Beardsley & Associates
International
Campbell, CA 95008

Beaufort Books, Inc.
9 E. 40th St.
New York, NY 10016

Bell Springs Publishers
P.O. Box 640
Laytonville, CA 95454

Bellavance, Diane. *See* Diane
Bellavance

The Benjamin Co.
1 Westchester Plaza
Elmsford, NY 10523

The Berkeley Publishing Group
200 Madison Ave.
New York, NY 10016

Betterway Publications
White Hall, VA 22987

Blackman, Kallick & Co., Ltd.
180 N. LaSalle St.
Chicago, IL 60601

Blackwell, Ltd.
108 Crowley Rd.
Oxford OX4 1JF
England

Blagrove Publications
P.O. Box 584
Manchester, CT 06040

Boardroom Books
63 E. Willow St.
Millburn, NJ 07041

Bookman House
No. 2 Shadow Lane
Houston, TX 77055

Books in Focus, Inc.
160 E. 38th St.
New York, NY 10016

Bowker, R.R., Co. *See* R.R. Bowker
Co.

Bradford's Directory of Marketing
Research Agencies and
Manufacturing Consultants
Department B-15
P.O. Box 276
Fairfax, VA 22030

Broadman Press
127 Ninth Ave., N.
Nashville, TN 37203

Brookfield Publishing Co., Inc.
Old Post Rd.
Brookfield, VT 05036

Brooks/Cole Publishing Co.
555 Abrego St.
Monterey, CA 93940

Brown, William C., Co., Publishers.
See William C. Brown Co.,
Publishers

Bryant College
Center for Management
Development
Smithfield, RI 02917

Bureau of Business and Economic
Research
School of Business
Administration
University of Mississippi
University, MS 38677

Bureau of Business Practice, Inc.
24 Rope Ferry Rd.
Waterford, CT 06385

Bureau of Business Research
University of Texas
Dept. F
P.O. Box 7459
Austin, TX 78713

Bureau of National Affairs, Inc.
1231 25th St., N.W.
Washington, DC 20037

Burwell Enterprises
5106 FM 1960 W, Suite 349
Houston, TX 77069

Business and Professional Women's
    Foundation
2012 Massachusetts Ave., N.W.
Washington, DC 20036

Business Books, Ltd.
17–21 Conway St.
London W1P 6JD
England

Business Financial Consultants, Inc.
3824 E. Indian School Rd.
Phoenix, AZ 85018

Business Marketing
740 Rush St.
Chicago, IL 60611

Business Press International, Ltd.
205 E. 42nd St.
New York, NY 10017

Business Publications, Inc.
13773 N. Central Expressway
Dallas, TX 75231

Business Publications Division
College of Business
    Administration
Georgia State University
University Plaza
Atlanta, GA 30303

Business Research and
    Communications
203 Calle del Oaks
Monterey, CA 93940

Business Week
McGraw-Hill Publications Co.
1221 Ave. of the Americas
New York, NY 10020

Butterworth Publishers, Inc.
80 Montvale Ave.
Stoneham, MA 02180

Buyout Publications
7124 Convoy Ct.
San Diego, CA 92111

CBI Publishing Co., Inc.
135 W. 50th St.
New York, NY 10020

C.L. Carter, Jr. and Associates
434 Banc Texas Bldg.
P.O. Box 5001
Richardson, TX 75080

Caddylack Publishing
201 Montrose Rd.
Westbury, NY 11590

Cahners Publishing
221 Columbus Ave.
Boston, MA 02116

California Continuing Education of
    the Bar
2300 Shattuck Ave.
Berkeley, CA 94704

Cambrian Financial Corp.
2775 Park Ave.
Santa Clara, CA 95050

Cambridge University Press
32 E. 57th St.
New York, NY 10022

Canadian Institute of Charter
    Accountants
150 Bloor St., W.
Toronto, Ontario M5S 2Y2
Canada

Capital Publishing Corp.
10 S. LaSalle St.
Chicago, IL 60603

Capitol Publications, Inc.
2430 Pennsylvania Ave., N.W.
Washington, DC 20037

Capricornus Press
P.O. Box 1023
Boulder, CO 80306

Center for Creative Leadership
5000 Laurinda Drive
P.O. Box P–1
Greensboro, NC 27402

Center for Entrepreneurial
Management
311 Main St.
Worcester, MA 01608

Center for Entrepreneurship and
Small Business Management
Wichita State University
P.O. Box 48
Wichita, KS 67208

The Center for Family Business
The University Press, Inc.
P.O. Box 24268
Cleveland, OH 44124

Center for Marketing
Communications
575 Ewing St.
P.O. Box 411
Princeton, NJ 08540

The Center for Small Business
1346 Connecticut Ave., N.W.
Washington, DC 20036

Center for Video Education, Inc.
103 S. Bedford Rd.
Mount Kisco, NY 10549

Central Services Offices of the
American Marketing
Association
250 S. Wacker Dr., Suite 200
Chicago, IL 60606

Century Communications, Inc.
5520 Touhy Ave., Suite G
Skokie, IL 60077

Chamber of Commerce of the
United States
Center for Small Business
1615 H St., N.W.
Washington, DC 20062

Charles E. Merrill Publishing Co.
1300 Alum Creek Dr.
Columbus, OH 43216

Charles Scribner's Sons
597 5th Ave.
New York, NY 10017

Chase Revel, Inc.
2311 Pontius Ave.
Los Angeles, CA 90064

Chilton Book Co.
201 King of Prussia Rd.
Radnor, PA 19089

City of Chicago
Department of Consumer
Services
121 N. LaSalle
Chicago, IL 60601

Cleaning Consultant Services, Inc.
P.O. Box 70261
Seattle, WA 98107

Coalition of Northeastern
Governors Policy Research
Center
400 N. Capitol St.
Washington, DC 20001

Coltrane and Beach, Book
Publishers
31129 Via Colinas
Westlake Village, CA 91362

Columbia Books, Inc.
1350 New York Ave., Suite 207
Washington, DC 20005

Columbia University Press
562 W. 113th St.
New York, NY 10025

Commerce Clearing House, Inc.
4025 W. Peterson Ave.
Chicago, IL 60646

Commodity Research Bureau
One Liberty Plaza
New York, NY 10006

The Conference Board, Inc.
845 Third Ave.
New York, NY 10022

Conference Board of Canada
Compensation Research Centre
25 McArthur Ave., Suite 100
Ottawa, Ontario K1L 6R3
Canada

Congressional Information Service,
Inc.
4520 East-West Hwy.,
Suite 800
Bethesda, MD 20814

Conservative Political Centre
32 Smith Square
London SW1
England

Consultants
Department B-15
P.O. Box 276
Fairfax, VA 22030

Consultants News
Templeton Rd.
Fitzwilliam, NH 03447

Contemporary Books, Inc.
180 N. Michigan Ave.
Chicago, IL 60601

Conway Publications
1954 Airport Rd., N.E.
Atlanta, GA 30341

Cornerstone Library
Simon & Schuster Bldg.
Rockefeller Center
1230 Ave. of the Americas
New York, NY 10020

Corporate Finance Sourcebook
163 W. 74th St.
New York, NY 10023

Council for Advancement and
Support of Education
11 DuPont Circle, Suite 400
Washington, DC 20036
Orders to: Publications Order Dept.
80 S. Early St.
Alexandria, VA 22304

Council for International Urban
Liaison
1120 G. St., N.W., Suite 400
Washington, DC 20005

Council of State Planning Agencies
Hall of the States
400 N. Capitol St.
Washington, DC 20001

Council on International and Public
Affairs
60 E. 42nd St.
New York, NY 10017

Crain Books. *See* Crain
Communications, Inc.

Crain Communications, Inc.
740 Rush St.
Chicago, IL 60611

Crain's Chicago Business
Crain Communications, Inc.
740 Rush St.
Chicago, Il 60611

Creative Strategies International
4340 Stevens Creek Blvd., Suite
275
San Jose, CA 95129

Cresheim Publications, Inc.
P.O. Box 27785
8300 Flourtown Ave.
Philadelphia, PA 19118

Croner Publications, Inc.
211-03 Jamaica Ave.
Queens Village, NY 11428

Croom Helm, Ltd.
Provident House
Burrell Row
Beckenham, Kent BR3 1AT
England

Crown Publishers, Inc.
1 Park Ave.
New York, NY 10016

Dame, Robert F., Inc. *See* Robert
F. Dame, Inc.

The Dartnell Corp.
4660 Ravenswood Ave.
Chicago, IL 60640

David McKay Co., Inc.
2 Park Ave.
New York, NY 10016

The Day
43–53 Eugene O'Neill Dr.
New London, CT 06320

Dekker, Marcel, Inc. *See* Marcel
Dekker, Inc.

Dell Publishing Co., Inc.
1 Dag Hammarskjold Plaza
New York, NY 10017

Delmar Publishers, Inc.
50 Wolf Rd.
Albany, NY 12205

Deloitte Haskins & Sells
1200 Travis
Houston, TX 77002

Deloitte Haskins & Sells
Small Business Services Dept.
1114 Ave. of the Americas
New York, NY 10036

Department of Labor
200 Constitution Ave., N.W.
Washington, DC 20210

Department of the Treasury
Internal Revenue Service
1111 Constitution Ave., N.W.
Washington, DC 20224

Diane Bellavance
c/o DBA Books
77 Gordon St.
Boston, MA 02135

Dilithium Press
11000 S.W. 11th St.
Beaverton, OR 97005

Direct Mail Marketing Association
Six E. 43rd St.
New York, NY 10017

Direct Marketing
Hoke Communications
224 7th St.
Garden City, NY 11530

Distribution Research and
Education Foundation
1725 K St., N.W.
Washington, DC 20006

Dorrance & Co., Inc.
828 Lancaster Ave.
Bryn Mawr, PA 19010

Doubleday & Co., Inc.
501 Franklin Ave.
Garden City, NY 11530

Dow Jones-Irwin
1822 Ridge Rd.
Homewood, IL 60430

Dowden, Hutchinson & Ross, Inc.
523 Sarah St., Box 699
Stroudsburg, PA 18360

The Dryden Press
CBS College Publishing
383 Madison Ave.
New York, NY 10017

Duke University Press
6697 College Station
Durham, NC 27708

Dun & Bradstreet, Inc.
Three Century Dr.
Parsippany, NJ 07054

Dun & Bradstreet International
99 Church St.
New York, NY 10007

Dun's Marketing Services
Dun & Bradstreet Corp.
Three Century Dr.
Parsippany, NJ 07054

Dutton, E. P., Inc. *See* E. P.
Dutton, Inc.

E. P. Dutton, Inc.
2 Park Ave.
New York, NY 10016

ETC Publications
Palm Springs, CA 92262

The Economist
Subscription Dept.
P.O. Box 904
Farmingdale, NY 11737-9804

Edge Enterprises, Inc.
P.O. Box 94473
Chicago, IL 60690

Elsevier North Holland Co., Inc.
Fulfillment Department
52 Vanderbilt Ave.
New York, NY 10017

Elsevier Science Publishing Co.,
Inc.
52 Vanderbilt Ave.
New York, NY 10017

Enterprise Publishing, Inc.
725 Market St.
Wilmington, DE 19801

The Entrepreneur Press
3422 Astoria Circle
Fairfield, CA 94533

European Journal of Marketing
MCB University Press, Ltd.
62 Toller Lane
Bradford, West Yorkshire BD8
9BY
England

Evans, M., and Co., Inc. *See* M.
Evans and Co., Inc.

Executive Enterprises Publications
Co., Inc.
33 W. 60th St.
New York, NY 10023

Executive Reports Corp.
210 Sylvan Ave., Dept. 200-B
Englewood Cliffs, NJ 07632

Expocon Management Associates,
Inc.
3695 Post Rd.
Southport, CT 06490

Facts on File, Inc.
Order Department
460 Park Ave., S.
8th Floor
New York, NY 10016

Fairchild Books
P.O. Box 818
New York, NY 10003

Farnsworth Publishing Co., Inc.
78 Randall Ave.
Rockville Centre, NY 11570

Financial Management Associates,
Inc.
3928 Iowa St.
San Diego, CA 92104

Financial Research Associates
1629 K St. N.W., Suite 520
Washington, DC 20006

Find/SVP
500 Fifth Ave.
New York, NY 10109

Fortune
541 N. Fairbanks Court
Chicago, IL 60611

Frances Pinter Publishers, Ltd.
5 Dryden St.
London WC2E 9NW
England

Franklin Watts, Inc.
387 Park Ave., S.
New York, NY 10016

Free Press
Division of Macmillan
Publishing Co., Inc.
866 Third Ave.
New York, NY 10022

Frost & Sullivan, Inc.
166 Fulton St.
New York, NY 10038

Future Shop
P.O. Box 111
Camarillo, CA 93010

Gale Research Co.
Book Tower
Detroit, MI 48226

Gale Research Co.
Grand River Books
Penobscott Bldg.
Detroit, MI 48226

George Allen & Unwin Publishers,
Ltd.
40 Museum St.
London, WC1A 1LU
England

Glencoe Publishing Co., Inc.
17337 Ventura Blvd.
Encino, CA 91316

Goldberg, James M. *See* James M.
Goldberg

Goodyear Publishing Co.
1640 Fifth St.
Santa Monica, CA 90401

Gordon Breach, Science Publishers,
Inc.
50 W. 23rd St.
New York, NY 10010

Gower Publishing Co.
Old Post Rd.
Brookfield, VT 05036

Gower Publishing Co., Ltd.
Gower House, Croft Rd.
Aldershot GU11 3HR
England

Graham & Trotman, Ltd.
Sterling House
66 Wilton Rd.
London SW1V 1DE
England

Grand River Books. *See* Gale
Research Co.

Granville Publications
10960 Wilshire Blvd.
Los Angeles, CA 90024

The Great 800 Directory Co.
P.O. Box 6944
Jackson, MS 39202

Grid, Inc. *See* Publishing Horizons,
Inc.

Grosset & Dunlap
51 Madison Ave.
New York, NY 10010

Gulf Publishing Co.
P.O. Box 2608
Houston, TX 77001

Gustafson Horseshoe Corp.
Distribution Office
1314 Monroe St.
Fort Calhoun, NE 68023

Hammond Farrell
105 Madison Ave.
New York, NY 10016

Harcourt Brace Jovanovich,
Publishers
1250 Sixth Ave.
San Diego, CA 92101

Harper & Row, Publishers
10 E. 53rd St.
New York, NY 10022

Harvard Business Review
Harvard University
Graduate School of Business
Administration
Soldiers Field
Boston, MA 02163

Harvard Business Review Reprint
Service
Soldiers Field
Boston, MA 02174

Hazelden Foundation
Box 176
Center City, MN 55012

Heinemann, William, Ltd. *See*
William Heinemann, Ltd.

Hills-Bay Press
P.O. Box 5221
San Mateo, CA 94402

Hoke Communications
224 Seventh St.
Garden City, NY 11530–5726

Holmes & Meier Publishers, Inc.
Import Division
IUB Bldg.
30 Irving Place
New York, NY 10003

Holt, Rinehart & Winston
383 Madison Ave.
New York, NY 10017

Houghton Mifflin Co.
One Beacon St.
Boston, MA 02108

Howard W. Sams & Co., Inc.
4300 W. 62nd St.
Indianapolis, IN 46268

Huebner Publications
Solon, OH 44139

Human Sciences Research, Inc.
Westgate Research Park
McLean, VA 22110

INC. Executive Compensation
Study
38 Commercial Wharf
Boston, MA 02110

Inc. Publishing Co.
38 Commercial Wharf St.
Boston, MA 02110

Inc. Special Reports
38 Commercial Wharf
Boston, MA 02110

Inc./CBI Publications
286 Congress St.
Boston, MA 02110

Industry Book Publishing, Inc.
1437 Tuttle Ave.
Wallingford, CT 06492

Institute for Business Planning, Inc.
IBP Plaza
Englewood Cliffs, NJ 07632

The Institute for Economic and
Financial Research
P.O. Box 4526
Albuquerque, NM 87196

Institute for Information Studies
200 Little Falls St., Suite 104
Falls Church, VA 22046

The Institute of Electrical and
Electronics Engineers, Inc.
345 E. 47th St.
New York, NY 10017

Institute of Real Estate
Management
430 N. Michigan Ave.
Chicago, IL 60611

Institute of Real Estate of the
National Association of
Retailers. *See* National
Association of Retailers
Institute of Real Estate
Management

Instrument Society of America
P.O. Box 12277
67 Alexander Dr.
Research Triangle Park, NC
27709

Insurance Institute of America
Providence Rd.
Malvern, PA 19355

Intempo Communications, Inc.
23802 Cassandra Bay
Laguna Niguel, CA 92677

Inter-Action Imprint
15 Wilkin St.
London NW5 3NG
England

InterFinance Corp.
511 11 Ave., S.
Minneapolis, MN 55415

Intermediate Technology
Publications, Ltd.
9 King St.
London WC2E 8HN
England

Internal Revenue Service. *See*
Department of the Treasury
Internal Revenue Service

International Advertising
Association
475 Fifth Ave.
New York, NY 10017

International Association of
Business Communicators
870 Market St., Suite 928
San Francisco, CA 94102

International Association of
Personnel in Employment
Security
1801 Louisville Rd.
Frankfort, KY 40601

International Entrepreneurs'
Association
631 Wilshire Blvd.
Santa Monica, CA 90401

International Ideas
1627 Spruce St.
Philadelphia, PA 19103

International Labour Office
1750 New York Ave., N.W.,
Suite 311
Washington, DC 20006

International Monetary Fund
Publications Unit,
Room C-200
700 19th St., N.W.
Washington, DC 20431

International Publications Service
114 E. 32nd St.
New York, NY 10016

International Self-Counsel Press,
Ltd.
Head and Editorial Office
306 W. 25th St.
North Vancouver, British
Columbia V7N 2G1
Canada

International Thompson Publishing,
Ltd.
Elm House
10–16 Elm St.
London WC1X OBP
England

International Wealth Success, Inc.
P.O. Box 186
Merrick, NY 11566

Irwin, Richard D., Inc. *See* Richard
D. Irwin, Inc.

JLA Publications
50 Follen St., Suite 507
Cambridge, MA 02138

Jai Press
36 Sherwood Place
Greenwich, CT 06836

James M. Goldberg
1828 L St., N.W., Suite 660
Washington, DC 20036

Jamieson Press
(Subsidiary of Business
Succession Resource Center,
Inc.)
P.O. Box 909
Cleveland, OH 44120

John Wiley & Sons, Inc.
605 Third Ave.
New York, NY 10158

The Johns Hopkins University
Press
701 W. 40th St., Suite 275
Baltimore, MD 21211

Jossey-Bass, Inc., Publishers
433 California St.
San Francisco, CA 94104

Journal of Business Research
Elsevier North Holland, Inc.
Fulfillment Dept.
52 Vanderbilt Ave.
New York, NY 10017

Journal of Commerce
99 Wall St.
New York, NY 10005
For orders:
445 Marshall St.
Phillipsburg, NJ 08865

Journal of Commerce
Twin Coast Newspapers, Inc.
110 Wall St.
New York, NY 10005

Journal of Finance
Graduate School of Business
New York University
100 Trinity Place
New York, NY 10006

*Journal of Small Business
Management*
Bureau of Business Research
West Virginia University
P.O. Box 6025
Morgantown, WV 26506–6025

Ken–Books
1932 Ocean Ave.
San Francisco, CA 94127

Kendall/Hunt Publishing Co.
2460 Kerper Blvd.
Dubuque, IA 52001

Kent Publishing Co.
20 Park Plaza
Boston, MA 02116

Kentwood Publications
P.O. Box 2787
Alameda, CA 94501

Kluwer-Nijhoff Publishing
190 Old Derby St.
Hingham, MA 02043

Knopf, Alfred A., Inc. *See* Alfred A.
Knopf, Inc.

Knowledge Industry Publications,
Inc.
701 Westchester Ave.
White Plains, NY 10604

Krieger, Robert E., Publishing Co.
See Robert E. Krieger
Publishing Co.

Kumarian Press, Inc.
630 Oakwood Ave., Suite 119
West Hartford, CT 06110

L. Stuart, Inc.
120 Enterprise Ave.
Secaucus, NJ 07094

La Cumbre Management, Inc.
3887 State S. Bar
Santa Barbara, CA 93110

Law & Business, Inc.
757 Third Ave.
New York, NY 10017

Lawyers & Judges Publishing Co.
3130 N. Dodge Blvd.
P.O. Box 42050
Tucson, AZ 85733

The Lawyers Co-operative
Publishing Co.
Aqueduct Bldg.
Rochester, NY 14694

Lebhar–Friedman Books
Chain Store Publishing Corp.
425 Park Ave.
New York, NY 10022

Legal Management Services, Inc.
250 W. 94th St.
New York, NY 10025
Book orders:
Route One
Stoddard, WI 54658

Lewis Publishing Co.
Fessenden Rd.
Brattleboro, VT 05301

Lexington Books
Division of D. C. Heath & Co.
125 Spring St.
Lexington, MA 02173

Lifetime Learning Publications
10 Davis Dr.
Belmont, CA 94002

Linden Press. *See* Simon &
Schuster, Inc.

Little, Brown & Co.
34 Beacon St.
Boston, MA 02106

Littlefield, Adams & Co.
81 Adams Dr.
Totowa, NJ 07511

Logistics Management Institute
4701 Sagamore Rd.
Washington, DC 20016

Longman, Inc.
95 Church St.
White Plains, NY 10601

Longman, Ltd.
Longman Group
Longman House
Burnt Mill
Harlow, Essex CM20 2JE
England

Lord Publishing
46 Glen St.
Dover, MA 02030

M/A Press
P.O. Box 606
Beaverton, OR 97075

M. Evans and Co., Inc.
216 E. 49th St.
New York, NY 10017

MCB Publications
198/200 Keighley Rd.
Bradford, West Yorkshire BD9
4JQ
England

MCB University Press, Ltd.
62 Toller Lane
Bradford BD8 9BY
England

MV Publishing, Inc.
1000 Quail, Suite 120
Newport Beach, CA 92660

MWJ Publications Group
P.O. Box 1421
Paramount, CA 90723

Macmillan Publishing Co., Inc.
866 Third Ave.
New York, NY 10022

Macro Communications
150 W. 58th St.
New York, NY 10022

Management Information Studies
One Mission Plaza
Monterey, CA 93940

Management World
AMS Bldg.
2360 Maryland Rd.
Willow Grove, PA 19090

Marcel Dekker, Inc.
270 Madison Ave.
New York, NY 10016

Marketing Board
8170 Corporate Park Dr., Suite
100
Cincinnati, OH 45242

Marketing for Profit, Inc.
Box 1087
St. Charles, IL 60174

Marketing News
American Marketing Association
International Headquarters
250 S. Wacker Dr., Suite 500
Chicago, IL 60606–5819

Marketing Publications Inc.
National Press Bldg.
Washington, DC 20045

Marketing Science Institute
1000 Massachusetts Ave.
Cambridge, MA 02138

Mason/Charter Publishers, Inc.
641 Lexington Ave.
New York, NY 10022

Matthew Bender & Co., Inc.
245 E. 45th St.
New York, NY 10017

Maxwell Sroge Publishing
731 N. Cascade, The Sroge Bldg.
Colorado Springs, CO
80903–3205

McGraw Hill Book Co.
1221 Ave. of the Americas
New York, NY 10020

McGraw-Hill Ryerson, Ltd.
330 Progress Ave.
Scarborough, Ontario
M1P 2Z5
Canada

McKay, David, Co., Inc. *See* David
McKay Co., Inc.

Meridional Publications
Wake Forest, NC 27587

Merrill, Charles E., Publishing Co.
See Charles E. Merrill
Publishing Co.

Monarch
Simon & Schuster Bldg.
1230 Ave. of the Americas
New York, NY 10020

Moody's Investors Service
99 Church St.
New York, NY 10007

Moore Publishing Co., Inc.
701 S. Gunderson Ave.
Oak Park, IL 60304

Morrow, William, & Co., Inc. *See*
William Morrow & Co., Inc.

Multinational Executive, Inc.
Subscription Dept.
Harvard Square, Box 92
Cambridge, MA 02138

Municipal Finance Officers
Association
180 N. Michigan Ave.
Chicago, IL 60601

NCC Publications
The National Computing Centre,
Ltd.
Oxford Rd.
Manchester M1 7ED
England

NYU Institute of Retail
Management
202 Tisch Hall
Washington Square
New York, NY 10003

National Association of
Accountants
919 Third Ave.
New York, NY 10022

National Association of College and
University Business Officers
One Dupont Circle, Suite 500
Washington, DC 20036–1178

National Association of Credit
Management
Publications Division
475 Park Ave. S.
New York, NY 10016

National Association of Purchasing
Agents
49 Sheridan Ave.
Albany, NY 12210

National Association of Realtors
777 14th St. S.W.
Washington, DC 20024

National Association of Realtors
Institute of Real Estate
Management
430 N. Michigan Ave.
Chicago, IL 60611

National Association of Securities
    Dealers, Inc.
1735 K St., N.W.
Washington, DC 20006

National Association of Small
    Business Investment
    Companies
1156 15th St., N.W.
Washington, DC 20005

*National Business Employment
    Weekly*
Dow Jones & Co., Inc.
The Wall St. Journal
    Headquarters
420 Lexington Ave.
New York, NY 10170

National Chamber Foundation
1615 H St., N.W.
Washington, DC 20062

National Federation of Independent
    Business
600 Maryland Ave., S.W., Suite
    695
Washington, DC 20024

National Institute for Work &
    Learning
1211 Connecticut Ave., N.W.,
    Suite 301
Washington, DC 20036

National Register Publishing Co.
5201 Old Orchard Rd.
Skokie, IL 60077

National Retail Merchants
    Association
100 W. 31st St.
New York, NY 10001

National Safety Council
444 N. Michigan Ave.
Chicago, IL 60611

The National Science Foundation
Office of Small Business R&D
1800 G St., N.W.
Washington, DC 20550

National Small Business Association
1604 K St., N.W.
Washington, DC 20006

National Technical Information
    Service
5285 Port Royal Rd.
Springfield, VA 22161

National Underwriter Co.
420 East Fourth St.
Cincinnati, OH 45202

Nation's Business
Chamber of Commerce of the
    U.S.
1615 H St., N.W.
Washington, DC 20062

Nelson-Hall, Inc., Publishers
325 W. Jackson Blvd.
Chicago, IL 60606

New American Library, Inc.
1633 Broadway
New York, NY 10019

New Century Publishers, Inc.
220 Old New Brunswick Rd.
Piscataway, NJ 08854

New Harbinger Publications
2200 Aldine, Suite 305
Oakland, CA 94607

New York Institute of Finance
70 Pine St.
New York, NY 10270

New York University
Graduate School of Business
100 Trinity Place
New York, NY 10006

New York University Institute of
    Retail Management. *See* NYU
    Institute of Retail
    Management

Newman Books, Ltd.
48 Poland St.
London W1V 4PP
England

Newspaper Enterprise Association, Inc.
200 Park Ave.
New York, NY 10017

Nichols Publishing Co.
P.O. Box 96
New York, NY 10024

North American Communications, Inc.
1377 K St., N.W., Suite 663
Washington, DC 20005

Northwood Books. *See* International Thompson Publishing, Ltd.

Norton W. W., & Co., Inc. *See* W. W. Norton & Co., Inc.

OECD Publications and Information Center. *See* Organization for Economic Cooperation & Development

Oasis Press
1287 Lawrence Station Rd.
Sunnyvale, CA 94089

Office Publications, Inc.
1200 Summer St.
Stamford, CT 06904

Omega Centre
21166 N. Pheasant Trail
Barrington, IL 60010

Organization for Economic Cooperation & Development
OECD Publications and Information Center
1750 Pennsylvania Ave., N.W., Suite 1207
Washington, DC 20006

The Oryx Press
2214 N. Central Ave.
Phoenix, AZ 85004

Oxford University Press
Walton St.
Oxford OX2 6DP
England

Pages To Go!!
2140 N. Iris Lane
Escondido, CA 92026

Paladin Press
Paladin Entreprises, Inc.
P.O. Box 1307
Boulder, CO 80306

Parker Publishing Co., Inc.
Route 59 at Brookhill Dr.
West Nyack, NY 10995

Paulist Press
545 Island Rd.
Ramsey, NJ 07446

Penguin Books, Inc.
40 W. 23rd St.
New York, NY 10010

Penton Publishing Co.
680 N. Rocky River Dr.
Cleveland, OH 44017

Pergamon Press, Inc.
Maxwell House
Fairview Park
Elmsford, NY 10523

Personnel Journal, Inc.
P.O. Box 2440
Costa Mesa, CA 92626

Persuasive Press
Executive Learning Division
Box 3479
Redwood City, CA 94064

Peter Peregrinus, Ltd.
P.O. Box 26
Hitchin Herts SG5 1SA
England

Petrocelli Books, Inc.
1101 State Rd., Bldg. D
Princeton, NJ 08540

Pilot Books
Pilot Industries, Inc.
347 Fifth Ave.
New York, NY 10016

Pinter, Francis, Publishers, Ltd. *See* Francis Pinter Publishers, Ltd.

Playboy Paperbacks
1633 Broadway
New York, NY 10019

Playboy Press
919 N. Michigan Ave.
Chicago, Il 60611

Pollyanna Press
422 Route 206, Suite 177
Somerville, NJ 08876

Power & Systems Training, Inc.
P.O. Box 388
Prudential Station
Boston, MA 02199

Practising Law Institute
810 7th Ave.
New York, NY 10019

Praeger Publishers
521 Fifth Ave.
New York, NY 10175

Predicasts, Inc.
11001 Cedar Ave.
Cleveland, OH 44106

Prelude Press
Box 69773
Los Angeles, CA 90069

Premier Publishers
16254 Wedgwood
Fort Worth, TX 76133

Prentice-Hall, Inc.
Rte. 9 W.
Englewood Cliffs, NJ 07632

Price Waterhouse
1251 Ave. of the Americas
New York, NY 10020

Probus Publishing Co.
118 N. Clinton St.
Chicago, IL 60606

Prudential Publishing Co.
311 California, 7th Floor
San Francisco, CA 94104

Pt. Pleasant Publishing Co.
P.O. Box 1309
Pt. Pleasant, NJ 08742

Publications Press
Division of T.I.S. Enterprises
P.O. Box 1998
Bloomington, IN 47402

Publishing Horizons, Inc.
2950 N. High St.
P.O. Box 02190
Columbus, OH 43202

Purchasing World
6521 David Industrial Pkwy.
Solon, OH 44139

Quality Circle Institute
Red Bluff, CA 96080

Quorum Books
88 Post Rd., Box 5007
Westport, CT 06881

R. R. Bowker Co.
205 E. 42nd St.
New York, NY 10020

Rand McNally & Co.
P.O. Box 7600
Chicago, IL 60680

Random House, Inc.
Sales Dept.
201 E. 50th St.
New York, NY 10022

Rauch Associates
P.O. Box 6802
Bridgewater, NJ 08807

Rawson Associates Publishers, Inc.
597 5th Ave.
New York, NY 10017

Regnery, Henry, Co. *See* Contemporary Books, Inc.

Renouf USA, Inc. *See* Brookfield
Publishing Co., Inc.

Research Corp. of the Association
of School Business Officials of
the United States and Canada
720 Garden St.
Park Ridge, IL 60068

Research Institute of America
589 Fifth Ave.
New York, NY 10164

Reston Publishing Co., Inc.
11480 Sunset Hills Rd.
Reston, VA 22090

Reymont Associates
29 Reymont Ave.
Rye, NY 10580

Richard D. Irwin, Inc.
1818 Ridge Rd.
Homewood, IL 60430

Richards Rosen Press, Inc.
29 E. 21st St.
New York, NY 10010

Robert E. Krieger Publishing Co.
P.O. Box 9542
Melbourne, FL 32901-9542

Robert F. Dame, Inc.
1905 Huguenot Rd.
Richmond, VA 23235

Ronald Press
605 Third Ave.
New York, NY 10016

Running Press
125 S. 22nd St.
Philadelphia, PA 19103

SBR Update
1 Mission Plaza
Monterey, CA 93940

S.I.R. Educational Fund of the
Society of Industrial Realtors
of the National Association of
Realtors. *See* National
Association of Realtors

Sage Publications, Inc.
275 S. Beverly Dr.
P.O. Box 5024
Beverly Hills, CA 90212

Sales Management, Inc.
Bill Communications, Inc.
633 Third Ave.
New York, NY 10017

Sams, Howard W., & Co., Inc. *See*
Howard W. Sams & Co., Inc.

Saunders, W. B., Co. *See* W. B.
Saunders, Co.

Scarecrow Press, Inc.
52 Liberty St.
P.O. Box 656
Metuchen, NJ 08840

Science Research Associates, Inc.
155 Wacker Dr.
Chicago, IL 60606

Scope Books, Ltd.
3 Sandford House, Kingsclere
Newbury, Berkshire
RG15 8PA
England

Scott, Foresman & Co.
1900 E. Lake Ave.
Glenview, IL 60025

Scribner's. *See* Charles Scribner's
Sons

Secretary of State's Office
(Vermont)
109 State St.
Montpelier, VT 05602

Self-Counsel Press, Inc.
1303 N. Northgate Way
Seattle, WA 98133

Sharratt & Co.
P.O. Box 2171 SGB
Littleton, CO 80161

Shepard's/McGraw-Hill
P.O. Box 1235
Colorado Springs, CO 80901

208 Small Business: An Information Sourcebook

Shippers National Freight Claim
Council, Inc., Publishers
120 Main St., Box Z
Huntington, NY 11743

Simon & Schuster, Inc.
Mass Merchandise Sales Co.
1230 Ave. of the Americas
New York, NY 10020

Skinner, Thomas, Directories, Ltd.
See Thomas Skinner
Directories, Ltd.

Small Business Administration. See
U.S. Small Business
Administration

Small Business Monitoring &
Research Co., Inc.
Monterey, CA 93940

Small Business Publications, Inc.
Drawer 330
Osterville, MA 02655

Small Business Report
Business Research &
Communications
203 Calle Del Oaks
Monterey, CA 93940

Smaller Business Association of
New England
Small Business News
69 Hickory Dr.
Waltham, MA 02154

Society for Intercultural Education,
Training, and Research
1414 22nd St., N.W.
Washington, DC 20037

Society of Industrial Realtors
S.I.R. Educational Fund
National Association of Realtors
777 14th St., N.W.
Washington, DC 20005

South-Western Publishing Co.
5101 Madison Rd.
Cincinnati, OH 45227

Special Libraries Association
105 W. Madison St.
Chicago, IL 60606

St. Martin's Press, Inc.
175 Fifth Ave.
New York, NY 10010

Stargate Consultants, Ltd.
P.O. Box 46167
Stn. G.
Vancouver, British Columbia
V6R 4G5
Canada

The Stephen Greene Press
P.O. Box 1000
Brattleboro, VT 05301
Distributed by:
Viking Penguin, Inc.
40 W. 23rd St.
New York, NY 10010

Sterling Publishing Co., Inc.
Two Park Ave.
New York, NY 10016

Sterne Profit Ideas
8361 Vickers, Suite 304
San Diego, CA 92111

Stuart, Lyle, Inc. See L. Stuart, Inc.

Summit Books
Simon & Schuster Bldg.
Rockefeller Center
1230 Ave. of the Americas
New York, NY 10020

Superintendent of Documents. See
U.S. Government Printing
Office

TPR Publishing Co.
81 Montgomery St.
Scarsdale, NY 10583

TPW Publishing Co.
2483 Old Middlefield Way, Suite
130
Mountain View, CA 94043

Tab Books, Inc.
Blue Ridge Summit, PA 17214

Third Party Publishing Co.
P.O. Box 13306
Montclair Station
Oakland, CA 94661-0306

Thomas Publishing Co.
One Penn Plaza
250 W. 34th St.
New York, NY 10117

Thomas Skinner Directories, Ltd.
Windsor Ct.
East Grinstead House
East Grinstead, West Sussex
RH19 1XE
England

Till Press
P.O. Box 27816
Los Angeles, CA 90027

Time, Inc.
541 N. Fairbanks Ct.
Chicago, IL 60611

The Traffic Service Corp.
1435 G St., N.W.
Washington, DC 20005

Twin Coast Newspapers, Inc.
110 Wall St.
New York, NY 10005

UMI Research Press
300 N. Zeeb Rd.
Ann Arbor, MI 48106

United Nations Educational,
Scientific and Cultural
Organization
7, Place de Fontenoy
Paris 75700
France

United Nations Publications
Room A-3315
New York, NY 10017

United States Council for
International Business
1212 Ave. of the Americas
New York, NY 10036

U.S. Department of Commerce
International Trade
Administration
Trade Information and Analysis
Trade Development
Room 2217
Washington, DC 20230

U.S. Department of Commerce
Minority Business Development
Agency
14th St. between Constitution
Ave. and E St., N.W.
Washington, DC 20230

U.S. Department of Health and
Human Services
Public Health Service
Food and Drug Administration
5600 Fishers Lane
Rockville, MD 20857

U.S. Government Printing Office
Dept. 33
Washington, DC 20402

U.S. Screen Print Industries, Inc.
7755 E. Gelding Dr., Suite
103-04
Scottsdale, AZ 85260

U.S. Small Business Administration
1441 L St., N.W.
Washington, DC 20416

U.S. Small Business Administration
Investment Division
1441 L St., N.W.
Washington, DC 20416

U.S. Small Business Administration
Office of Advocacy
1441 L St., N.W.
Washington, DC 20416

U.S. Small Business Administration
Office of International Trade
1441 L St., N.W.
Washington, DC 20416

U.S. Small Business Administration
Office of Management Assistance
1441 L St., N.W.
Washington, DC 20416

U.S. Small Business Administration
Office of Management
Information and Training
1441 L St., N.W.
Washington, DC 20416

U.S. Small Business Administration
Office of Women's Business
Ownership
Interagency Committee on
Women's Business Enterprise
1441 L St., N.W.
Washington, DC 20416

U.S. Small Business Administration
Public Communications Division
1441 L St., N.W.
Washington, DC 20416

Universe Books, Inc.
381 Park Ave., S.
New York, NY 10016

University Associates
8517 Production Ave.
P.O. Box 26240
San Diego, CA 92126
or
7596 Eads Ave.
LaJolla, CA 92037

University of California–Riverside
Graduate School of
Administration
Riverside, CA 92521

University of California Press
2120 Berkeley Way
Berkeley, CA 94720

University of Chicago Press
5801 Ellis Ave.
Chicago, IL 60637

University of Massachusetts Press
P.O. Box 429
Amherst, MA 01004

University of Michigan
Graduate School of Business
Administration
Ann Arbor, MI 48109

University of Mississippi
Small Business Development
Center and Bureau of Business
Administration
University, MS 38677

University of Tokyo Press
7-3-1 Hongo
Bunkyo-ku, Tokyo 113-91
Japan

University Press of America
P.O. Box 19101
Washington, DC 20036

Uniworld Business Publications,
Inc.
50 E. 42nd St.
New York, NY 10017

Unlimited Marketing Publications
190 Angell St.
Box 944 Annex Station
Providence, RI 02901

Upstart Publishing Co., Inc.
The Small Business Publishing
Co.
P.O. Box 323
Portsmouth, NH 03801

VGM Career Horizons
8259 Niles Center Rd.
Skokie, IL 60077

Vallancey Reference Books, Ltd.
P.O. Box 280
Guernsey, British Isles

Van Nostrand Reinhold Co., Inc.
135 W. 50th St.
New York, NY 10020

Vance Bibliographies
P.O. Box 229
Monticello, IL 61856

Vantage Press
516 W. 34th St.
New York, NY 10001

Venture Magazine, Inc.
35 W. 45th St.
New York, NY 10036

Viking Press
40 W. 23rd St.
New York, NY 10010

W. B. Saunders Co.
West Washington Square
Philadelphia, PA 19105

W. W. Norton & Co., Inc.
500 Fifth Ave.
New York, NY 10010

Wall St. Journal
Dow-Jones Corp.
22 Courtland St.
New York, NY 10007
Subscriptions:
200 Burnell Rd.
Chocopee, MA 01021

Warner Books
666 Fifth Ave.
New York, NY 10103

Warner Software/Warner Books
666 Fifth Ave.
New York, NY 10103

Warren, Gorham & Lamont
210 S. St.
Boston, MA 02111

Watts, Franklin. *See* Franklin Watts

Waveland Press, Inc.
P.O. Box 400
Prospect Heights, IL 60070

West Publishing Co.
50 West Kellogg Blvd.
P.O. Box 43526
St. Paul, MN 55165

West Virginia University
Bureau of Business Research
Morgantown, WV 26506

Weybridge Publishing Co.
16911 Brushfield Dr.
Dallas, TX 75248

Wiley, John, & Sons, Inc. *See* John
Wiley & Sons, Inc.

William C. Brown Co., Publishers
2460 Kerper Blvd.
Dubuque, IA 52001

William Heinemann, Ltd.
10 Upper Grosvenor St.
London W1X 9PA
England

William Morrow & Co., Inc.
105 Madison Ave.
New York, NY 10016

Woodherd-Faulkner
17 Market St.
Cambridge CB2 3PA
England

Word Power, Inc.
Box 17034
Seattle, WA 98107-0734

Work in America Institute
700 White Plains Rd.
Scarsdale, NY 10583

World Bank Headquarters
1818 H St., N.W.
Washington, DC 20433

World Trade Academy Press
50 E. 42nd St.
New York, NY 10017

Appendix B
Small Business
Administration Programs*

Created by Congress in 1953 as an independent federal agency, the U.S. Small Business Administration (SBA) assists and counsels the millions of American small businesses. Its mission is to help people enter and remain in business. In order to fulfill this mission, the SBA offers programs to small business people that can help them succeed. Special efforts are made by this organization to assist women, minorities, the handicapped, and veterans in their business ventures.

The SBA consists of three operational levels: the Central Office in Washington, DC, Regional Offices (Boston, New York, Philadelphia, Atlanta, Kansas City, Dallas, Denver, Chicago, Seattle, and San Francisco), and District Offices located throughout the country (see Appendix F). Assistance is also available through the Service Corps of Retired Executives (SCORE), Small Business Institutes (SBIs), and Small Business Development Centers (SBDCs).

Some of the services offered by the Small Business Administration are listed below:

ADVOCACY

The Office of Advocacy performs five basic duties for small businesses: (a) to serve as a base for complaints, criticism, and suggestions regarding policies and activities of the executive branch of the federal government that affects small business; (b) to act as counsel to small businesses in resolving problems with the federal government; (c) to suggest possible changes in the executive branch to better carry out the mandate of the Small Business Act; (d) to act as

Based on material from *Your Business and the U.S. Small Business Administration.* Washington, DC: U.S. Government Printing Office, 1985; and *The United States Government Manual 1985–86.* Washington, DC: U.S. Government Printing Office, 1985. pp. 621–24.

representative of small businesses before other federal agencies whose actions may affect small business; (e) and to seek help from government and private groups to provide information on programs and services of the federal government.

INNOVATION AND RESEARCH

The SBA monitors and supervises the Small Business Innovation Development Act (1982) which requires that federal agencies too must direct more research and development opportunities to small, high-tech firms. In addition, it encourages participation by small businesses in various federal research and development programs, and encourages the participation of small manufacturing businesses and research and development firms to participate in these programs.

LOANS

A variety of loan programs are available to small businesses who often cannot borrow from conventional lenders without government help. Guaranteed direct or immediate loans such as local development company loans, small general contractor loans, seasonal line of credit, energy loans, handicapped assistant loans, disaster loans, pollution control loans, equipment, facilities, machinery, supply or materials loans, and surety bonds are all available through the SBA.

MANAGEMENT ASSISTANCE

The Management Assistance Program provides free individual counseling, courses, conferences, workshops, problem clinics, and numerous publications for small businesses. Some of the programs are:

SCORE and ACE—designed to help executives and managers solve operating problems by one-on-one counseling relationships.

Small Business Institutes—on over 500 university and college campuses, on-site management counseling is provided by senior and graduate students of business administration and their faculty advisors.

Small Business Development Centers (SBDCs)—by drawing from the local and state resources as well as federal government programs, the private sector, and university facilities, managerial and technical help and other types of specialized assistance important to the small business person is available through this program.

Business Management Courses—these business courses are co-sponsored by SBA in conjunction with educational institutions,

Chambers of Commerce and trade associations to offer help in planning, organization, and control of a business.

International trade counseling and training—for those planning to enter the overseas market or expand overseas operations, the SBA works closely with the U.S. Department of Commerce and other government agencies and private organizations to provide help in developing programs to aid the small firm sell abroad.

Management, marketing, and technical publications—numerous publications are issued by SBA on specific management problems and various aspects of business operations.

MINORITIES

Special programs to help members of minority groups (Blacks, Native Americans, and Hispanics) start or expand their own small business are offered by the SBA. These programs are often combined with those of private industry, banks, local communities, and other federal agencies. These latter groups can work through the Office of Minority Small Business and Capital Ownership Development. The SBA also offers financial assistance to public or private organizations to pay all or part of the cost for technical or management assistance to disadvantaged business persons.

PRIVATE SECTOR INITIATIVES

The primary objective of the private sector initiative program is to use the private sector to obtain maximum leverage in achieving goals of the agency and to meet the needs of the small business community. This program works toward maximum cooperation from state and local government entities in the programs in all agencies in order to utilize local initiatives to their best advantage for the small business.

PROCUREMENT ASSISTANCE

The SBA helps the small business person get a share of the billions of dollars in contracts with private companies. A computerized small business source referral system is maintained by the SBA which provides qualified sources for federal government and large business procurements using this system.

The SBA helps small business people get their share of these contracts as well as available government property. In addition, the SBA helps small business people benefit from research and development performed by government agencies or by corporations under government funding. Further, the SBA provides computerized literature searches to help the small company learn of the research information available to them.

SMALL BUSINESS INVESTMENT COMPANIES (SBICs)

The SBA also makes "venture" or "risk" investment money available to privately owned and operated Small Business Investment Companies (SBICs). SBA licenses a type of SBIC to help the socially or economically disadvantaged person who owns or manages a small business. The primary function of SBICs is to provide venture capital through equity financing, long-term loan funds and management services to small businesses.

VETERANS ASSISTANCE

Special efforts are made by SBA to help veterans who own or operate a small firm by sponsoring special business training workshops, and by offering the services of a veterans affairs specialist at each SBA office. The office helps in improving programs of finance, procurement, and management assistance for businesses owned or operated by veterans. It maintains a liaison with key executive agencies, state and local governments, and private organizations, to ensure that veterans make maximum use of existing programs.

WOMEN

Women make up more than half of America's population but own less than one-fourth of its businesses. The SBA offers loans, assistance programs, and counseling services to women.

The Office of Women's Business Ownership (OWBO) develops and coordinates a national program designed to increase the strength, profitability, and visibility of women-owned businesses by making complete use of government and private sector resources. This office acts as liaison with nonfederal business, educational organizations, and community resources in order to help the growth and development of women-owned businesses.

In addition, the OWBO develops and recommends programs to provide training and counseling in the starting, management, and financing of women-owned businesses. This group is also responsible for negotiating with federal agencies to set government-wide goals that will increase federal prime contracts with women-owned businesses.

Appendix C
Small Business
Administration—Field
Offices*

(RA: Regional Administrator, DD: District Director; BM: Branch Manager; OC: Officer in Charge)

Region	Officer in Charge	Address/Telephone
I Boston, MA 02110	J.H. Angevine (RA)	60 Batterymarch, 617-223-6660
Boston, MA 02114	J.J. McNally, Jr. (DD)	150 Causeway St., 617-223-4074
Hartford, CT 06106	J.P. Burke (DD)	1 Hartford Sq. W., 203-722-2511
Providence, RI 02903	J.A. Hague (DD)	380 Westminster Mall, 401-528-4580
Augusta, ME 04330	T.A. McGillicuddy (DD)	40 Western Ave., 207-622-8378
Concord, NH 03301	W. Phillips (DD)	55 Pleasant St., 603-224-4724
Montpelier, VT 05602	D.C. Emery (DD)	87 State St., 802-832-4422
Springfield, MA 01103	M. Record (OC)	1550 Main St., 413-785-9268
II New York, NY 10278	P.P. Neglia (RA)	26 Federal Plaza, 212-264-1450
	B.X. Haggerty (DD)	26 Federal Plaza, 212-264-1318
Syracuse, NY 13260	J.W. Harrison (DD)	100 S. Clinton St., 315-423-5371
Buffalo, NY 14202	F.J. Sciortino (BM)	111 W. Huron St., 716-846-4305

*The United States Government Manual 1985–86 Washington, DC: U.S. Government Printing Office, 1985, pp. 625–26.

Region	Officer in Charge	Address/Telephone
Camden, NJ 08104	J. Fernicola (OC)	1800 E. Davis St., 609-757-5183
Elmira, NY 14901	J.J. Cristofaro (BM)	333 E. Water St., 607-733-6610
Melville, NY 11747	W. Leavitt (BM)	35 Pinelaw Rd., 516-454-0764
Rochester, NY 14614	P. Flihan (OC)	100 State St., 716-263-6700
St. Thomas, VI 00801	L. Baptiste (OC)	Federal Office Bldg., Veterans Dr., 809-774-8530
Hato Key, PR 00919	W.B. Robles (DD)	Federal Bldg., Carlos Chardon Ave., 809-753-4003
St. Croix, VI 00820	C. Christensen (OC)	4A LaGrande Princesse Chrostoamsted, 809-733-3480
III Bala Cynwyd, PA 19004	R.T. Lhulier (RA) W.T. Gennetti (DD)	231 St. Asaphs Rd., 215-596-5901
Charleston, WV 25301	E.G. Zimmerman (BM)	Charleston National Plaza, 304-347-5220
Harrisburg, PA 17101	K.J. Olson (BM)	100 Chestnut St., 717-782-3846
Wilkes-Barre, PA 18702	J. Sokolowski (BM)	20 N. Pennsylvania Ave., 717-826-6446
Wilmington, DE 19801	J.J. Giannini (BM)	844 King St., 302-573-6294
Richmond, VA 23240	C.S. Marschall (DD)	400 N. 8th St., 804-771-2741
Washington, DC 20036	J.E. Wolfe (DD)	1111 18th St. N.W., 202-634-1805
Pittsburgh, PA	J.M. Kopp (DD)	960 Penn Ave., 412-722-4306
Towson, MD 21204	J.A. Feldman (DD)	8600 LaSalle Rd., 301-962-2054
Clarksburg, WV 26301	M.P. Shelton (DD)	168 W. Main St., 304-623-3706
Newark, NJ 07102	A.P. Lynch (DD)	60 Park Pl., 201-645-3580
IV Atlanta, GA 30367	M.A. Widemire (RA)	1375 Peachtree St. N.E., 404-881-4999
Atlanta, GA 30309	C.B. Barnes (DD)	1720 Peachtree Rd. N.W., 404-881-4749
Birmingham, AL 35256	J.C. Barksdale (DD)	908 S. 20th St., 205-254-1341
Charlotte, NC 28202	G.A. Keel (DD)	230 S. Tryon St., 704-371-6561

Region	Officer in Charge	Address/Telephone
Columbia, SC 29201	J.C. Patrick, Jr. (DD)	1835 Assembly St., 803-765-5373
Jackson, MS 39269	J.K. Spradling (DD)	100 W. Capitol St., 601-960-4363
Jacksonville, FL 32202	D.E. McAllister (DD)	400 W. Bay St., 904-791-3103
Louisville, KY 40202	B.R. Wells (DD)	600 Federal Pl., 502-582-5971
Coral Gables, FL 33134	J.L. Carey (DD)	222 Ponce de Leon Blvd., 305-350-5533
Nashville, TN 37219	R.M. Hartman (DD)	404 James Robertson Pkwy., 615-251-5850
Biloxi, MS 39530	C.A. Gillis (BM)	111 Fred Haise Blvd., 601-435-3676
Statesboro, GA 30458	C. Henderson (OC)	52 N. Main St., 912-489-8719
Tampa, FL 33602	E. Moore (OC)	700 Twiggs St., 813-228-2594
West Palm Beach, FL 33407	R. Cosper (OC)	3500 45th St., 305-689-2223
V Chicago, IL 60604	R.D. Durkin (RA)	230 S. Dearborn St., 312-353-0357
	J.L. Smith (DD)	219 S. Dearborn St., 312-353-4508
Cincinnati, OH 45202	C.G. Boatright (BM)	550 Main St., 513-684-2814
Cleveland, OH 44199	C. Hemming, Jr. (DD)	1240 E. 9th St., 216-522-4182
Columbus, OH 43215	F.D. Ray (DD)	85 Marconi Blvd., 614-469-7310
Detroit, MI 48226	R.L. Harshman (DD)	477 Michigan Ave., 313-226-6075
Eau Claire, WI 54701	T. Jernigan (OC)	500 S. Barstow St., 715-834-9012
Indianapolis, IN 46204-1584	R.D. General (OC)	575 N. Pennsylvania St., 315-269-7272
Marquette, MI 49885	P. Jacobson (OC)	220 W. Washington St., 906-225-1108
Madison, WI 53703	C. Charter (DD)	212 E. Washington Ave., 608-264-5205
Milwaukee, WI 53203	R.C. Miller (BM)	310 W. Wisconsin Ave., 414-291-1488
Minneapolis, MN 55403	C.C. Moreno (DD)	100 N. 6th St., 612-349-3530
Springfield, IL 62701	J.N. Thomson (BM)	4 N. Old State Capitol Plaza, 217-492-4416
South Bend, IN 46601	E.L. Harris (OC)	River Glen Office Plaza, 219-236-8361

Region	Officer in Charge	Address/Telephone
VI Dallas, TX 75235-3391	R.H. Lopez (RA)	8625 King George Dr., 214-767-7643
Dallas, TX 75242	J.S. Reed (DD)	1100 Commerce St., 214-767-0600
Fort Worth, TX 76102	G. Box (BM)	819 Taylor St., 817-334-3777
Albuquerque, NM 87110	P. Ramos (DD)	5000 Marble Ave., N.E., 505-766-3430
Austin, TX 78701	J. Perez (DD)	300 E. 8th St., 512-482-7811
Corpus Christi, TX 78401	M.A. Cavazos (BM)	400 Mann St., 512-888-3301
El Paso, TX 79902	H. Zuniga (DD)	10737 Gateway W., 915-541-7676
Houston, TX 77054	D.D. Grose (DD)	2525 Murworth, 713-660-4409
Little Rock, AR 72201	M. Britt (DD)	320 W. Capitol Ave., 740-378-5277
Harlingen, TX 78550	R. Martin (DD)	222 E. Van Buren, 512-423-4533
Lubbock, TX 79401	P.J. O'Jibway (DD)	1611 10th St., 806-743-7462
Marshall, TX 75670	G. Lewis (OC)	100 S. Washington St., 214-935-5257
New Orleans, LA 70112	T.A. Aboussie (DD)	1661 Canal St., 504-589-6885
Shreveport, LA 71101	R. Windham (OC)	500 Fannin St., 318-226-5196
Oklahoma City, OK 73102	R.K. Ball (DD)	200 N.W. 5th St., 405-231-5237
San Antonio, TX 78206	J. Perez (DD)	727 E. Durango, 512-730-6105
VII Kansas City, MO 64106	W.A. Powell (RA)	911 Walnut St., 816-374-3316
	P. Smythe (DD)	1103 Grand Ave., 816-374-5557
Des Moines, IA 50309	C.E. Lawlor (DD)	210 Walnut St., 515-284-4567
Omaha, NE 68102	R.S. Budd (DD)	19th and Farnam Sts., 402-221-3620
Springfield, MO 65806	S.C. Slaughter (BM)	309 N. Jefferson, 417-864-7670
St. Louis, MO 63101	R.L. Andrews (DD)	815 Olive St., 314-425-6600
Wichita, KS 67202	C. Hunter (DD)	110 E. Waterman St., 316-269-6566
Cedar Rapids, IA 52402	R.W. Potter (DD)	373 Collins Rd. NE., 319-399-2571

Region	Officer in Charge	Address/Telephone
Cape Girardeau, MO 63701	G.L. Martin (OC)	339 Broadway, 314-335-6039
VIII Denver, CO 80202-2395	C.R. Suarez (RA)	1405 Curtis St., 303-844-5441
Denver, CO 80202-2599	E. Uccellini (DD)	721 19th St., 303-844-2607
Casper, WY 82602-2839	P. Nemetz (DD)	100 East B St., 307-261-5761
Fargo, ND 58102	R.L. Pinkerton (DD)	657 2d Ave. N., 701-237-5771
Salt Lake City, UT 84138-1195	R.K. Moon (DD)	125 S. State St., 801-524-5804
Sioux Falls, SD 57102-0577	C. Leedom (DD)	101 S. Main Ave., 605-336-2980
Helena, MT 59626	J.R. Cronholm (DD)	301 S. Park, 406-449-5381
Billings, MT 59101	J. Labatt (OC)	2601 1st Ave. N., 406-657-6047
IX San Francisco, CA 94102	I. Castillo (RA)	450 Golden Gate Ave., 415-556-7487
San Francisco, CA 94105	L.J. Wodarski (DD)	211 Main St., 415-974-0642
Santa Ana, CA 92701	J.S. Waddell (BM)	2700 N. Main St., 714-836-2494
Agana, GU 96910	Jose M.L. Lujan (BM)	238 O'Hara St., 671-472-7277
Fresno, CA 93721	P. Bergin (DD)	2202 Monterey St., 209-487-5189
Honolulu, HI 96850	D.K. Nakagawa (DD)	300 Ala Moana, 808-546-8950
Las Vegas, NV 89101	R.S. Garrett (DD)	301 E. Stewart, 702-385-6611
Los Angeles, CA 90071	G.Y. Morita (DD)	350 S. Figueroa St., 213-688-2956
Phoenix, AZ 85012	W. Fronstein (DD)	3030 N. Central Ave., 602-241-2206
Reno, NV 85505	R. Davis (OC)	50 S. Virginia St., 702-784-5268
Sacramento, CA 95814	(Vacancy) (BM)	660 J St., 916-440-2956
San Diego, CA 92188	G.P. Chandler, Jr. (DD)	880 Front St., 714-293-5430
San Jose, CA 95113	P. Calleja (OC)	111 W. St. John St., 408-291-7584
Tucson, AZ 85701	R.A. Schulze (OC)	301 W. Congress, 602-792-6715
X Seattle, WA 98121	S.J. Hall (RA)	2615 4th Ave., 206-442-5677

Region	Officer in Charge	Address/Telephone
Seattle, WA 98174	J.J. Talerico (DD)	915 2d Ave., 206-442-5534
Anchorage, AK 99501	F. Cox (DD)	8th and C Sts., 907-271-4022
Boise, ID 83702	J.G. Kaeppner (DD)	1020 Main St., 208-334-1696
Fairbanks, AK 99701	S. Carter (BM)	101 12th Ave., 907-456-0211
Portland, OR 97204-2882	(Vacancy) (DD)	1220 S.W. 3d Ave., 503-294-5221
Spokane, WA 99210	V.W. Cameron (DD)	651 U.S. Courthouse, 509-456-3781

Appendix D
Small Business Innovation
Research Agencies*

DEPARTMENT OF AGRICULTURE
Dr. W. K. Murphey, Office of Grants and Program Systems, West Auditors
Bldg., Room 112, 15th & Independence Ave., S.W., Washington, DC
20251, (202) 475-5022

DEPARTMENT OF COMMERCE
Mr. James P. Maruca, Director, Office of Small and Disadvantaged Business
Utilization, 14th & Constitution Ave., N.W., Room 6411, Washington,
DC 20230, (202) 377-1472

DEPARTMENT OF DEFENSE
Mr. Horace Crouch, Director, Small Business and Economic Utilization,
Office of Secretary of Defense, Room 2A340–The Pentagon,
Washington, DC 20301, (202) 697-9383

DEPARTMENT OF EDUCATION
Dr. Edward Esty, SBIR Program Coordinator, Office of Educational Research
and Improvement, Mail Stop 40, Washington, DC 20208, (202)
254-8247

DEPARTMENT OF ENERGY
Ms. Gerry Washington, c/o SBIR Program Manager, Washington, DC 20545,
(301) 353-5867

DEPARTMENT OF HEALTH & HUMAN SERVICES
Mr. Richard Clinkscales, Director, Office of Small and Disadvantaged
Business Utilization, 200 Independence Ave., S.W., Room 513D,
Washington, DC 20201, (202) 245-7300

DEPARTMENT OF THE INTERIOR
Dr. Thomas Henrie, Chief Scientist, Bureau of Mines, 2401 E Street, N.W.,
Washington, DC 20241, (202) 634-1305

---

*The Small Business Answer Desk Directory. Washington, DC: Office of the
Chief Counsel for Advocacy, U.S. Small Business Administration, 1985, p.
112.

DEPARTMENT OF TRANSPORTATION
Mr. George Kovatch, SBIR Program Manager, Transportation Systems
   Center, Kendall Square, Cambridge, MA 02142, (617) 494-2051

ENVIRONMENTAL PROTECTION AGENCY
Mr. Walter H. Preston, Office of Research and Development, 401 M Street,
   S.W., Washington, DC 20460, (202) 382-5744

NATIONAL AERONAUTICS AND SPACE ADMINISTRATION
Mr. Carl Schwenk, SBIR Office–Code RB, 600 Independence Ave., S.W.,
   Washington, DC 20546, (202) 453-2848

NATIONAL SCIENCE FOUNDATION
Mr. Roland Tibbetts, Mr. Ritchie Corvell, SBIR Program Managers, 1800 G
   St., N.W., Washington, DC 20550, (202) 357-7527

NUCLEAR REGULATORY COMMISSION
Mr. Wayne Batson, Office of Nuclear Regulatory Research, Washington, DC
   20460, (301) 427-4250

Appendix E
U.S. Government Toll Free Numbers*

Agency	Number
Agriculture Fraud Hotline	800/424-9121
Commerce Department Fraud Hotline	800/424-5197
Consumer Product Safety Commission	800/638-2772
Defense Fraud Hotline	800/424-9098
EPA Hazardous Waste Hotline	800/424-9346
EPA Industry Assistance Hotline	800/424-9065
EPA Small Business Hotline	800/368-5888
Energy Inquiry and Referral (Energy Dept.)	800/523-2929
Export-Import Bank	800/424-5201
Fair Housing and Equal Opportunity (HUD)	800/424-8590
Federal Crime Insurance	800/638-8780
Federal Deposit Insurance Corporation	800/424-5488
Federal Home Loan Bank Board	800/424-5405
Flood Insurance	800/424-5405
General Accounting Office Fraud Hotline	800/424-5454
Health Info Clearinghouse (HHS)	800/336-4797
Highway Traffic Safety Administration	800/424-9393
Housing Discrimination Hotline (HUD)	800/424-8590
Interior Dept. Fraud Hotline	800/424-5081
Internal Revenue Service	(see state lists)
Labor Fraud Hotline	800/424-5409
National Consumer Co-Op Bank	800/424-2481
National Health Info Hotline (HHS)	800/424-2481
Overseas Private Investment Corporation	800/424-6742
Small Business Answer Desk	800/368-5855
Talking Books Program (Lib. of Congress)	800/424-9100
Veterans Administration (by state)	(refer to operator)
Women's Economic Development Corps	800/222-2933

*The Small Business Answer Desk Directory, Washington, DC: Office of the Chief Counsel for Advocacy, U.S. Small Business Administration, 1985, p. 113.

Appendix F
U.S. Department of Commerce District Office Directory*

International Trade Administration
U.S. and Foreign Commercial Service

Paula Unruh, Acting Director General
U.S. and Foreign Commercial Service, Room 3804, HCH Building
14th & Constitution Ave., N.W. Washington, DC 20230
Area Code 202 Tel. 377-0725 FTS 377-0725

ALABAMA
Birmingham – Gayle Shelton, Jr., Director, Third Floor, Berry Bldg.,
2015–2nd Ave., N., 35302, 205-254-1331, FTS 229-1331

ALASKA
Anchorage – Richard Lenahan, Director, 701 C St., P.O. Box 32, 99513,
907-271-5041, FTS 8 907 271-5041

ARIZONA
Phoenix – Donald W. Fry, Director, Federal Bldg. & U.S. Courthouse, 230 N.
First Ave., Room 3412, 85025, 602-261-3285, FTS 261-3285

ARKANSAS
Little Rock – Lon J. Hardin, Director, Suite 635, Savers Federal Bldg., 320
W. Capitol Ave., 72201, 501-378-5794, FTS 740-5794

CALIFORNIA
Los Angeles – Daniel J. Young, Director, Room 800, 11777 San Vincente
Blvd., 90049, 213-209-6707, FTS 793-6707
Santa Ana – 116–A W. 4th St., Suite 1, 92701, 714-836-2461, FTS 799-2461
San Diego – P.O. Box 81404, 92138, 619-293-5395, FTS 895-5395
San Francisco – Betty D. Neuhart, Director, Federal Bldg., Box 36013, 450
Golden Gate Ave., 94102, 415-556-5860, FTS 556-5868

---

*Business America 8 (October 28, 1985), p. 6–7.

COLORADO
Denver – Samuel J. Cerrato, Director, Room 119, U.S. Customhouse, 721-19th St., 80202, 303-844-3246, FTS 564-3246

CONNECTICUT
Hartford – Eric B. Outwater, Director, Room 610-B, Federal Office Bldg., 450 Main St., 06103, 203-722-3530, FTS 244-3530

DELAWARE
Serviced by Philadelphia District Office

DISTRICT OF COLUMBIA
Serviced by Baltimore District Office

FLORIDA
Miami – Ivan A. Cosimi, Director, Suite 224, Federal Bldg., 51 S.W. First Ave., 33130, 305-350-5267, FTS 350-5267
Clearwater – 128 North Osceola Ave., 33515, 813-461-0011
Jacksonville – 3 Independent Drive, 32202, 904-791-2796, FTS 946-2796
Orlando – 75 E. Ivanhoe Blvd., 32802, 305-425-1247
Tallahassee – Collins Bldg., Room G-20, 107 W. Gaines St., 32304, 904-488-6469, FTS 946-4320

GEORGIA
Atlanta – (Vacant) Suite 504, 1365 Peachtree St., N.E., 30309, 404-881-7000, FTS 257-7000
Savannah – James W. McIntire, Director, 27 E. Bay St., P.O. Box 9746, 31401, 912-944-4204, FTS 248-4204

HAWAII
Honolulu – Stephen K. Craven, Director, 4106 Federal Bldg., P.O. Box 50026, 300 Ala Moana Blvd., 96850, 808-546-8694, FTS 8 808-546-8694

IDAHO
Boise – (Denver, Colorado District) Statehouse, Room 113, 83720, 208-334-2470

ILLINOIS
Chicago – Joseph F. Christiano, Director, 1406 Mid Continental Plaza Bldg., 55 E. Monroe St., 60603, 312-353-4450, FTS 353-4450
Palatine – W. R. Harper College, Algonquin & Roselle Rd., 60067, 312-397-3000, Ext. 532
Rockford – 515 N. Court St., P.O. Box 1747, 61110-0247, 815-987-8100

INDIANA
Indianapolis – Mel R. Sherar, Director, 357 U.S. Courthouse & Federal Office Bldg., 46 E. Ohio St., 46204, 317-269-6214, FTS 331-6214

IOWA
Des Moines – Jesse N. Durden, Director, 817 Federal Bldg., 210 Walnut St., 50309, 515-284-4222, FTS 862-4222

KANSAS
Wichita (Kansas City, Missouri District) – River Park Place, Suite 565, 727 N. Waco, 67203, 316-269-6160, FTS 752-6160

KENTUCKY
Louisville – Donald R. Henderson Director, Room 636B, U.S. Post Office and Courthouse Bldg., 40202, 502-582-5066, FTS 352-5066

LOUISIANA
New Orleans – Paul Guidry, 432 International Trade Mart, No. 2 Canal St., 70130, 504-589-6546, FTS 682-6546

MAINE
Augusta (Boston, Massachusetts District) – 1 Memorial Circle, Casco Bank Bldg., 04330, 207-622-8249, FTS 833-6249

MARYLAND
Baltimore – LoRee P. Silloway, Director, 415 U.S. Customhouse, Gay and Lombard Sts., 21202, 301-962-3560, FTS 922-3560
Rockville – 101 Monroe St., 15th Floor, 20850, 301-251-2345

MASSACHUSETTS
Boston – Francis J. O'Connor, Director, 10th Floor, 441 Stuart St., 02116, 617-223-2312, FTS 223-2312

MICHIGAN
Detroit – George R. Campbell, Director, 445 Federal Bldg. 231 W. Lafayette, 48226, 313-226-3650, FTS 226-3650
Grand Rapids – 300 Monroe N.W., Room 409, 49503, 616-456-2411, FTS 372-2411

MINNESOTA
Minneapolis – Ronald E. Kramer, Director, 108 Federal Bldg., 110 S. 4th St., 55401, 612-349-3338, FTS 787-3338

MISSISSIPPI
Jackson – Mark E. Spinney, Director, Jackson Mall Office Center, Suite 328, 300 Woodrow Wilson Blvd., 39213, 601-960-4388, FTS 490-4388

MISSOURI
St. Louis – Donald R. Loso, Director, 120 S. Central Ave., 63105, 314-425-3302, ext. 4, FTS 279-3302
Kansas City – James D. Cook, Director, Room 635, 601 E. 12th St., 64106, 816-374-3142, FTS 758-3142

MONTANA
Serviced by Denver District Office

NEBRASKA
Omaha – George H. Payne, Director, Empire State Bldg., 1st Floor, 300 S. 19th St., 68102, 402-221-3664, FTS 864-3664

NEVADA
Reno – Joseph J. Jeremy, Director, 1755 E. Plumb Lane, #152, 89502, 702-784-5203, FTS 470-5203

NEW HAMPSHIRE
Serviced by Boston District Office

NEW JERSEY
Trenton – Thomas J. Murray, Director, Capitol Plaza, 8th Floor, 240 W. State St., 08608, 609-989-2100, FTS 483-2100

NEW MEXICO
Albuquerque – William E. Dwyer, Director, 517 Gold, S.W., Suite 4303, 87102, 505-766-2386, FTS 474-2386

NEW YORK
Buffalo – Robert F. Magee, Director, 1312 Federal Bldg., 111 W. Huron St., 14202, 716-846-4191, FTS 437-4191
Rochester – 121 East Ave., 14604, 716-263-6480, FTS 963-6480
New York – Milton Eaton, Director, Room 3718, Federal Office Bldg., 26 Federal Plaza, Foley Square, 10278, 212-264-0634, FTS 264-0600

NORTH CAROLINA
Greensboro – Joel B. New, Director, 203 Federal Bldg., 324 W. Market St., P.O. Box 1950, 27402, 919-378-5345, FTS 699-5345

NORTH DAKOTA
Serviced by Omaha District Office

OHIO
Cincinnati – Gordon B. Thomas, Director, 9504 Federal Office Bldg., 550 Main St., 45202, 513-684-2944, FTS 684-2944
Cleveland – Zelda W. Milner, Director, Room 600, 666 Euclid Ave., 44114, 216-522-4750, FTS 942-4750

OKLAHOMA
Oklahoma City – Ronald L. Wilson, Director, 4024 Lincoln Blvd., 73105, 405-231-5302, FTS 736-5302
Tulsa – 440 S. Houston St., 74127, 918-581-7650 FTS 745-7650

OREGON
Portland – Lloyd R. Porter, Director, Room 618, 1220 S.W. 3rd Ave., 97204, 503-221-3001, FTS 423-3001

PENNSYLVANIA
Philadelphia – Robert E. Kistler, Director, 9448 Federal Bldg., 600 Arch St., 19106, 215-597-2866, FTS 597-2866
Pittsburgh – William M. Bradley, Director, 2002 Federal Bldg., 1000 Liberty Ave., 15222, 412-644-2850, FTS 722-2850

PUERTO RICO
San Juan (Hato Rey) – J. Enrique Vilella, Director, Room 659, Federal Bldg., 00918, 809-753-4555, Ext. 555, FTS 8-809-753-4555

RHODE ISLAND
Providence (Boston, Massachusetts District) – 7 Jackson Walkway, 02903, 401-528-5104, Ext. 22, FTS 838-5104

SOUTH CAROLINA
Columbia – Johnny E. Brown, Director, Strom Thurmond Federal Bldg., Suite 172, 1835 Assembly St., 29201, 803-765-5345, FTS 677-5345
Charleston – 17 Lockwood Dr., 29401, 803-724-4361, FTS 677-4361

SOUTH DAKOTA
Serviced by Omaha District Office

TENNESSEE
Nashville – Jim Charlet, Director, Suite 1427, One Commerce Place, 37239, 615-251-5161, FTS 852-5161
Memphis – 3876 Central Ave., 38111, 901-521-4826, FTS 222-4826

TEXAS
Dallas – C. Carmon Stiles, Director, Room 7A5, 1100 Commerce St., 75242, 214-767-0542, FTS 729-0542
Austin – P.O. Box 12728, Capitol Station, 78711, 512-472-5059
Houston – Felicito C. Guerrero, Director, 2625 Federal Courthouse, 515 Rusk St., 77002, 713-229-2578, FTS 526-4578

UTAH
Salt Lake City – Stephen P. Smoot, Director, U.S. Courthouse, 350 S. Main St., 84101, 801-524-5116, FTS 588-5116

VERMONT
Serviced by Boston District Office

VIRGINIA
Richmond – Philip A. Ouzts, Director, 8010 Federal Bldg., 400 N. 8th St., 23240, 804-771-2246, FTS 925-2246

WASHINGTON
Seattle – C. Franklin Foster, Director, Room 706, Lake Union Bldg., 1700 Westlake Ave., N., 98109, 206-442-5616, FTS 399-5615
Spokane – P.O. Box 2170, 99210, 509-838-8202

WEST VIRGINIA
Charleston – Roger L. Fortner, Director, 3000 New Federal Bldg., 500 Quarrier St., 25301, 304-347-5123, FTS 930-5123

WISCONSIN
Milwaukee – Patrick A. Willis, Director, Federal Bldg., U.S. Courthouse, 517 E. Wisconsin Ave., 53202, 414-291-3473, FTS 362-3473

WYOMING
Serviced by Denver District Office

Appendix G
Government Printing Office
Book Stores*

ALABAMA
Birmingham, 9220-B Parkway East, 205-254-1056

CALIFORNIA
Los Angeles, ARCO Plaza, 505 S. Flower St., 213-688-5841
San Francisco, 450 Golden Gate Ave., 415-556-0643

COLORADO
Denver, 1961 Stout St., 303-837-3964
Pueblo, 720 N. Main, Majestic Bldg., 303-544-3142

FLORIDA
Jacksonville, 400 W. Bay St., 904-791-3801

GEORGIA
Atlanta, 275 Peachtree St., N.E., 404-221-6947

ILLINOIS
Chicago, 219 S. Dearborn St., 312-353-5133

MASSACHUSETTS
Boston, John F. Kennedy Federal Bldg., Sudbury St., 617-223-6071

MICHIGAN
Detroit, 477 Michigan Ave., 313-226-7816

MISSOURI
Kansas City, 601 E. 12th St., 816-374-2160

OHIO
Cleveland, 1240 E. 9th St., 216-522-4922
Columbus, 200 N. High St., 614-469-6956

*The Small Business Answer Desk Directory. Washington, DC: Office of the Chief Counsel for Advocacy, U.S. Small Business Administration, 1985, p. 98.

PENNSYLVANIA
Philadelphia, 600 Arch St., 215-597-0677
Pittsburgh, 1000 Liberty Ave., 412-644-2721

TEXAS
Dallas, 1100 Commerce St., 214-767-0076
Houston, College Center, 9319 Gulf Freeway, 713-229-3515

WASHINGTON
Seattle, 915 Second Ave., 206-442-4270

WASHINGTON, DC area:
Main Bookstore, 710 N. Capitol St., 202-275-2091
Commerce Department, 14th and E Sts., N.W., 202-377-3527
HHS, 330 Independence Ave., S.W., 202-472-7478
Retail Sales Branch, 8660 Cherry Lane, Laurel, MD, 301-953-7974
Pentagon Bldg., Main Concourse, 703-557-1821

WISCONSIN
Milwaukee, 519 E. Wisconsin Ave., 414-291-1304

Note: Publications may be ordered by phone and charged to a major credit card.

Author Index

Numbers refer to citation numbers, not page numbers.

Title Index

Subject Index